Volume 16

Advances in
Librarianship

Volume 16

Advances in
Librarianship

Edited by

Irene P. Godden

The Libraries
Colorado State University
Fort Collins, Colorado

Academic Press, Inc.
Harcourt Brace Jovanovich, Publishers
San Diego   New York   Boston   London   Sydney   Tokyo   Toronto

Copyright © 1992 by ACADEMIC PRESS, INC.
All Rights Reserved.
No part of this publication may be reproduced or transmitted in any form or by any
means, electronic or mechanical, including photocopy, recording, or any information
storage and retrieval system, without permission in writing from the publisher.

Academic Press, Inc.
1250 Sixth Avenue, San Diego, California 92101-4311

United Kingdom Edition published by
Academic Press Limited
24–28 Oval Road, London NW1 7DX

Library of Congress Catalog Number: 79-88675

International Standard Book Number: 0-12-024616-3

PRINTED IN THE UNITED STATES OF AMERICA
92 93 94 95 96 97   BC   9 8 7 6 5 4 3 2 1

Contents

Strategic Quality Management in Libraries
Donald E. Riggs

Digital Technology: Implications for Library Planning
Karen Horny

Buying Publishers' Trade Paperbacks versus Hardbacks: A Preventive Conservation Strategy for Research Libraries
Randy Silverman and Robert Speiser

The Future of Library Science in Higher Education: A Crossroads for Library Science and Librarianship

C. D. Hurt

The European Communities: Reference Works and Documentary Sources of the Spanish Parliament

Rosa María Grau and Miguel Angel Gonzalo

Contributors

Numbers in parentheses indicate the pages on which the authors' contributions begin.

Patricia B. Culkin (83), CARL Systems, Inc., Denver, Colorado 80210

Miguel Angel Gonzalo (183), Research and Documentation Library, Congress of Deputies, 28014 Madrid, Spain

Rosa María Grau (183), Research and Documentation Library, Congress of Deputies, 28014 Madrid, Spain

Karen Horny (107), Northwestern University Library, Evanston, Illinois 60208

C. D. Hurt (153), School of Library Science, University of Arizona, Tucson, Arizona 85721

Carol A. Mandel (33), Columbia University Libraries, New York, New York 10027

Donald E. Riggs (93), University Library, University of Michigan, Ann Arbor, Michigan 48109

Randy Silverman (127), Harold B. Lee Library, Brigham Young University, Provo, Utah 84602

Robert Speiser (127), Department of Mathematics, Brigham Young University, Provo, Utah 84602

Julie Wessling (1), University Libraries, Colorado State University, Fort Collins, Colorado 80523

Preface

The past few years have been characterized by changes in almost any field one may care to name. Certainly, there have been profound changes in the ways we approach and manage libraries and provide basic library services, such as bibliographic control, document delivery, preservation, and planning for physical facilities. The profession has also become more and more aware of changes in the international world of librarianship, which are beginning to affect us as communications networks link us more closely to the world beyond the American continent. In addition, most practitioners in the profession are probably aware of the ongoing and often painful changes in librarianship's educational process.

Articles in this volume of *Advances in Librarianship* address aspects of some of these changes, placing them in historical context, bringing forward new facets, or suggesting new goals or directions.

In the lead article, *Wessling* discusses the accelerating evolution of traditional interlibrary loan services into a full range of document delivery options. She suggests a model for the future in which all available avenues for document acquisitions and all available delivery options, from traditional to "high tech," will be utilized, with the most efficient pathway defined by the user within desired cost and time parameters.

Cooperative cataloging programs, credited with improving access to information while greatly reducing costs, have generally been accepted as one of the most successful collaborative library projects in the history of librarianship. *Mandel*, after restating underlying premises, provides a detailed history of the development, successes, and as yet unresolved problems of a program that has profoundly affected the art and science of bibliographic control, ending with a review of current goals and models that will need to be aligned in order to realize its still greater potential.

Claiming that its economic benefits have been eroded by an antiquated distribution system, *Culkin* takes to task one of the major structures underpinning cooperative cataloging efforts. In discussing the MARC format, the record structure developed by the Library of Congress to facilitate communication and transfer of bibliographic data, she suggests that a more automated distribution model, by forcing change in the distribution paradigm, would gain efficiencies in local processing while freeing funds for increased direct procurement of materials—a win–win situation for all players, except perhaps the utilities.

At a time when increases in information and knowledge resources coupled with budget cuts push libraries to expand services, even while staff size is stable or even decreasing, "inventing the future and strategic directions for the library and making them happen are awesome responsibilities," according to *Riggs*. He discusses how strategic management, coupled with the concepts of TQM (total quality management), provides an approach or "way of life" which, while no panacea, promises an opportunity for improving job satisfaction, and library services and products, in favorable as well as unfavorable financial climates.

Digital technology and its implications for library planning, and particularly space planning, are discussed by *Horny*, who reviews current projects which attempt to measure the costs and quality of conversion and storage utilizing various methodologies. She covers access, retrieval, and communication issues and concludes by listing a series of questions that need to be addressed by those planning for future library buildings and/or the "virtual library" of the future.

While preservation activities in libraries have generally been accepted as necessary and beneficial, there are few examples in the literature of actual cost models which provide formulae for translating general benefits into actual dollars and cents savings. *Silverman* discusses a preventive conservation strategy that suggests a conceptual shift in using existing resources—buying and reinforcing trade paperbacks versus buying hardbacks—that has resulted in savings at a particular institution that benefit both collection development and preservation efforts.

Library education has arrived at a crossroad in the last few years, with many graduate library programs closing, some being rethought and revitalized, and the entire present accreditation process coming under severe criticism. *Hurt*, dean of the graduate library school at the University of Arizona, after reviewing the history of library education in the United States, incisively bares current problems and presents the challenging choices we have in moving ahead—or becoming obsolete.

A European perspective is provided by *Grau* and *Gonzalo*, who, in discussing documentary sources and reference works in the library/documentation department of the Spanish parliament, open a window on the sophisticated information networks emerging in the European Communities. The detail provided will suggest comparisons, and will also make this article a useful source for further research.

Document Delivery: A Primary Service for the Nineties

Julie Wessling
University Libraries
Colorado State University
Fort Collins, Colorado 80523

I. Introduction

Stories told at professional meetings, some of them published (Carpenter, 1991; Jackson, 1991; Johnson, 1991; Martin, 1989), have it that there is a crisis in interlibrary loan (ILL) operations. They say numbers of requests have escalated beyond a manageable quantity for even the largest operations (or especially for the largest operations) and that requests are being turned away. They even claim the whole ILL process is outdated and is no longer capable of supporting user demand—that it is far too slow to support expectations in a computerized age. It is true that the number of requests is rising dramatically, whereas the resources supporting ILL operations are showing only modest, if any, increase. It is therefore necessary for librarians to focus on the overall picture to identify a positive, manageable pathway to a solution that allows effective delivery of needed material.

Advances in technology, especially in the past 2 years, promise to revolutionize ILL service and transform it into a service of primary importance, a service that can support the growing information needs of library users. It is the purpose of this article to show that the only aspect of ILL in danger of becoming obsolete is its name, which implies emphasis on library-to-library activity. ILL service must reach beyond traditional interlibrary lending and provide users with comprehensive access to documents from a variety of sources. This enhanced ILL service should offer "one-stop-shopping" for the user and provide the link between libraries and other sources of documents and information. If libraries act cooperatively and aggressively to expand document delivery options, they will prove that they can play a leadership role in meeting the information needs of users in the 1990s.

ADVANCES IN LIBRARIANSHIP, VOL. 16
Copyright © 1992 by Academic Press, Inc.

II. Evolution of ILL into Library Document Delivery

Automation of library catalogs, along with computerized indexes and abstracts, puts bibliographic access on the desks of a variety of users including academic faculty, students, researchers, business entrepreneurs, telecommuters, distance learners, school children, and hobbyists. This facilitated access to bibliographic information enhances awareness of library resources and increases expectation for delivery of indentified material. New attention is focused on the inadequacy of traditional services, which require the user to travel to a library to use resources or to request an interlibrary loan for items not held at the local library. Computers and technology give command to the individual and move emphasis away from institutions and organizations. *Megatrends 2000* (Naisbitt and Aburdene, 1990) devotes an entire chapter to the "triumph of the individual," emphasizing the newly found understanding in the 1990s that the success of society is based on the composite accomplishments of individuals. The combination of technology, which provides instant gratification, and the recognition of individual contributions sets the stage for users to expect a timely response that is specific to each separate need. It is no longer acceptable to treat all customers the same; institutions that continue to offer only one level of service, or only one type of access, are at risk of becoming obsolete. (Naisbitt and Aburdene, p. 333).

The response of libraries to this computerized age of the individual has concentrated on improved automated access to local holdings and enhanced bibliographic access to resources outside the library. There is an expanding trend, especially among academic research libraries, to include access to resources in the same equation as building collections, using acquisition funds to purchase access to electronic resources and databases. However, a plan for document delivery of electronically identified material has been alarmingly absent. Although the telecommunication path for bibliographic access to the individual is being strengthened, there is little attention being given to the development of a corresponding document delivery path. The delivery link is critical if libraries are to maintain a leadership role in providing information.

ILL provides a model of successful transfer of resources among libraries to serve individual user needs. It is important to expand this traditional role to include planned delivery of identified resources held not only in libraries, but also in electronic databases or distributed through commercial services. Expanded ILL service, more appropriately called *library document delivery*, acts as an electronic guide to the user and equips a library with the means to offer simple and predictable access to needed documents; it broadens the current library-to-library lending system and provides a single electronic access point for users to obtain direct delivery of needed items. Libraries are at varying stages of offering this expanded service, with some of the large research libraries currently providing a full range of options. Librarians in charge of the lending branch of the National Agricultural Library (NAL) describe current document delivery service provided by NAL as including full-text retrieval, networking, outreach, the use of document delivery vendors, and a wide range of technological innovation (Ditzler, 1990). The overwhelming increase in the use of new technologies for information dissemination, as well as the overwhelming amount of information now available, dictates the need for libraries to provide facilitated access to alternatives for document delivery.

An example of movement in this direction is the MELDOC program at the University of California at Irvine. It allows dial-in users of MELVYL (the University of California nine-campus online union catalog) to request electronically campus document delivery of identified items or to request an ILL when the item is not held locally. The newest module adds another option for users by linking directly with commercial document delivery suppliers and permitting the user, for a fee, to select rapid direct delivery of selected titles (Smith and Lynch, 1990). The MELVYL document delivery request system includes special files such as the MEDLINE database. A user is able to transfer a citation identified in MELVYL MEDLINE to an electronic message, which is routed to his or her home campus library collection, where it is either filled from that collection or referred to another campus to be filled by ILL. Linkage to an outside vendor is planned to support delivery of items not available within the University of California system (Horres, Starr, and Renford, 1991). This integrated service provides the individual user with facilitated access to several options for document delivery. It is easy and predictable, with the cost and expected turnaround time defined at the point of access, and it eliminates the frustration of mastering a different procedure for accessing each of the increasing number of choices to obtain a needed item. The process of merging traditional ILL service with a full range of document delivery options allows provision of the single-point access service that is desired by the user. Only libraries possess retrospective holdings, a critical element in the information access equation. Gateways and interfaces are needed to facilitate document retrieval from library collections as well as from commercial document sources. The speed at which librarians move to create these links will determine the ultimate place of libraries in the information arena. A library document delivery service provides the connection between an identified bibliographic citation and the specified document. Where the requested material is obtained, whether from the local library, another library, an electronic information bank, or a commercial supplier, is not of concern to the patron as long as requirements of time and cost are met.

The 1990s find most large libraries with the technology and expertise to focus attention on diminishing the existing barriers between users and needed material. The evolution of ILL into an enhanced library-based document delivery service requires a close review of existing library-to-library delivery mechanisms, application of technology to transfer of facsimiles of materials, and facilitated use of existing fee-based document sources. What tools do libraries currently have to address delivery demand, and how may these be merged successfully into a first class document delivery service?

III. Delivery Options

A close look at delivery methods, comparing their advantages and disadvantages, helps to identify the options for libraries to take a more proactive posture in meeting the information needs of users. Five factors are important in analyzing the desirability of each delivery mode; these are cost, speed, reliability, ease of use, and, in the case of fascimile, the quality of the received document.

A. Traditional Methods

Traditional methods of mail and courier delivery are critical for transport of loaned material. Physical movement of either the user or the material is necessary to successfully match an individual patron with a monograph not held locally. It is unlikely, if not impossible, that a day will come when all materials will be scanned digitally into electronic databases for remote access. Traditional delivery methods remain significant to library users, especially for access to the enormous retrospective collections; these unique materials may never be available electronically.

1. Mail Services

The United States Postal Service (USPS) offers the advantages of being familiar and delivering almost anywhere. Despite the significant increase of library rates in 1991, the special library rate category, enacted by Congress in 1928, keeps traditional mail service a cost-effective option for delivery of loaned material between libraries. Speed is a different story. In 1978, library-rate packages took 5 days to be delivered, and photocopies mailed first class took 2 days (Kaya and Hurlebaus, 1978). Experience today is not greatly different, although actual delivery time varies with geographic location. For instance, in Colorado, libraries located along the Denver ubran metroplex, or "front range," receive mail in 2 days from other "front range" locations, but libraries located on the "western slope," on the other side of the Continental Divide, average 5 days to receive mail from the Denver area. United Parcel Service (UPS) offers an alternative for most libraries, although accessibility is still not as widespread as the USPS. UPS shaves 2 to 3 days off postal service delivery time, depending on geographical location, but required insurance keeps the per-item cost higher.

Reliability of USPS is high based on the tradition of "the mail goes through"; however, it is a rare individual who cannot relate a personal experience that transforms this tradition to the status of a myth. The same record of inconsistent reliability is true with UPS. Nonetheless, mail services continue to play a role in delivery of loaned library items by offering an economical transport system, especially for libraries outside a local or regional courier loop. Most importantly, express services offered by USPS and UPS, along with Federal Express, offer the only current option for same day or overnight rush delivery of physical items. Although local courier arrangements may fill the need for rush delivery of selected loans, mail services are the sole source for very rapid service on a regional, national, or international level.

2. Courier Services

Courier services are common in universities among main campuses and branches or other off-campus sites. In addition, many formal and informal courier services serve multitype libraries in close geographic vicinity. Well-planned courier systems benefit users with fast economical delivery of materials. Cooperative efforts allow libraries to negotiate highly efficient and economical transport systems among libraries in a specific region; this is a clear advantage over independent document delivery suppliers. Several states, including Pennsylvania and Colorado, have courier systems that connect libraries across the entire state. In Pennsylvania, the courier utilizes the services of UPS with a negotiated contract; Colorado service is a combination of state-operated courier routes and a commercial carrier (Deekle, 1990; Campbell, 1990; Fayad, 1990). Some library couriers cross state lines; the Colorado courier, for instance, includes stops at libraries in Laramie and Cheyenne, Wyoming. An ambitious multistate library courier is under discussion by members of the Association of Big Eight Universities (ABEU), covering libraries stretching from Missouri to Colorado, New Mexico to Iowa. Courier systems offer libraries the opportunity to match user expectation with predictable delivery options. For instance, a courier service could move people, in addition to or instead of, books. Delivery times may be matched with different levels of demand at different libraries, and time-consuming wrapping requirements are streamlined. Formal and informal courier services continue to augment USPS and UPS routine delivery options and provide an important mechanism for libraries to share materials. Efficient use of couriers demands close attention to both schedules and appropriate materials for transport. Time and cost factors need periodic review against alternative mail or commercial services. Advances in technology, offering improved delivery options for a portion of materials traditionally moved by courier, may change the definition of a desirable schedule or route. For instance, if transmission of time-sensitive material is resolved by electronic delivery, the primary focus of a courier might become ease of use, security of materials, and delivery cost.

B. Advances in Technology

Technology provides users with a solution to their need for speedy delivery, but also creates new, sometimes overwhelming, hardware or software requirements for utilization. The user's need for high-resolution documents, along with his or her time and technological limitations, will determine how a document is transmitted by ILL staff. However, it is important for libraries to assist users in sorting through the available delivery choices and also to serve as a relay center, when necessary, to equalize access to the more sophisticated, high-quality document delivery technologies.

1. Telefacsimile

Telefacsimile (fax) machines transmit copies of documents over telephone lines. The use of fax is now commonplace in libraries to meet the increased demands of users for rapid document delivery. Advances in speed of transmission, increased memory for storing and sending documents overnight, improved copy quality, and lower cost have all made fax more acceptable for library applications. It is unfortunate that the concept of *rush* has been so tightly bound to the word *fax*. This has inhibited the development of fax as an accepted, and expected, routine document delivery method for libraries. Fax, or any other new technology, may or may not allow the most rapid possible delivery of a specific item. To reach maximum efficiency, any technology should be merged on an equal basis with existing options.

For fax to be fully integrated into a library's document delivery service, it is critical that high-end equipment be used. This benefits both a lender and a borrower and promotes routine use of fax for article delivery. Important features for a fax machine from the standpoint of a lender include: a scanner to eliminate the need to photocopy first, a large memory for storing documents and taking advantage of off-hour phone rates, memory to accommodate frequently used phone numbers, resolution and half-tone adjustment for sending high-quality copy, fast scan and transmittal speed for efficiency, and automatic error reports. These features support efficient use of staff and allow provision of quality fax at the lowest possible cost. Use of a fax machine that combines these features may allow a library to transmit fax copies to other libraries at a lower cost than supplying them through the mail or even on the courier. High prone charges are frequently cited as a reason libraries hesitate to use fax routinely. However, the cost quoted to transmit a five-page article from Philadelphia to Baltimore in 1988 was only ninety-nine cents (Jackson, 1988). Participants in a Washington state project report an average thirty-six cents per page transmission cost (Moore, 1988). During a recent telefacsimile document delivery project, the Center for Research Libraries (CRL) found that the addition of 20 MB (megabytes) of memory to their fax machine, permitting overnight transmission of documents, reduced telecommunication costs by 48%. The actual cost averaged less than sixteen cents per page (Davis and Simpson, 1991). These studies indicate that communication charges, even during prime afternoon hours, compare favorably with mailing the article and paying postage cost, envelope and mailing label cost, and staff time to prepare the article for mailing. When a fax with a direct-copy scanner is used, eliminating the photocopy cost, the fax transmission becomes even more cost effective. Lenders concerned with phone costs might also consider use of a secure polling network for high-volume borrowers. This permits the lender to store articles that are accessible only by the requesting library. The borrowing fax calls the lending fax during off-rate phone hours, and by giving a coded handshake, or password, has waiting articles transmitted to it, along with the incurred telecommunication charges. This approach is limited to a relatively small group of cooperating libraries; it is currently used by a consortium of health science libraries in the eastern part of the United States. (Divens, 1991).

From the standpoint of a borrower, the use of plain paper is the single most important feature in a fax machine. This is critical to the quality of the received copy and to patron satisfaction. Thermal paper is unacceptable for all but very temporary information. Users dislike it and immediately copy it onto plain paper for actual use. A high quality printer, preferably a laser printer, and storage to accommodate incoming pages when paper or toner is depleted are also important borrowing features. There are several sophisticated fax machines available that combine these desirable features for both a lender and a borrower; they include the Canon L920, the Fujitsu 7800, and the Xerox 3010. Although these machines involve a larger investment initially, they permit a library to provide high quality fax copy to its users and to transmit fax copies to other libraries in an efficient, cost-effective manner. The borrower benefits from rapid, quality transmission, and the lender trims delivery costs.

Some sophisticated Group III fax machines, such as the Canon L920, have an RS232 serial port allowing cable link to a microcomputer and interface with Group IV fax units. This addresses the need for additional memory in a large volume fax operation, and also provides opportunity for combining fax with digital transmission.

2. Digital Transmission

a. RLG Ariel. The Research Libraries Group (RLG) has beta tested a document transmission workstation, Ariel, in the ILL departments of six university research libraries: Colorado State University, Dartmouth College, University of California at Berkeley and at Davis, University of Michigan, and University of Pennsylvania. Ariel supports digital transmission of articles over the Internet, a network of hundreds of computer networks connecting universities and research institutions across the United States, Canada, Europe, and Asia (Matthews, 1991). It does this by combining RLG application software with off-the-shelf hardware, including an IBM-compatible microcomputer, a document scanner, and a laser printer. Staff can scan articles directly from a bound volume at the lending library. The articles are compressed to less than 10% of their original size for rapid transmission in digital form, conveyed over the Internet, and then printed out on a laser printer at the receiving library. Operation is menu-driven and use is facilitated by function keys.

Because it is nondedicated equipment, Ariel offers all the advantages of an extra microcomputer in the office. The microcomputer, scanner, and printer may be used for any application when not being used to scan or print articles. RLG is developing a link between Ariel and fax that will support communication with Group III or Group IV fax machines. This will further expand the flexibility of Ariel and permit interfacing with a greater number of libraries as well as more individual users.

From the receiving viewpoint, high-quality, high-resolution copy printed with a laser printer on plain paper at 300×300 dpi (dots per inch) is one of the most striking advantages of Ariel; it is especially impressive for graphs, chemical or mathematical formulas, illustrations, and photographs. No human intervention is required to receive materials. Articles automatically print out on the laser printer attached to Ariel. Should paper or toner run out during receipt, articles are stored in the microcomputer until supplies are replenished. High-volume users may wish to purchase a duplex laser printer, allowing printing on both sides of each sheet of paper.

Ariel is a modular workstation; a receive-only station is possible by combining the software with a microcomputer and laser printer. This increases the options for affordable direct delivery to users, either individuals or groups, such as an academic department. To address the concern of a department or individual making infrequent use of Ariel and not placing the microcomputer in a receive mode on a regular basis, RLG is planning a feature to make it possible to hold the file in the ILL department and just message to the individual that material has arrived; the user could then pull the file over from the ILL microcomputer when desired.

To the lender, Ariel offers the advantage of direct scanning from a bound volume; there is no need to photocopy articles first. A supplier saves not only the photocopy charges but also direct telecommunication charges because transmission is over the Internet. Scanning directly from journals may require a different staffing pattern for the supplying library, but it is a very cost-effective way to provide copies of articles. The article is scanned in once and then, unlike using a fax machine, there are an unlimited number of automatic tries until transmission is successful. To avoid perpetual attempts at delivery when the requesting end is out of commission for a lengthy time, RLG is including an expiration-date feature in production software. After 2 or 3 days, or whatever time period is assigned by the lender, an undelivered article automatically prints out on the lender's printer and then may be sent by fax or through the mail. The document storage capacity on Ariel is very large, much greater than that of available fax machines. A fax machine with 32 MB of memory reaches capacity at less than 100 pages of journal text. In contrast, a microcomputer with an 80-MB hard drive accommodates in excess of 600 pages of journal text as a result of Ariel's compression of material to one tenth its original size. A larger hard disk may be added to handle higher storage needs.

Ariel also may be configured as a send-only station by combining the software with a scanner and microcomputer. This application could handle transmission of articles from a storage facility, or branch library, to the main library and reduce turnaround time below that of courier delivery. Wear and tear on the physical volumes would also diminish.

Scanning technology as of this date does not adequately support all library applications. Affordable scanners, such as the Hewlett-Packard (HP) Scanjet Plus or Panasonic FS-RS506 used with Ariel, have uncomfortably long scan times (16 to 18 minutes per page on the HP Scanjet) and lack scanning beds to easily accommodate tightly bound volumes. A shorter scan time, and provision of a flatbed that comes clear to the edge of the scanner, would facilitate document delivery applications and also offer better protection for library materials. Slow scanning is not unique to the HP and Panasonic scanners; the University of California, Berkeley, library staff feels the scan time with the Canon L920 fax machine makes it unacceptable for large-scale daily use. The staff at Berkeley photocopies articles before faxing rather than utilize the direct book-copying feature (Smith and Lynch, 1990). It is important that the library community make its scanning needs known and work cooperatively toward making an impact on industry priorities and standards.

The general availability of Ariel to non-RLG libraries provides opportunity for digital transmission to be merged into routine document delivery operations of a large number of libraries. Ariel is especially attractive for consortiums; a cooperating group of libraries with access to the Internet could provide economical, rapid delivery of high-quality copy for users. RLG is cooperating with project directors of other Internet projects, including the Ohio State University fax link and the North Carolina State University/NAL project for digital transmission. Supported interface with each of these projects is the ideal for greatest benefit to all sizes of libraries, as well as users, each with dissimilar equipment configurations and varying telecommunication access capabilities. The Internet Engineering Task Force (IETF) is developing standards for image transmission on the Internet. This promises to facilitate interface of technological advances in each project and make digital transmission a mainstream form of document delivery.

b. NCSU/NAL Digital Text Transmission Project.   North Carolina State University (NCSU) libraries and the NAL are involved in a joint project for transmission of digitized text over the Internet. It is similar to the RLG project in that it uses a microcomputer linked to a scanner and printer at each participating location. However, it has been developed in a Macintosh microcomputer environment rather than using the IBM-compatible microcomputers maintained in the Ariel configuration. In addition, this project uses a host computer, usually a mainframe, at the recipient site. The file is transmitted in compressed form, similar to the Ariel system, and is reduced to approximately one tenth of its original size for rapid transmission over the Internet. Inclusion of a host computer requires that ILL staff at the receiving library check the file server of the mainframe computer periodically to see if items have arrived, just as one might check for receipt of electronic mail. When an article arrives, ILL staff retrieves it via an ethernet connection to the library's local area network (LAN) and then, after decompressing the file, has a choice of printing it out at a local printer, downloading it to a floppy diskette, or transmitting it to the user's workstation. The environment promotes the ability to display an image of text on a high resolution monitor and then import it into any software program that supports bit-mapped images (Casorso, 1991). High quality, high resolution documents are mentioned in this project as an outstanding benefit. It also takes advantage of the Internet for efficient, cost-free transmission. The variation of delivering the article to a host computer, rather than directly to a microcomputer in the library, offers potential for direct, unmediated delivery to the individual user. It would be just as easy for an individual user, rather than ILL staff, to call up the file on the mainframe and select delivery to a local printer or downloading to a floppy diskette. Staff at North Carolina State University libraries is testing this capability in a pilot project. North Carolina State's Electronic Document Delivery Service (EDDS) automatically notifies the user when an article arrives; the document number is matched with the user's e-mail address and triggers an electronic message announcing receipt. The individual researcher then retrieves the article from a university mainframe computer via the campus network (Casorso, 1992). The NCSU/NAL project is moving into expanded testing with the inclusion of 12 additional libraries in 1991–1992: Clemson University, University of Delaware, Iowa State University, University of Maryland at College Park, Michigan State University, University of Minnesota, North Carolina Agricultural and Technical State University, Ohio State University, Pennsylvania State University, Utah State University, Virginia Polytechnic Institute and State University, and Washington State University. Other hardware and software combinations will be evaluated, and attention will be given to merging the system into a library's ILL operation (NAL, 1991). The availability of user-direct delivery, including file import capability for use in other software programs, is an interesting variation to watch.

c. Ohio State University Internet/Fax Delivery. The Big Ten library project, based at Ohio State University, is being beta tested at Ohio State University, University of Cincinnati, and Indiana University. It differs from the other two projects in that it links fax technology, using a microcomputer as mediator, with Internet transmission. Off-the-shelf microcomputer and fax components are combined with public domain software. The project addresses concern with high long-distance charges for fax transmission, reportedly reaching several thousand dollars per year at Ohio State and other Big Ten institutions. In this configuration, a fax machine takes the place of the scanner and printer required with Ariel and the NCSU/NAL design. An article is scanned into the fax machine at the supplying library, and a file transfer protocol is used to send the article over the ethernet to a microcomputer, with a fax board, located in the same room. The article is then transmitted over the Internet with a communication protocol, transfer control protocol/Internet protocol (TCP/IP), which supports data exchange between different computing environments. It is received by a microcomputer, with a fax board, in the requesting library and is transmitted to a nearby fax machine for actual printing of the article (Kennedy, 1991). Some participants in this project report that the process is cumbersome because of the in-library transfer between the fax machine and the microcomputer in the supplying library and then from the microcomputer to the fax machine in the receiving library. An advantage to this system is that it allows interface with an existing fax operation and it is likely that an individual user would have access to fax technology. The fax machine can continue to work over telephone lines for deliveries and receipts to and from libraries without Internet gateways. Project directors report on the "ILL-L: Interlibrary Loan discussion group" electronic bulletin board that the addition of a scanner and laser printer to the basic microcomputer would allow interface with Ariel. They are also interested in flexible delivery options, including file delivery over local area networks (Kalal, 1991).

d. Other Projects. Local projects at libraries of various sizes highlight the marked interest in electronic document delivery. The most innovative of these share in common recognition of the need to meet information demands of remote users and further recognition of the library's role to serve as mediator between the user and alternative delivery mechanisms.

Lehigh University in Bethlehem, Pennsylvania, uses a campus-wide network to electronically support library services in the remote Mountaintop campus. Users may electronically submit requests for photocopy or ILL, place recalls, make recommendations for book or journal purchases, ask reference questions, and consult a number of full-text, locally produced databases of reference tools. A number of compact disk (CD–ROM) databases are also available, and an expert system offers use instruction. Fax machines are used for document delivery, and plans call for merging fax technology with the campus-area network to support downloading an article file to the user's microcomputer so that it may be read on the screen or printed out on a laser printer. The proposed system would allow the user, or the library, to send an article request to a commercial document delivery supplier and have the article faxed directly to the requestor. The plan also includes provision for electronic notification of the user when a fax is waiting and allows the file to be downloaded or printed at the user's workstation (Richards and Johnson, 1990).

Geographic barriers in Alaska are decreased by an innovative document delivery system. Requested articles are scanned at the University of Alaska, Fairbanks, using a Kurzweil machine, a sophisticated instrument designed to translate text into speech for visually impaired users; the article is then converted to American Standard Code for Information Interchange (ASCII) text and uploaded for transmission by electronic mail to the requestor. When the file is received by the requestor's IBM-compatible microcomputer, it is printed out on a local printer. Because the article is transmitted as ASCII data, only the text is included, not illustrations, graphs, or pictures (Taber, 1991). Information gleaned from projects such as this may provide valuable information for future document delivery configurations.

C. End-User Services

1. Databases with Document Delivery Components

In response to increased user demand, online search services are increasing the number of document delivery options available, and are facilitating users' ability to retrieve documents. For instance, DIALOG Information Retrieval Services (DIALOG) links the user with over 70 document delivery services; once a citation to a needed document has been identified, an order can be placed for direct delivery without rekeying bibliographic information. Hundreds of thousands of publications are ordered this way each year through online services (Bourne, 1990). Search services, such as DIALOG or BRS Information Technologies (BRS), provide gateways to support menu-driven, end-user searching. Use of these services is facilitated by libraries that provide direct telecommunication access for their clientele. For example, the Pikes Peak Library District in Colorado Springs, Colorado, has an extensive computer system called Maggie's Place. One component of Maggie's Place is LINK, which allows users to connect through any terminal on Maggie to remote computers and telecommunication networks such as DIALOG (Westin and Finger, 1991). This link supports user access to the full range of document delivery sources embedded in online search services. However, no online service provides delivery of all indexed items; it remains important to include an alternative path for items not supplied through commercial services. An option would be to permit users to download citations for items not available through direct delivery service or for items the user prefers to obtain in some other, possibly less costly, manner to them and support uploading into a local library document delivery service.

UnCover 2, a joint project of CARL Systems, Inc. (CSI) and the Colorado Alliance of Research Libraries (CARL), demonstrates a specialized document delivery service tailored to provide delivery from local or coordinated holdings in libraries. The UnCover database, begun in 1988, includes the table of contents of the combined serial holdings of CARL Member Libraries. The delivery component of UnCover promises article delivery by fax within 24 hours. The service includes optical scanning and storage of the article when first requested and immediate fax delivery of subsequent requests. CARL staff is placed in CARL Member Libraries to retrieve and scan articles requested for the first time. Like other online links to document delivery suppliers, article copyright fees are included in the delivery cost and the user is provided with "one-stop-shopping" by the ability to locate, order, and receive documents at a remote terminal. UnCover is available as a gateway service to libraries not belonging to CARL. The gateway may be customized to include local holdings and call-number information. For instance, the UnCover gateway at the California State University system includes 17 California State campuses, 12 of which plan to customize their versions to reflect local library holdings. California State also plans to use CARL as a platform to include other online databases and commercial document delivery options for users ("ON TRACK," 1991). CARL Member Library users of UnCover are advised online that articles are available through ILL as well as delivery by UnCover2. To facilitate the alternative of ILL for article delivery, some CARL users are interested in developing an electronic link from the database to the user's ILL or library document delivery service to support user-generated requests for ILL. CARL-identified locations would be attached to the request; the borrowing library could then arrange the order of the lending string as appropriate for automatic referral among CARL lenders. Requests not satisfied by a CARL library could be sent on to other libraries. This system is planned for a workstation environment to allow interface with the Online Computer Library Center (OCLC), or another system, for those libraries wishing to upload requests for transmission beyond the CARL group.

Access is planned by OCLC in 1992 through the OCLC EPIC online reference system and its end-user service, FirstSearch, to a table of contents database covering journals in science, engineering, business, and medicine. FirstSearch, a user-friendly menu-driven program, will allow users to search by subject for books and other material included in OCLC's bibliographic database as well as a variety of indexing and abstracting tools. The table of contents service, Faxon Finder, will include delivery of needed articles by fax or Faxon XPress, Faxon Research Services' document delivery service. Future plans for the service include direct document delivery to a user's computer (Faxon's Journal, 1991; Wilson, 1991a). Journal contents information services, linked directly with speedy delivery systems, provide the individual user with a full circle of access to identification of needed information and delivery of the actual document. It is important that libraries remain visible in this environment by providing easy access to local holdings and alternative access to actual documents. Ideally, a searcher on FirstSearch will be able to identify which needed articles are available locally and receive ready assistance in identifying other local holdings to meet his or her information needs. OCLC indicates intention to provide a link from the bibliographic databases on FirstSearch to the holdings file of the OCLC Online Union Catalog; this will provide the link for users at OCLC libraries to know if a journal identified in any of the FirstSearch databases is held locally. An electronic link to local ILL services is necessary to provide library-mediated access for the user to items not locally owned.

An excellent example of linking the user electronically, regardless of location, to the holdings of the primary library and also an extended group of libraries exists in the medical library community. The National Library of Medicine's (NLM) Grateful Med system allows an individual user to search and identify articles in any of the more than 40 NLM databases including MEDLINE, which indexes 3500 medical journals (Colaianni, 1990). Actual delivery of the article is now facilitated with a recent link to Grateful Med, called Loansome Doc, which allows the user to generate an electronic request to his or her primary library for document delivery of specific articles. If the request cannot be filled in the host library, it may be referred to another participating library without rekeying the bibliographic information. Loansome Doc supports library document delivery service to health care professionals, regardless of geographical location; charges and service are the same as for users who come to the library, or call, for ILL assistance (Gadzikowski, 1991). Based on wide-spread interest in the NLM databases, a variety of commercial end-user searching systems have been developed to facilitate use. PaperChase is a computer program that provides a user-friendly interface for searching MEDLINE, the largest of the NLM databases. This commercially available computer program allows users to successfully retrieve citations in MEDLINE without knowledge of the NLM medical subject headings (MeSH) and with very little or no training. PaperChase is a popular interface when MEDLINE is provided in a network environment to a variety of users. In addition to enhanced, user-friendly searching capabilities, PaperChase permits the user, with a single keystroke, to order a full-text photocopy of any of the citations identified on MEDLINE. Most articles are mailed first class the next business day for a flat fee; express mail or fax delivery is available for an additional charge (King, 1990; Lawson, 1990). MEDLINE offers the best example of a database with linkages to alternative delivery systems, library delivery through Loansome Doc, and commercial delivery through PaperChase.

   Table of contents level indexing for books is also emerging on electronic systems. For instance, Meckler Publishing is producing table of contents indexing for its technology books, as well as journals, and makes the service available through an electronic connection with Princeton University's JvNCNET, linked to the Internet. Users may order facsimile copies of chapters from books as well as articles from journals (Nelson, 1991). Another major player, Blackwell North America, is also planning chapter level indexing for monographs.

2. Full-Text Article Services

There are a growing number of online services available that link citations with full-text articles that may be transmitted directly to a user's computer or printed out and faxed or mailed to the requester. Examples include the Information Access Company's *Magazine ASAP* and *Trade & Industry ASAP*. These products may be accessed through a number of sources including

BRS, DIALOG, Dow Jones, Mead Data Central (NEXIS), and CARL. It is troublesome to the user that each source for the service provides different coverage dates for the journals and newspapers included, and also variations in the actual titles indexed. Time lag for inclusion on each system also varies, sometimes by as much as 5 weeks. In addition, actual material included in full-text coverage varies by the service. Most deal with only text, not graphics, and some drop even more than that, for instance, letters to the editor or columns. There is also inconsistency about inclusion of special issues. (Quint, 1991; Tenopir, 1991). As options proliferate, it becomes more important for users to have a single source for assistance in identifying choices. Libraries are in an excellent position to facilitate use of these services for patrons with time-sensitive needs and also to provide alternatives as necessary. The libraries of the University of Tennessee, Knoxville (UTK) have developed an innovative method to manage this expanding number of alternatives by development of the Electronic Journal List (EJL). EJL is a database developed using dBASE III +; it identifies journals available electronically including host system, file name, time coverage of the online journal, and UTK library subscription information. Although much of the information is duplicated in the publication *Fulltext Sources Online*, a reference tool published by Biblio-Data, UTK library staff feels EJL is valuable because of its quarterly update and linkage with local subscription information. As appropriate, articles needed by users are ordered by library staff from full-text services. Most articles obtained this way involve modest costs; some articles are less than $2. The most expensive are those citations that demand complex search strategy to identify in the supplying database; the highest article cost experienced by UTK is less than $20. UTK currently obtains journal articles, free of charge to the patron, from electronic sources as a regular ILL function (Gillikin, 1990). In addition to fast access to the text of requested articles, this approach avoids copyright restrictions linked to ILL acquisition. Electronic document delivery from full-text sources for immediate computer printout is currently limited to text; charts, graphs, tables, and illustrations are not included. This limitation makes it important to provide alternative delivery, which includes full graphics.

Progress beyond the text-only limitation is possible with document storage on CD–ROM, as demonstrated by the European Article Delivery Over Network Information Systems (ADONIS) project. Journals are sent directly from publishers to the ADONIS office in Amsterdam, indexed by Excerpta Medica, assigned a specific ADONIS number, and scanned on a weekly basis; copies of articles are stored and supplied on CD–ROM. ADONIS allows storage of both text and graphics by use of two different scanning modes—threshold for text and dither for graphics. Use of dithering while scanning an article allows shades and textures in the color or gray-scale original to be reflected in shades of gray or black and white in a computer display or print version. Access to articles is currently through document supply services; in the United States suppliers are Information on Demand (IOD) in Berkeley, California, and University Microfilms, Inc. (UMI) in Ann Arbor, Michigan (Stern and Campbell, 1989). The software used with ADONIS is being improved to increase the number of pages stored on one CD–ROM from the original 7,000 pages per disc to 15,000 pages per disc, the actual number varying with the density of graphics. The retrieval software is being enhanced for speed and user friendliness, and the number of titles included exceeds 400 in 1991. The updated product is designed to operate on off-the-shelf hardware rather than requiring a specialized workstation, and use of jukeboxes allows facilitated access to a very large number of disks (Stern and Compier, 1990). This increased capacity and flexibility makes it a more attractive option for on-demand delivery of articles.

ADONIS likely served as a model for UMI's image workstation for searching and printing articles stored in four full-text image databases contained on compact disk: Business Periodicals Ondisc, General Periodicals Ondisc, Social Sciences Index/Full Text, and IEE/IEEE Periodicals Ondisc. Articles may be retrieved by searching the database or by paging through individual copies of journals on the disk. A desired article can then be displayed on the screen and enlarged or printed out on an attached laser printer. The price for such a product is high and is likely to be beyond the reach of many individual libraries. For example, one database, Business Periodicals Ondisc, is priced close to $20,000 (King, 1991).

These products may be networked, using the Image Print Server, so that multiple users can search the databases and request prints of articles. A large scale installation of the UMI image print server is being tested at Carnegie-Mellon University (CMU) in Pittsburgh. Multiple jukeboxes are linked and mounted on the Library Information System II campus network and provide faculty and students at CMU with instant access to over 7 million pages of text; articles, complete with graphs and illustrations, may be printed on demand (Carnegie Mellon, 1991). The ability to successfully include graphics in full-text storage makes it a superior choice for on-demand document delivery. With the addition of network capability, there is potential for it to be the prevailing source in article document delivery.

Another project looking at networking electronic sources is based at Cornell University. This experiment uses a Xerox DocuTech, a machine that works like a photocopier and is able to print 160 pages a minute from electronic files; networked electronic sources can be accessed, and printed, as needed by users in remote locations (Gherman, 1991). Networking agreements for electronic sources are critical for libraries to offer a full range of access to documents; this is another area where cooperative resource sharing can promote equality in access for all users.

3. Electronic Publishing

Electronic journals are composed of text, just like paper journals, and are transmitted over computer networks to individual subscribers who may read issues online or download desired parts for a print copy. Most electronic publications do not include graphs, charts, or illustrations; however, a recent American Association for the Advancement of Science (AAAS) journal *Current Clinical Trials* includes sophisticated graphs and illustrations that may be viewed by users with a high resolution graphics monitor and Windows 3.0 software, along with at least 2 MB of random access memory (RAM). Only a very small percentage of published journal titles are currently available in electronic format, but there is considerable interest in and discussion about these products. Electronic journals boast very rapid turnaround time for publication and provide opportunity for immediate reaction and exchange among readers. For instance, the refereed electronic journal *PSYCOLOQUY* promotes immediate peer review by refereeing each original comment entered on the network, usually within hours of receipt, in an attempt to maintain high interest and rapid interaction of ideas. Electronic journals are currently available on Bitnet, the interuniversity communications network; issues are sent electronically to each individual subscriber's electronic mailbox. Some are also available over Internet, where journals are transmitted to subscribed sites rather than individuals (Electronic Journal, 1991; Wilson, 1991b). For libraries linked to Internet, there is opportunity to provide access to these journals through centralized library terminals. Copyright issues need to be resolved for widespread growth to occur in electronic publishing. Unlike their paper counterparts, however, current electronic journals do not request exclusive copyright and allow authors to retain control of their material, promoting easy access and copying on the networks. Probably a bigger concern is the technology and hardware that end users currently have available. Very few users have the high resolution monitors and state-of-the-art color printers necessary to view and produce quality copies of needed articles. It is unlikely that consumers will be willing to accept mediocre copies as the only print access to publications (Weber, 1990). Although it is likely that individual libraries will not be able to afford equipment with the advanced capabilities required for quality print copies from electronic documents, it may be an area where cooperative library initiatives can fill the gap and provide relayed delivery of required articles to requestors.

4. Information Brokers

Information brokers are willing and able to deliver requested documents to users in virtually any geographic location. These services first appeared in the early 1970s; since then, especially since 1989, there has been a rapid increase in the number of such operations in the United States (Maxwell, 1990). The fourth edition of *Document Retrieval Sources and Services* (1987) lists over 200 organizations providing these services. This includes libraries that provide document delivery services for users beyond the library's basic community, nonprofit organizations, which provide services from their collections for nonmembers, database producers, who maintain a collection of the material they abstract and index, and commercial services, which are privately based. High-paying clients of information brokers list speed as the primary concern; frequently these are users who find traditional library services too time-consuming to utilize. Information brokers make frequent use of electronic ordering services such as those provided by DIALOG and BRS; they also take advantage of full-text articles, including titles stored in the ADONIS project and, more recently, UnCover2 delivery features. However, commercial document suppliers also rely on libraries for many, perhaps the majority, of the documents supplied to their clients. Holdings are identified through the national bibliographic utilities and the many library catalogs now accessible on the Internet, such as MELVYL, CARL, and ILLINET. Retrieval of documents is done by a combination of "runners" in major libraries and participation in traditional ILL services. The relationship between commercial services and libraries is strained at times when libraries view these services as parasitic on their collections rather than providing a needed service to clientele with time requirements libraries are not able to meet. The balance of dependence, however, is currently shifting, and a closer, more cooperative alliance is developing. The enormous increase in quantity of ILL activity and the increasing expectations of users have forced use of all available options, including use of commercial suppliers. This is facilitated by the many document suppliers now accessible on the ILL subsystems of the bibliographic utilities. The Research Libraries Information Network (RLIN) includes access to Engineering Information Inc. (Ei) Document Delivery Service (EiDDS), and OCLC provides a link to UMI, IOD, Chemical Abstracts Services (CAS), National Technical Information Services (NTIS), the ERIC Document Reproduction Service (EDRS), and the Institute for Scientific Information's "Genuine Article" document delivery service. Indeed, in recent years, UMI has ranked as the largest lender on the OCLC ILL subsystem (Jackson, 1990a). The Engineering Information service on RLIN includes searchable citations based on the tables of contents of over 3,000 engineering journals and conference proceedings and boasts availability on RLIN 6 weeks earlier than Ei's abstracts index, Compendex Plus. It provides the same immediate ordering function at the article level as provided by a service such as DIALOG's DIALORDER, but promotes use by library staff because of its facilitated inclusion in the regular ILL workflow.

IV. Future Trends for Library Document Delivery

Libraries will be able to provide "one-stop-shopping" for its users by the incorporation and management of all delivery options within a library document delivery service. Libraries will become switching centers that will supply information and material from a variety of sources. Expanding networks will allow library services to be provided electronically to users in remote locations; they also will provide gateways to access services located around the world. Many libraries, including major research libraries, will be linked directly into the national telecommunication backbone, currently represented by the Internet, and will be in a position to supplement the services of smaller libraries. It will become increasingly important for even the smallest libraries, while specializing in immediate information needs of its clientele, to acquire knowledge on entry points for users to obtain access to a broad range of information sources (Beiser, 1991).

A. Delivery to Individuals

The standards document "Standards for university libraries: Evaluation of performance" (1989), jointly adopted by the Association of College and Research Libraries (ACRL) and the Association of Research Libraries (ARL), addresses underlying assumptions for access and states

> With the development of online catalogs, telefacsimile transmission, and other forms of information transfer, many users are now able to conduct their bibliographic research outside the library. In such instances, providing access implies the delivery of information, whether in printed or electronic format, by the library to the user at the user's location. This process should be reflected in the policies and procedures of the library. (p. 684)

There is evidence that direct delivery to patrons of photocopy received by ILL is occurring; respondents to a question posed in August 1991 on the "ILL-L: Interlibrary Loan discussion group" electronic bulletin board overwhelmingly indicate this practice. Variations arise in whether articles are mailed to off-campus addresses where postage charges are incurred and requirement for patrons to retrieve articles when there is a fee involved. However, there is also recognition by many ILL offices that mailing photocopy directly to the requester speeds receipt of the article and also saves staff effort by reducing patron interaction time.

ILL offices around the country have made countless changes to streamline procedures within their own operations in an attempt to handle the exponential growth in the number of requests. There are further opportunities to look beyond the walls of each individual operation and examine the circle of interaction between the borrowing and lending library. A close look at this interchange makes it readily apparent that there is unnecessary, duplicated effort. Once a request is filled by a lender, there is no reason for the borrowing library to put further effort into that request. Delivery of a requested item to the borrowing library, rather than directly to the individual requester, demands matching of paperwork and file updating; in addition, it requires resolving problem items that cannot be matched with requests, frequently a result of misfiling at the beginning of the process. The borrowing library needs only notification of unfilled requests; these do require additional effort by the requesting library to acquire material for the user. The ability to transmit a requested document electronically from the supplying library directly to another library's patron is noted by Jackson (1990b) as a potential benefit of a delivery system such as Ariel. It is logical to combine the proven efficiency of ILL offices sending photocopy directly to their own users with the goal of electronic delivery to support direct transmission from the lending library to the requesting individual. There is no reason to wait for technology to facilitate this concept.

Elimination of duplicate handling by the supplier and the borrowing library at the delivery end of the cycle is beneficial and promotes more rapid receipt of requested material. It is desirable, and likely, that direct delivery to the user will become accepted practice for requests involving copy. This transfer could be by mail, courier, fax, or digital transmission. It may be appropriate for borrowing libraries to continue to relay documents to individuals lacking appropriate hardware for electronic receipt; however, the predominant traffic pattern for efficient article delivery must eliminate unnecessary passage back through the requesting library. Elimination of this procedure for books or other loaned material involves more complex concerns. Yet, for easily replaceable items, it might be cost effective to allow direct delivery of loaned items to individuals. Books could be mailed in containers with reversible labels to facilitate user return. Borrowing libraries could continue to accept responsibility for lost or damaged items. As long as the borrowing library acts as mediator for placement of loan requests, it is possible to screen patron eligibility and also identify appropriate material for requests. Rare or expensive books could continue to be sent to the borrowing library and handled as "library use only" loans. Involvement of ILL service or library document delivery service at the beginning of the operation facilitates the process for patrons by providing one access point for alternative delivery sources; it also places the burden of tracking the request, and redirecting it to additional sources, on the library staff rather than the user. Security of the process is maintained by the borrowing library's ability to monitor appropriateness of requests as well as patron eligibility; this initial involvement is an efficient use of both staff and user time.

The benefit of early interaction with library staff to request material from other sources is demonstrated by the unwillingness of most participating libraries to use the patron module of the Illinois Library Network (ILLINET). The ILLINET patron-generated request module is designed to allow a user to route a request automatically to an identified holding library and have material shipped to a local library for use. Only two Illinois libraries, the University of Illinois at Urbana-Champaign and Lake Forest College Library, allow patrons to initiate a request directly. Other libraries require staff intervention to transmit the order (Newsome, 1991). The recognition that needed material may be available locally, that alternative sources may exist in the local library, and the desire to obtain the material from other sources when the request is not satisfied during the automated referral process, all combine to make libraries hesitant to turn the request process over to patrons. For maximum efficiency, ILL patterns must evolve that maintain initial patron interaction with the borrowing library, although this might be transparent to the user, but eliminate the need for duplicating work done by the lending library or other document supplier.

B. Link with Document Suppliers

Cooperation between libraries and commercial document delivery services will continue to expand in response to user demand. OCLC and RLIN will increase the number of document suppliers accessible through those utilities; in addition, there will be more libraries that provide users with telecommunication links to commercial suppliers, as exemplified by Maggie's Place in the Pikes Peak Library District, and also more frequent inclusion of direct document delivery modules through public access catalogs, similar to MELDOC in the University of California System. RLG has announced a variation on the link between the user and commercial suppliers. Individual users at institutions with campus-wide access to RLIN will be able to search commercial files of citations and, when a citation to a needed article is found, automatically send an order to their interlibrary loan department, which can then get it from another library or a commercial source (RLIN citations, 1991). Recognition of the natural inclusion of delivery from commercial sources in ILL services is demonstrated by the ARL request, when reporting 1990/91 ILL borrowing activity, to include the number of requests filled by document delivery services. It is essential for libraries to utilize all sources when identifying alternative locations for requests to meet patron demand. Telecommunication links must be nurtured to support direct ordering by users as appropriate, yet these links must provide gateways for requestors to utilize librarians' expertise, to navigate more easily the complex, expanding universe of electronic access to desired information and documents. Patrons identifying needed materials electronically should not have to rekey bibliographic information; the ability to automatically request document delivery must be supported. Users must be presented with choices linked to predictable outcomes. This should include direct links to fee-based document suppliers for time-sensitive material, and facilitated requests for loaned material held in other library collections.

C. Link with Collection Development

There is a need to plan the entire circle of access to information and delivery of identified documents. Increased access to citations, such as availability of databases on CD–ROM, is diminished in usefulness when the document delivery half of the circle is missing. New Mexico State Library recently introduced a new resource sharing program called PICLIST that allows easy bibliographic access to available materials held at the State Library. The program produces 200 to 300 requests per day coming from libraries throughout the state. Despite the obvious success and popularity of the project, it is likely the program will cease at the end of the year because of the lack of staff to handle the demand. No funds were set aside for staff to actually fill incoming requests when the program was planned (Fischer, 1991). Document delivery must be considered as an integral part of any enhanced access.

User expectations and the increasing complexities for obtaining identified items demand that access and delivery be considered as a single piece. Without this focus in evaluation of access, libraries will lose credibility with users and increase the opportunity for commercial sources to price the average requestor out of the information link. It is impossible to ensure equal support, equal communication, and equal ability for all patrons, but planned information access, including a delivery component, promotes more equitable access regardless of the location of the user. To negotiate successfully with other libraries and document suppliers, it is necessary for a library to make a commitment to purchase, catalog, and maintain collections in designated disciplines; cooperative collection development must be more than just a myth. Despite numerous articles and discussions on the benefits of cooperative collection development, a working, active role model is impossible to find. The closest examples of cooperative effort occur as a result of forced weeding or serial cancellation projects; a healthy, successful program of active cooperative purchasing on a comprehensive level is yet to be identified. Some of the tools are in place; certainly the *RLG Conspectus* (1985–1988) for identifying strengths in a collection is a valuable tool for supporting such endeavors. Yet, how much planning is currently occurring to fill the gaps that already exist and will surely get worse as a result of massive serial cuts? How will libraries meet demand years down the road for the increasing number of rarely held items?

There is need right now to address this issue locally, statewide, regionally, and nationally. Binding commitments must be made by libraries to maintain these lesser held items, to provide bibliographic access on regional and national databases, and to make provision for actual delivery of requested material. It is critical that national bibliographic utilities be maintained. Self-contained stand-alone databases mean no one else outside the system knows what is available. There is need to lobby for government assistance, such as Library Services Construction Act (LSCA) funds, to encourage and support participation in national utilities, including OCLC and RLIN. As libraries achieve success in this area, they possess an invaluable bartering tool for maintaining leadership and control in the delivery of information. Commercial services, an essential element in any equation for successful document delivery, will correctly remain as a support enterprise in this scenario.

Nonexistent or incomplete access to serial holdings information remains a serious impediment to efficient resource sharing. A significant number of libraries contributing to RLIN provide holdings information, and the system supports easy access for the searcher to library-specific journal holdings information. This situation greatly facilitates ILL activity by resulting in high fill rates on the initial try. Perhaps the best example of cooperative control of serials is DOCLINE, the NLM-automated ILL system for medical libraries, where 80% of the contributing libraries report specific serial holdings. Because of this high level of participation, DOCLINE boasts an impressive ILL fill rate of 92% to 99%; the majority of requests are satisfied on the first or second location. DOCLINE links directly with SERHOLD, which indicates the specific holdings of each library owning a bibliographic title. This permits ILL requests to be routed automatically to libraries coded for the needed issue. Importance of standardized serials holdings information is demonstrated by the markedly lower fill rates among the medical libraries with nonstandardized holdings information (not in ANSI standard 1980, level 3). When a library has nonstandardized data, DOCLINE assigns a request based on whether a journal is currently published and whether the library has a current subscription. Even when these two requirements are met, up to 8% of the routed requests are unfilled because of incomplete holdings (Colaianni, 1990; Hill, 1989). It is imperative that holdings information be included in all state, regional, and national bibliographic efforts. The efficiency rate drops dramatically for any cooperative sharing of journal titles without this critical information, and it becomes impossible to guarantee that all volumes of a journal are available long term when libraries are forced to enter into serial cancellation efforts.

D. Telecommunication Environment

The entire telecommunication environment is becoming increasingly complex. Growth in the number of users, increase in the amount of use by each individual, and the development of more intensive applications, such as digital transmission of documents, have stretched current networks to their limits. Between 100,000 and 200,000 computers are currently connected directly to the Internet with six times as many users. By the end of the decade at least 1 million computers will be connected to the Internet with even more users (Weber, 1990). In response to this mushrooming need for higher capacity telecommunication lines, national legislation has been passed to establish a high speed Research and Education Network (NREN) by 1996 capable of transmitting data at 1 gigabit per second or greater. A national research network with high-speed optic fiber cable would allow researchers to exchange text, graphics, and even video information more rapidly and with a dependable response time. NREN would greatly enhance opportunities for predictable reliance on rapid document delivery from a remote site to a requester. The establishment of such a network is critical for achieving success in meeting the growing user demand for instant delivery of documents and information. A major concern in this area, however, is the lack of adequate telecommunication lines in some parts of rural America to support even voice phone or fax machines. How can these isolated but significant segments of the country be included in the rapid advances planned for the electronic highways? Prohibitive costs to connect the more remote areas of the country may exasperate the gap between the information rich and the information poor. Overall, technology helps to bridge these differences, both real and perceived, by facilitating some level of access to the major library resources. This partial access, however, may only serve to "whet the appetite" and make what one does not have available more obvious. Efforts should be made on a state and regional basis to assist in equalizing benefit from improved telecommunication networks. For instance, on a state or regional basis, relay stations in areas with access to optic fiber cables might facilitate transfer of documents to areas with minimal or no telecommunication connections. It is also possible that use of high-density storage media, such as CD–ROMs, may aid in alleviating the immediate need for high-speed telecommunication in sparsely populated areas. Indeed, the ultimate document delivery system serving a user in the future may well involve a linked combination of high-density storage devices and high-speed telecommunication lines; in some situations, it might be most efficient and likely much less expensive simply to transfer, perhaps by courier, an entire full-text database on CD–ROM (Kountz, 1991).

V. Conclusion

Predictions for library services in the future have a common theme of forecasting increased digitized information, increased electronic services, and a greater emphasis on services to the customer. This sets the stage for ILL, expanded into a library document delivery service, to become a primary service. As electronic information sources not only increase rapidly in number but also become increasingly decentralized, it will be critical to maintain a single gateway for the user to access the full range of available resources. Although this should rightly be the focus of the entire public service arm of a library, it will fall largely to the document delivery area to maintain a clear, unobstructed highway between an identified information source and the user; and this document delivery path will provide a highly visible evaluation tool for measuring the value of library services.

A model library document delivery service should do the following:

1. *Include campus-based or local library-based delivery from the home institution library, and also a full menu of options for delivery from other sources such as electronic databases, high-density storage discs, and other libraries.* Whether material is provided from a library's own collection or from a remote source is of little concern to the user in an electronic environment. Assisted document delivery decreases time the user must spend navigating complex bioliographic choices and increases the study time available once needed items are in hand. The need for facilitating placement of identified material in the hands of the user is recognized as a desirable goal (Kilgour, 1972; Gorman, 1991). A user in 1972 feeling frustration with the slow, complex access for obtaining library materials accepted the only service an institution provided; in the 1990s, however, this same patron simply abandons libraries as a source and looks elsewhere for satisfaction of information needs.

2. *Provide online bibliographic access for identifying materials linked with rapid document delivery of needed items.* Online databases including library catalogs will support the patron's ability to generate a request electronically, without rekeying bibliographic information, for delivery of an identified item. Routing of this request will include the option of transmission to a commercial document supplier as well as transmission to the document delivery service of the user's primary library.

3. *Allow the user to define cost and time parameters; the library document delivery service should then facilitate transfer of the request to the most efficient path allowed by these parameters, offering alternatives when the stipulated requirements cannot be met.* A user-provided indication of cost and time requirements will determine the appropriate path for a request. For example, a patron willing to pay a fee and needing an item quickly will have a request automatically routed to a commerical document supplier, whereas a student with limited funds but sufficient time will have a request routed to the ILL office for handling. The role of the library document delivery unit includes sorting through available options to provide the most efficient, rapid delivery of requested items and also merging the increasing number of items available from electronic or commercial sources or both with the ongoing stream of requests requiring traditional loans from other library collections. Document sources will include electronic databases and high-density disk storage of full-text articles as well as library collections.

4. *Include the capability to route requests automatically to the most appropriate source, based on electronically stored holdings or availability information.* A successful example of automatic routing of requests is DOCLINE, the ILL system used by medical libraries, which automatically links to citations in the NLM databases by use of a unique identifier (UI). This permits a user to request a document identified in MEDLINE without rekeying the bibliographic information. The link is further enhanced by SERHOLD, which permits automatic routing of requests based on issue-specific holdings information at each library. This automatic link to library holdings is supplemented by the option for direct ordering from a commercial supplier through PaperChase.

5. *Support direct delivery to the individual, whether the item is supplied by the local collection or obtained from a remote source.* Processing by the requesting library after a request is filled delays getting the material to a user. ILL protocol must be modified to support direct delivery from the supplying library to the requesting individual. This will allow ILL delivery to approach the delivery speed and efficiency of commercial services.

6. *Include a range of technology-based delivery mechanisms such as electronic transfer and fax and, also, traditional methods such as courier, USPS, and UPS; mechanisms will change as technology changes.* Libraries are in a position to take advantage of the range of available technology for direct document delivery to the user. It is important to maintain a variety of options to meet the information demands of the full population of users.

7. *Take advantage of interfaces and gateways to link databases and delivery options, facilitating the ability for a user to order materials directly and, at the same time, maintaining access to a full range of library-initiated delivery alternatives.* Document delivery will include direct end-user requests, resulting from services such as CARL's UnCover2 or OCLC's FirstSearch databases; it will

include library-facilitated end-user ordering, as demonstrated by MELDOC's direct link to commercial suppliers; it will also include requests sent by libraries on behalf of users, as exhibited by increased availability of document delivery suppliers on the ILL subsystems of OCLC and RLIN.

8. *Take into account the different ways users want to interact with information, and provide appropriate options for access to materials.* Libraries cannot assume that they know what is needed; patron demand has demonstrated that needs vary by discipline and by individuals within the discipline. For instance, rapid delivery of current information in the sciences does not address the need for source material in the humanities (Farrell, 1991; Wiberley, 1991). The age of the individual mandates that a library document delivery service be designed to accomodate very different, sometimes competing, needs for access to information.

9. *Utilize all available avenues for document acquisition.* The primary challenge for the document delivery librarian in the coming years will be to orchestrate an increasing number of demands at varying rhythms, simultaneously. It is no longer possible to handle all requests in the same manner; efforts to provide a single access for patrons will succeed only if there is acceptance of the need to utilize all available sources for document acquisition.

10. *Receive support from funding formulas that include access as an element of library collections.* Funding formulas, now expanding the definition of collections to include access, must be stretched even further to accomodate the actual delivery in the most cost-effective manner of the identified source. Areas of collecting responsibility to meet the needs of a library's primary clientele must determine the subsidy assigned to support delivery of documents in a specific discipline. Efficient, planned use of document delivery sources in these areas will provide the user will full service in a defined collecting range. Needs falling outside a library's primary focus might more appropriately be charged to the individual requester, but facilitated, rapid access to the item must be supported.

11. *Provide access to all materials.* It is important not to lose sight of information that will likely never be available electronically. Such items include very specialized or esoteric publications aimed at small audiences and large numbers of retrospective materials currently held in libraries and not demonstrating high-level demand. This is where successful cooperative collection development and cooperative collection weeding is most critical. These items are at high risk of becoming "lost" from both the access and delivery paths.

The 1990s promise to make the term ILL obsolete, but traditional ILL will continue to exist as an essential arm of a greatly augmented library document delivery service, a service that provides direct delivery to individuals of identified resources whether they are held in the local library, another library, or available from the growing number of electronic sources. The service provided by this area of the library furnishes the link between users and information sources, a user expectation of primary importance in the 1990s.

References

Beiser, K. (1991). Library technology through a wide-angle lens. *Wilson Library Bulletin* **65**, 48–50.

Bourne, C. P. (1990). A review of technology and trends in document delivery services. In *Riding the Electronic Wave: Proceedings of the Library of Congress Network Advisory Committee Meeting, November 29–December 1, 1989* (Network Planning Paper, No. 20), pp. 9–28. Library of Congress, Washington, D.C.

Campbell, J. (1990). The serendipitous courier. *Colorado Libraries* **16**, 19–20.

Carnegie Mellon/UMI state-of-the-art installation. (1991). *Library Hotline* **24** June, p. 4.

Carpenter, M. (1991). If we say resource sharing is a good thing, let's mean it. *Journal of Academic Librarianship* **17**, 230–231.

Casorso, T. (1991). The North Carolina State University Libraries and the National Agricultural Library joint project on transmission of digitized text: Improving access to agricultural information. *RSR: Reference Services Review* **19**, 15–22.

Casorso, T. (1992). Research materials: Now only keystrokes away. *College and Research Libraries News* **53**, 128.

Colaianni, L. A. (1990). DOCLINE: The National Library of Medicine experience. In *Riding the Electronic Wave-Document Delivery: Proceedings of the Library of Congress Network Advisory Committee Meeting, November 29–December 1, 1989.* (Network Planning Paper, no. 20), pp. 33–36. Library of Congress, Washington, D.C.

Davis, E. S., and Simpson, D. B. (1991). *Final Performance Report for a Combination Grant Authorized by College Library Technology and Cooperation Grants Program Higher Education Act, Title II-D U.S. Department of Education Washington, D.C. from the Center for Research Libraries Chicago, IL for the project "Establishing a Telefacsimile Document Delivery Service"* (unpublished). Center for Research Libraries, Chicago.

Deekle, P. (1990). Document delivery comes of age in Pennsylvania. *Wilson Library Bulletin* **65**, 31–33.

Ditzler, C. J., Lefebvre, V., and Thompson, B. G. (1990). Agricultural document delivery: Strategies for the future. *Library Trends* **38**, 377–396.

Divens, W. C., Jr. (1991). Electronic message on "ILL-L: Interlibrary Loan Discussion Group" (ILL-L@UVMVM.bitnet) dated 2 May.

Document Retrieval, Sources & Services, 4th ed. (1987). Information Store, San Francisco.

Electronic Journal. (1991). *Association of Research Libraries Newsletter* 8 May, p. 2.

Farrell, D. (1991). The humanities in the 1990s: A perspective for research libraries and librarians. *Library Hi Tech* **9**, 69–71.

Faxon's Journal table of contents and document delivery services to be available on OCLC. (1991). *Action for Libraries* August, p. 3.

Fayad, S. (1990). Document delivery: You can get it there from here. *Colorado Libraries* **16**, 13–14.

Fischer, N. (1991). *"New Mexico News."* Presentation made at 1991 Colorado Interlibrary Loan Workshop, 3 May, Durango, Colorado.

Fulltext Sources Online. (1989–). BiblioData, Needham, Massachusetts

Gadzikowski, C. (1991). Loansome Doc: New option for document delivery. *Octasphere* **18**, 55.

Gherman, P. M. (1991). Setting budgets for libraries in electronic era. *Chronicle of Higher Education* 14 August, A36.

Gillikin, D. P. (1990). Document delivery from full-text online files: A pilot project. *Online* **14**, 27–32.

Gorman, M. (1991). Scholarship, teaching, and libraries in an electronic age. *Library Hi Tech* **9**, 73–75.

Hill, S. (1989). Growth of communication systems among biomedical libraries. In *Research Access through New Technology* (M. E. Jackson, ed.), pp. 47–55. AMS Press, New York.

Horres, M., Starr, S. S., and Renford, B. L. (1991). MELVYL MEDLINE: A library services perspective. *Bulletin of the Medical Library Association* **79**, 309–320.

Jackson, M. E. (1988). Facsimile transmission: The next generation of document delivery. *Wilson Library Bulletin* **62**, 37–43.

Jackson, M. E. (1990a). Library to library: Trends in resource sharing (part II). *Wilson Library Bulletin* **64**, 99–100.

Jackson, M. E. (1990b). The online environment in the 1990s: A challenge for resource sharing. In *Proceedings of the Fifth Integrated Online Library Systems Meeting, New York, May 2–3, 1990*, pp. 91–101. Learned Information, Inc., Medford, New Jersey.

Jackson, M. E. (1991). Library to library: Are our ILL systems ill? *Wilson Library Bulletin* **66**, 82–85.

Johnson, C. (1991.) New realities in interlibrary cooperation: Report on an ALA conference program. *Journal of Interlibrary Loan & Information Supply* **2**, 73–76.

Kalal, B. (1991). *OSU Internet/Fax Library Project Update*. Electronic message on "ILL-L: Interlibrary Loan Discussion Group" (ILL-L@UVMVM.bitnet) dated 20 June.

Kaya, B., and Hurlebaus, A. (1978). Comparison of United Parcel Service and United States Postal Service delivery speed and cost for interlibrary loan. *Bulletin of the Medical Library Association* **66**, 345–346.

Kennedy, K. (1991). Conference reports: Cause90: "Challenges and opportunities of information technology in the 90s"—Two reports. *Library Hi Tech News* March, 1–2.

Kilgour, F. (1972). Evolving, computerizing, personalizing. *American Libraries* **3**, 141–147.

King, A. (1991). Full text & CD–ROM: Variations on a theme. *Online* **15**, 107–108.

King, N. S. (1990). Search characteristics and the effects of experience on end users of PaperChase. *College and Research Libraries* **52**, 360–374.

Kountz, J. (1991). High density data storage, the Sony data discman electronic book, and the unfolding multi-media revolution. *Library Hi Tech* **9**, 77–90.

Lawson, R. (1990). PaperChase: A user-friendly program for searching the biomedical literature. *BioTechniques* **8**, 680–683.

Martin, N. P. (1989). Information transfer, scholarly communication, and interlibrary loan: Priorities, conflicts, and organizational imperatives. In *Research Access through New Technology* (M. E. Jackson, ed.), pp. 1–21. AMS Press, New York.

Matthews, J. R. (1991). Conference reports: Computers in libraries '91. *Library Hi Tech News* June, 1–4.

Maxwell, C. (1990). Information on Demand: Information broker services—the IOD experience. In *Riding the Electronic Wave-Document Delivery: Proceedings of the Library of Congress Network Advisory Committee Meeting, November 29–December 1, 1989* (Network Planning Paper, no. 20), pp. 53–61. Library of Congress, Washington, D.C.

Moore, M. Y. (1988). Fax it to me: A library love affair. *American Libraries* **19**, 57–59.

Naisbitt, J., and Aburdene, P. (1990). *Megatrends 2000: Ten New Directions For the 1990's*. Avon Books, New York.

NAL joins NC State in image transmission project. (1991). *National Agricultural Library Annual Report for 1990*, p. 6. National Agricultural Library, Beltsville, Maryland.

Nelson, N. (1991). Electronic message on "ILL-L: Interlibrary Loan Discussion Group" (ILL-L@UVMVM.bitnet) dated 19 September.

Newsome, K. (1991). Electronic message on "ILL-L: Interlibrary Loan Discussion Group" (ILL-L@UVMVM.bitnet) dated 5 June.

ON TRACK. . .New uncover gateways. (1991). *ON CARL* Winter, p. 2.

Quint, B. (1991). Flipping for full-text. *Wilson Library Bulletin* **66,** 82–85.

Richards, B. G., and Johnson, J. M. (1990). Electronic delivery of information via a campus-wide network. *Science and Technology Libraries* **11,** 5–17.

RLG Conspectus. (1985–1988). Research Libraries Group, Stanford, California.

RLIN citations file plus document delivery tapped for major expansion (1991). *The Research Libraries Group News* Fall, 6–7.

Smith, D., and Lynch, C. A. (1990). Document delivery systems at the University of California: An overview. In *Riding the Electronic Wave-Document Delivery: Proceedings of the Library of Congress Network Advisory Committee Meeting, November 29–December 1, 1989* (Network Planning Paper, no. 20), pp. 41–48. Library of Congress, Washington, D.C.

Standards for university libraries: Evaluation of performance. (1989). *College and Research Libraries News* **50,** 679–691.

Stern, B., and Campbell, R. (1989). International document delivery: The ADONIS project. *Wilson Library Bulletin* **63,** 36–41.

Stern, B. T., and Compier, H. C. J. (1990). ADONIS—Document delivery in the cd–rom age. *Interlending and Document Supply* **18,** 79–87.

Taber, S. (1991). *Resource Sharing in Alaska.* Presentation made at 1991 Colorado Interlibrary Loan Workshop, 3 May, Durango, Colorado.

Tenopir, C. (1991). Online databases: The same databases on different systems. *Library Journal* 1 May, p. 59.

Weber, R. (1990). The clouded future of electronic publishing. *Publishers Weekly* 29 June, 76–80.

Westin, A. F., and Finger, A. L. (1991). *Using the Public Library in the Computer Age: Present Patterns, Future Possibilities.* American Library Association, Chicago.

Wiberley, S. T., Jr. (1991). Habits of humanists: Scholarly behavior and new information technologies. *Library Hi Tech* **9,** 17–21.

Wilson, D. L. (1991a). Researchers get direct access to huge database. *Chronicle of Higher Education* 9 October, A24–A28.

Wilson, D. L. (1991b). Testing time for electronic journals. *Chronicle of Higher Education* 11 September, A22–A24.

Cooperative Cataloging: Models, Issues, Prospects

Carol A. Mandel
Columbia University Libraries
New York, New York 10027

I. Introduction

Cooperative cataloging is a widely accepted practice in American librarianship. Its acceptance is based on two straightforward and well-proven premises: (1) libraries can extend database coverage (and thus access to information) by pooling catalog records; and (2) libraries can lower cataloging costs (and thus improve services) by sharing catalog records. These premises have undergirded cataloging efforts for nearly a century, proving as sound in today's world of international computerized databases as they were when the Library of Congress began its distribution of printed catalog cards in 1901. The size of shared databases and the use of shared cataloging copy continue to grow. The path, however, from actual library operations to the idealized notion of cooperative cataloging is neither short nor straight. As with many of society's undertakings, the good of the many sometimes conflicts with the good of the one—and there is not always clear agreement on what constitutes a common good.

Recent developments have called into question some long-held assumptions about cooperative cataloging. A number of major efforts to share records on a large scale between and among databases have been unsuccessful. The Linked Systems Project (LSP) has not achieved its goals. Although operational for transmitting authority data between the Library of Congress (LC) and the Research Libraries Information Network (RLIN) and the Online Computer Library Center (OCLC), LSP does not include a component for exchanging bibliographic records, and no work is in progress. A 1991 initiative to merge and coordinate the content of the OCLC and RLIN databases was stillborn ("RLG and OCLC," 1991), and the leadership of both organizations foresee no further effort along this line. There is growing concern, and possibly some demonstrable evidence, that the widespread use of local (i.e., in-house) library systems will result in decreased contribution of records to shared databases (e.g., Lowell, 1990; Reid, 1990; Wetherbee, 1991). As budgets tighten, issues of balance and equity in distributing the costs of contribution to shared databases take on greater visibility. In response to questioning by both catalogers and administrators (Gregor and Mandel, 1991) standards for national-level cooperative cataloging are undergoing scrutiny. And the carefully observed and evaluated struggles of the National Coordinated Cataloging Project pilot phase, completed in 1991, have raised a number of central issues about the appropriate models for cooperative cataloging.

The definition of cooperative cataloging is, perhaps deceptively, straightforward. The *ALA Glossary* (1983) describes it as "The original cataloging of bibliographic items through the joint action of a group of independent libraries which make bibliographic records accessible to group members and sometimes to non-participating libraries as well. Sometimes called shared cataloging because the cataloging responsibility and cataloging product are shared" (pp. 39, 59). This definition is distinguished from "centralized cataloging" in which one agency creates catalog records that others use. In practice, the distinction is less clear, because the degree of centralization and central coordination varies greatly from project to project. In the United States, a key element in program design has often revolved around the role of LC, and the extent of LC's responsibility and oversight has often shifted during the course of a program. The goals and objectives of cooperative endeavors have been equally variable, and long-running programs have often made significant shifts in direction and operation as the projects evolved. The formula for success in a cooperative cataloging effort is not self-evident, but is derived from a set of complex, interacting issues. As Burger (1990) notes, "In an era when funds for libraries are tight and library staffs are stretched thinly, cooperative efforts are seen as the salvation. . . . But we should not assume that every cooperative program is a good one. We should be ruthless in examining all our assumptions underlying the policy, the macro and micro systems, and the policy's purported results" (p. 64). This article provides an analysis of significant projects and attendant issues to identify critical success factors for well-designed models of cooperative cataloging. At a time when the resources allocated to providing bibliographic access are strained, it is essential to insure that cooperative programs are carefully shaped and tuned to meet their desired objectives.

II. Cooperative Cataloging before MARC

A. Coordination by the Library of Congress

The initiation of cooperative cataloging in the United States is usually traced to 1901 when LC began distributing its cataloging data to other libraries via the sale of printed cards. This was conceived as a cooperative endeavor from the outset. Writing in his annual report for the fiscal year 1901, then Librarian of Congress, Herbert Putnam noted

> It is fully recognized by the Library of Congress that next in importance to an adequate exhibit of its own resources, comes the ability to supply information as to the resources of other libraries. As steps in this direction may be mentioned:
> First. The acquisition of printed catalogues of libraries, both American and foreign.
> Second. An alphabetic author catalogue on cards of books in department and bureau libraries in Washington.
> Third. A similar catalogue of books in some of the more important libraries outside of Washington.
> The Library . . . hopes to receive a copy of every card printed by the New York Public Library, the Boston Public Library, the Harvard University Library, the John Crerar Library, and several others. (Cited in Immroth, 1976, p. 183)

Implementation of the cooperative elements came in 1902 when the Library began to print and distribute catalog records submitted by other government agencies; by 1909 exchange arrangements for catalog cards had been made with several American libraries.

The next landmark in cooperative cataloging stemmed from a 1931 study by the ALA's (American Library Association) Cooperative Cataloging Committee showing that LC cards were available for only about 70% of English language books acquired by large research libraries and only 54% of foreign language acquisitions. (Noted in LC, 1991, p.3) This led to the initiation of a project targeted to increase the amount of contributed copy processed through LC for foreign materials and analytics for monographic series. The ALA Committee established an office at the Library in 1932 that in turn developed into a LC Division, the Cooperative Cataloging and Classification Service, in 1934. The Service appears to have been largely focused on LC's role in accepting, editing, and distributing copy rather than on the coordination and encouragement of other libraries to contribute it. As Hanson and Daily note (1970), "Efforts at cooperative cataloging were never as intense as those directed toward centralization, which would afford more concentration of staff and tools, maximum standardization of procedures and codification of rules, and substantially improved supervision and administration" (p.280).

Yee (1987) provides an insightful and informative account of this program and its transition in 1941 to absorption by the Library's Descriptive Cataloging Division. She attributes the demise of the separate division in part to the sharp decline in purchases of foreign books by participating libraries during the depression and in part because revision of cooperative cataloging was more costly than anticipated. Writing in the Library's annual report for 1940, then Chief of the Cooperative Cataloging and Classification Service, David Haykin, explained the need for costly revision because (among other reasons) not all catalogers from cooperating libraries "were sufficiently familiar with the cataloging practices of the Library of Congress, which was the standard adopted for the work" (Yee, 1987, p. 14). In recommending the reorganization of the cooperative service, the Librarian's Committee on Cooperative Cataloging compared the relative success of the work done in the Card Division for distribution of cards from District of Columbia libraries to the high cost of work in the Cooperative Cataloging and Classification Service, noting that the output of the Service had amounted to an average of only one entry per reviser per working day. The group recommended that LC begin to use cooperatively supplied copy when it subsequently acquired the same title, rather than cancelling the contributed copy, and that it reduce its revision and editing of contributed copy. The Committee (excerpted in Yee, 1987) admonished

> "Above all, the staff of the subsection should avoid expressing mere personal opinion in making any changes either in the copy supplied by contributing libraries or in adapting printed cards with which to catalog Library of Congress books. Likewise, at any stage of the work time ought not to be spent debating nonessential matters. . . . In general, the revisers of outside copy should do much less 'authority work' than they have done in the past. . . . With respect to subject headings, the revisers should check only when the contributing library indicates the need for so doing. (p. 28)

The Committee also recognized the need to adjust outside cataloging copy to the large LC file. Copy from libraries lacking access to LC depository catalogs would need greater verification. New subject headings should be established in a manner enabling their future use for LC-acquired materials. In retrospect, the Committee's assessments can be viewed as the first in a long series of efforts by LC, and eventually other libraries, to strike an optimal balance in accepting other libraries' copy, maintaining local practices and preferences, and meeting perceived requirements for national distribution. Fifty years later, that balance has not yet been achieved.

The separate cooperative cataloging section was abolished in October of 1946, but relatively modest efforts in cooperative cataloging continued. Under the Farmington Plan, a postwar cooperative acquisitions program designed to obtain for American libraries European imprints that had been inaccessible during World War II, research libraries were asked to supply LC with cataloging copy for titles acquired through the plan. This program ended in 1948. Supplies of outside copy declined by 1949 and 1950. As described by Rather (1984, p. 9), the program was finally abandoned as unworkable in the early 1960s. Reviewing the complicated procedures for coordination between LC and the participating libraries, Yee posits, "one cannot but wonder whether the decline in copy received was not due in part to the complications and delays inherent in the administration of such a complex program" (Yee, 1987, p. 17). Rather (1984) offers a similar view, noting that "LC catalogers reviewed each catalog record completely and returned the updated version to the contributing library for concurrence before it was accepted for printing. . . . This tedious process was handled entirely by mail. Turn around time frequently exceeded a year" (p. 9) She also identifies a lack of agreement on standards as a factor contributing to the effort's demise, observing that "as late as 1960, some contributing libraries were still following the 1908 rules." According to one estimate (Kaplan, 1975, p. 253), American libraries contributed copy for only 14% of the cards printed and distributed by the Library of Congress during the period 1910–1965.

Although cooperative cataloging, as defined by a particular LC program, bogged down under the weight of revision and administration during the 1940s and 1950s, cooperative catalog building did not. At the same time that LC was carefully editing contributed copy for card printing, the Library's Union Catalog Division was industriously filing cards supplied by other libraries with minimal editorial review. The focus of the union catalog effort was comprehensive coverage. The catalog had begun with the 1909 exchange agreements with cooperative cataloging partners. In 1926, ALA was granted $250,000, to be expended over a 5-year period, from John D. Rockefeller, Jr. for the purpose of expanding the Union Catalog. During the grant period, over 6.3 million cards were added. (Described by Immroth, 1976.) As long as the Union Catalog existed solely as a card file at LC, its use was primarily for centralized reference and interlibrary loan. With the publication of the printed version in 1956, it was possible also to view the catalog as source of, at least partial, cataloging copy (subject headings were not always included for contributed copy). For the first time, American libraries could gain access to each others' records.

B. The Growing Interest in Copy Cataloging

However, it does not appear that the publication of the National Union Catalog (NUC) had a major impact on the practice of sharing cataloging copy. In the early 1960s, members of the Association of Research Libraries (ARL) became increasingly concerned about the unavailability of cataloging copy for what seemed to them a growing percentage of newly received materials. The Board noted that libraries were reporting that an average of 46% of their cataloging was for original records in 1963, and that arrearages of uncataloged materials were growing at an alarming rate. At ARL's request, James Skipper (1966) performed an in-depth study to document this trend. Analyzing a sample of current cataloging from nine large libraries, Skipper (pp. 61–64) found that although copy from NUC and LC was available for more than 80% of U.S. imprints, the percentage available for foreign materials was typically less than 70% for most countries. In all cases, there was a significant percentage of available copy not used. Overall, Skipper's analysis indicated

48% of current cataloging in the nine libraries was original and 52% based on copy. A more detailed breakdown (p. 58) of the 52% copy cataloging showed that 41% was standard LC copy, another 6% resulted from the PL480 program, only 2% came from cooperative cataloging distributed by LC (not surprising given the near demise of the LC-based cooperative cataloging program at this time), and only 3% of cataloging was based on non-LC copy from NUC. Skipper also found that another 8% of the records that had been cataloged represented original cataloging for which NUC copy was also available. He speculated (p. 65) on the reasons why libraries did not use this available copy, suggesting inability to locate the copy, need for more timely access to copy, and a lack of confidence in the quality of copy submitted to NUC.

To try to determine a trend, it is of interest to compare the situation documented by Skipper with that which obtained in 1931, when the ALA study showed that LC copy was available for 70% of English language and 54% of foreign titles in U.S. research libraries, Although a greater percentage of copy was in fact available in 1965 than in 1931, it appears that research libraries were doing just about as much original cataloging. Without figures for the intervening years, it is not possible to confirm the ARL Board's impression that the percentage of original cataloging was increasing, but it is probably safe to assume that the overall volume of original cataloging was larger as collections began to grow at an increasing rate. In 1965, the solution to this problem was not viewed as cooperative cataloging but as the need to increase the amount of LC copy centrally available. Reporting for ARL's Shared Cataloging Committee, Skipper concluded

> Despite the great amount of cooperative spirit and good will, the mechanics of cooperative cataloging generate too much friction and produce inordinate time delays, all of which seriously reduce the theoretical potential. . . . The Shared Cataloging Committee found that the evidence presented by the survey confirmed their recommendation that increased availability of catalog copy must come from centralized, rather than cooperative efforts and it seemed to be obvious that the Library of Congress was the most logical agency to implement the program. (p. 64)

The Committee's recommendations resulted in the creation of the National Program for Acquisitions and Cataloging (NPAC). Established in 1965 with funds provided by Congress via the Higher Education Act (HEA), the program focused on increasing LC's acquisition and cataloging of those foreign materials most needed by American research libraries. The program was incorporated generally into LC operations in 1972 when the funding was transferred from HEA to the Libraries' annual appropriation. Whereas NPAC's focus did little to encourage increased contributions of cooperative cataloging by research libraries, LC took advantage of the program to extend its cooperation with foreign national bibliographic centers and began adapting foreign cataloging copy through a Shared Cataloging Division established for this purpose. According to a Library report to Congress (LC, 1991), "the program was a major contribution to world-wide standardized cataloging practice and permitted the Library of Congress to double its cataloging output" (p. 4).

The fruits of this output were gratefully accepted by the rest of the library community, which continued to take advantage of LC cataloging via the distribution of printed cards. An investigation performed by Ishimoto in 1971 demonstrated that NPAC had the desired impact on research library cataloging in a relatively short time. She studied thirteen large research libraries and found that the amount and percentage of copy cataloging had increased so significantly that organization, staffing patterns and workflows in research library cataloging departments were undergoing dramatic change. Since eight of the libraries she studied were the same as those sampled by Skipper, it is possible to use her figures to judge the increase in LC copy cataloging for essentially the same group of libraries between 1965 and 1971. Based on figures shown by Ishimoto (p. 133) the eight ARL libraries used LC or NPAC copy for 66% of their cataloging in 1971; this compares with 49% in 1965.[1] Ishimoto notes that not all of the increase may be due to NPAC, because LC was also increasing its coverage of the Cataloging-In-Publication Program during the same period. In any case, improved centralized rather than cooperative cataloging was clearly a more successful approach to reducing research libraries' original cataloging workload in a pre-MARC era.

III. MARC and Shared Databases

A. The Development of Utility-Based Cooperative Cataloging

The development, adoption, and widespread use of the MARC Format for Bibliographic Data have been fundamental to cooperative cataloging. From its outset, MARC was conceived to enable the communication and *sharing* of bibliographic data, and it is a clear demonstration of how the use of a common standard can promote cooperative activity. Crawford (1984) notes that "At first, LC MARC was a vehicle for distribution of records from a single source. MARC has since become a vehicle for communication between systems . . . (p. 3)." This conceptual shift occurred virtually as soon as the first MARC records were introduced in 1967. In introducing the MARC II format, the

[1] This comparison assumes that Ishimoto included the use of LC-distributed cooperative and PL480 copy, and so uses the comparable figure from Skipper. If not, then the increase in use of copy from 1965 to 1971 is even slightly greater.

version of the format that was used for operational LC distribution after the pilot testing of MARC I, MARC's creators (Avram, Knapp, and Rather, 1968) stated that "One immediate result of the distribution of the MARC [I] tapes has been stimulation of interest in the concept of library data transmission. It has become evident that the MARC experiment has suggested to the library community the possibility that individual libraries can use a MARC-like system to contribute data from their own original cataloging for the use of others" (p. 2).

When LC began distributing its catalog records in machine-readable form in 1969, few individual libraries had the computer support capacity to take advantage of the service. The difficulty and expense of developing automated library systems prompted North American libraries to form consortia for using computerized cataloging services. Several of these organizations quickly grew into large, central union catalog databases of such scale and importance to library operations that they came to be known as "bibliographic utilities." Two utilities, OCLC and the Research Libraries Group's RLIN, have come to play a role akin to that of LC in promoting the sharing and distribution of cataloging data. Taken together, incorporating both the core of LC bibliographic tapes and member-contributed records, they constitute the functional NUC, displaying bibliographic and holdings records from some 5000 libraries.[2]

It is important to recognize that both OCLC and RLIN represent hugely successful and effective cooperative cataloging programs on a grand scale. Subsequent to their development, any U.S.-based cooperative program can realistically only be viewed as a subset of or adjunct to these enormous "projects." The OCLC database contains more than 24 million bibliographic records, and over the past 15 years, an increasing percentage of these have been supplied by participating member libraries as compared with LC records. A 1990 analysis of a sample drawn from the OCLC database and analyzed by Crook (Reid, 1990) indicated that since 1985, close to 80% of the records contributed for current cataloging (i.e., current or preceding year's imprints) are supplied by member libraries; this figure rose steadily from only 40% member contribution in 1974.

Encouragement of record contribution has taken aggressive effort on the part of RLG and OCLC. These organizations provide the means for libraries to contribute and distribute original cataloging with relative ease, but thoughtful design of both systems and policies has been necessary to maintain that ease. Because both technology and politics are continually changing, encouragement of participation is a dynamic, continual process. Several elements have evolved as standard aspects of the "utility" model of cooperative cataloging:

[2] Numbers of contributing libraries supplied by information centers at RLG and OCLC: 4500 provide cataloging to OCLC and ca. 500 to RLIN.

1. Contribution of records is encouraged by policy statements and membership requirements.

2. Standards for record creation are established so that records can be easily reused by other libraries. The standards review process is ongoing and involves extensive participation by member libraries.

3. Libraries "self-define" whether a record input to the database conforms to agreed-on standards. Libraries may also contribute records that do not meet standards, as long as they are identified as such.

4. Pricing incentives are used to encourage actions that will enhance the quality and usefulness of the database. These incentives are complex and vary in relation to such issues as technical requirements of the utility system, specific programmatic efforts designed to enlarge or enhance the database, and other program goals. A basic incentive is the reward of full standard cataloging through a credit system. Such credits are not provided for cataloging that does not meet standards.

5. System design attempts to be responsive to insure an efficient workflow for participating libraries. For example, workstations with added functionality have replaced terminals for online cataloging activities. The current challenge for both OCLC and RLIN is to provide cost-effective, efficient interaction with libraries' local systems and to avoid burdensome tape loading.[3]

6. No restrictions are placed on a library's selection of titles to catalog. Each library contributes records according to its local needs and priorities.

The success of these shared databases has resulted from a careful balance between the common good (i.e., a database of useful cataloging records) and local needs. Both the utility boards and their member libraries develop policies and practices with enlightened self-interest. Libraries will adjust local practices to meet a cooperative goal, but only if the adjustment is not unduly burdensome and if there is a perceived benefit, either direct or indirect, to the library and, therefore, to its clientele. Negotiating this balance requires continual adjustment. The great extent of libraries' contributions to RLIN and OCLC is evidence of the overall success of this dynamic process.

B. Patterns of Contribution and Use of Shared Databases by Research Libraries

The availability of such large databases of contributed records plays a significant role in libraries' cataloging operations. A 1990 survey by Mandel (Bibliographic Services Study Committee (BSSC), 1990, pp. 39, 44–45) of ARL

---

[3] Both OCLC and RLG have recently proclaimed such interaction with local systems as important strategic directions for their organizations. This can be seen, for example, in RLG's charge to it President's Commission on Technical Processing in June 1991 and in the OCLC flyer "Strategic Plan for Cataloging" distributed in January 1992.

university library members indicated that 26% of the libraries total cataloging output for 1989 was based on member copy; 54% was based on copy supplied by LC. Only 11% of the total output was full standard original cataloging (the median for these libraries was only 7.5%); the remaining 10% was a mix of minimal and other copy. These figures reveal a number of things about the importance of contributed cataloging. First, it is surprising to note that the match of LC copy to current cataloging needs of U.S. research libraries does not seem to have improved since the situation described by Skipper in 1965. In fact, the percentage of LC-based copy cataloging has dropped significantly since the 66% found by Ishimoto in 1971, either because LC is covering less of research libraries needs or because member copy is available more quickly. Although trends and causes cannot be projected because each study provides data for only a snapshot in time rather than tracing patterns over a number of years, the data indicate a continuing need for research libraries to supplement LC records with additional copy to catalog their current acquisitions. Second, member-contributed copy has enabled ARL libraries to reduce greatly their percentage of original cataloging, down from almost 50% in 1965 to close to 20% in 1989. But in many, if not most, research libraries, this also means that there is much less original cataloging activity taking place. The 89 ARL university libraries surveyed in 1990 reported a total of 358,940 titles given full original cataloging, with only three libraries creating more than 15,000 records and the median only 2,699 titles. Ishimoto's 1971 data showed all but three of the thirteen libraries surveyed with an original cataloging output of greater than 15,000 titles. Although the data in the two surveys are not strictly comparable, they match a general perception in the field that original cataloging departments are shrinking. Except for LC, the output of any individual library's original cataloging production is not great, either in percentage of total cataloging effort or in number. In most ARL university libraries, full standard original cataloging is a commodity in relatively short supply.

Because libraries have become so dependent on each others' cataloging copy, it is important to understand patterns of contribution and use of original cataloging records. Information about such patterns would help identify ways to optimize the overall system of shared cataloging and guide the development of appropriate cooperative programs. Unfortunately, the picture is quite complex and data are difficult to obtain. Whereas it is relatively easy to determine the source of catalog records in shared databases, it is more difficult to determine which copy—and which libraries—account for the records that are most used by others.

Analyses performed by Paul Kantor (1990; BSSC, 1990) in conjunction with the Council on Library Resources Bibliographic Services Study Committee provide some useful data on patterns in the OCLC database. One study

(BSSC, 1990, p. 38) analyzed a sample of OCLC records to determine the relative impact of LC/Cataloging-in-Publishing (CIP), LC, and ARL university library-contributed records in copy cataloging performed by ARL university libraries. That is, which group of records accounted for the most "derives" by ARL libraries and in what proportion. As would be expected, CIP records (i.e., records for titles produced by U.S. publishers participating in the CIP program) had the greatest effect and member copy the least. But the differences in impact are striking, with CIP accounting for close to 60% of the derives analyzed, other LC copy for approximately 30%, and ARL university copy for 10%. This percentage is not the same as the overall ratio of LC to member copy cataloging in ARL libraries because it does not take into account copy used from *non-ARL* libraries. What this analysis indicates is how relatively little copy ARL university libraries as a defined subgroup in OCLC derive from each other. In a related analysis (Kantor, 1990, p. 28) of the sample of ARL member copy records in OCLC, BSSC looked at the pattern of use of these records; about two thirds of the records were used by no other ARL library and only about 3.5% of these records were used by 10 or more ARL libraries.[4]

The lack of overlap in holdings among ARL libraries found in the Kantor analysis confirms results from earlier studies. A sample of current original cataloging from Indiana University Libraries studied by Crowe in 1978 showed that 56% of the records created had not been used by other libraries within a year of cataloging; most were records for foreign materials. Studies performed in a number of disciplines by RLG members to study collection overlap in the mid-1980s demonstrated a significant percentage of unique holdings in member libraries and many titles held by only one, two, or three libraries. Another RLG member study (Houbeck, Marko, and Richards, 1985) performed in conjunction with planning for a retrospective conversion project sampled overlap for titles in a mix of disciplines, languages, and imprint dates and found that 54% of the titles sampled were in only one to three libraries. Results were similar for both pre- and post-1968 imprints, so this is not only a phenomenon of historical collection building.

The inference that can be drawn from these analyses is that although member copy plays a substantial role in the copy-cataloging work at ARL university libraries, contributions of records from a large number of libraries, ARL and non-ARL, are required to satisfy the entire copy-cataloging needs of any particular research institution. However, within the universe of libraries providing original cataloging that other libraries need, there are clearly some

---

[4] Because this analysis could be performed only on the OCLC database, it does somewhat understate the degree of overlap that would be found if ARL RLIN libraries had also been included. It is reasonable to assume that if more research libraries are included, more overlap will occur.

libraries that provide a greater number of such records than others. Questions often asked are: "How many?" and "Which ones?" The success of the RLIN database demonstrates that at least this group of ca. 500 contributors, which includes a number of large original cataloging producers, can satisfy a high percentage of each others' copy cataloging needs. Studies of special subject cataloging within the database make this point quite clearly. The RLIN database is particularly rich in titles relating to art and architecture; the Art and Architecture Program (AAP) within RLG includes some 20 art and museum libraries as well as art library collections within larger institutions. Data analyzed by James Coleman (unpublished electronic memorandum, May, 1991) demonstrate that the special art libraries within RLIN gain between 73% and 97% of their cataloging needs from a combination of LC and other AAP member copy. Thus, the picture for this group of special libraries contrasts with the overall pattern of record use for general collections, indicating that subsets of libraries can be constructed in specialized subject areas that can supply a high percentage of each others' cataloging.

Preliminary analyses by Kantor (BSSC, 1990) of foreign language subsets in the OCLC database point to another possible trend: that for foreign language titles "a small set of libraries create records which are the sources for a large fraction of all the derives of the ARL university libraries using OCLC" (p. 36). Grover (1991) demonstrates the same pattern with data on the provision of catalog records for a sample of 298 Latin American titles searched several times between 1983 and 1985. Not all of the titles were cataloged during that period, and of those that were, approximately half of the records provided came from LC. The pattern of member contribution showed concentration in a relatively few libraries, with almost the same number cataloged on RLIN and OCLC, but not the same records. He summarizes, "A total of thirteen libraries in RLIN provided original cataloging to the system; but only six cataloged more than ten items. . . .In OCLC the total number of libraries was much higher (thirty-four), but only five libraries cataloged more than ten items" (p. 409).

Taken together, these studies point to a few general observation about ARL libraries' use of each other's cataloging. First, most ARL libraries will do some, in fact a significant amount of, original cataloging for the unique items they own; this cataloging will not be used by other libraries. Second, because of the lack of overlap in research library collections, research libraries need access to a database of records supplied by a relatively large number of libraries to gain access to all of the available copy that will match their collections. Third, the distribution of source libraries for cataloging copy is not level; some relatively small percentage of libraries supply a high percentage—but not all—of the copy, at least in selected specialized subjects and languages. Although this indicates that for a particular language or subject, a set of libraries can be defined as likely candidates to supply copy, confining cataloging to this group will not provide complete coverage of an area. The ideal shared cataloging environment supports maintenance of a large, central database with many contributors, and at the same time encourages, and even nurtures, original cataloging by key producers.

C. Linking Shared Databases

The current shared cataloging environment supports the needs of research libraries considerably better than in the pre-MARC era, but it is not ideal. While the RLIN and OCLC databases in combination with LC records may constitute a "virtual" national union catalog, operationally they are not one catalog. LC makes its records available on both systems, but the process for doing so is via tapeload, so that there are delays in libraries' access to LC records. RLIN and OCLC must each be searched separately; there is no link or gateway from one system to the other. As telecommunications and equipment costs decline, or at least rise more slowly than the costs of labor for original cataloging, a small but increasing number of libraries find it worthwhile to provide access to both systems; however, workflows that take advantage of both databases are still cumbersome and problematic. The separation of these two (three including LC) databases is widely viewed in the library profession as a barrier to optimal cooperative cataloging. The issue came to the fore of a 1979 meeting of ARL (ARL, 1979, p. 64) at which a panel representing the bibliographic utilities, LC, the Council on Library Resources (CLR), and ARL focused on the topic of national planning for bibliographic control. Although most participants endorsed a networked approach, OCLC's president at the time, Frederick Kilgour, expressed concern that the economics of linking were not well understood; if the OCLC cooperative were significantly harmed or the costs of linking too great, more damage than good would be done to the overall system. A subsequent study sponsored by CLR (Smalley, Griffith, Walker, and Wessells, 1980) on the costs and benefits of linking the utilities demonstrated the benefits to libraries of avoiding duplicative cataloging among the utilities, but did not resolve economic questions to everyone's satisfaction. The politics and potential economic impact of linking OCLC and RLIN were just as controversial a decade later, as negotiations between the two organizations to coordinate and link databases collapsed in June 1991.

Even before the 1979 ARL meeting, LC had identified the linking of bibliographic networks to be a national priority. Based on the results of an LC-commissioned study (Buckland and Basinski, 1978), LC established its Network Development Office and in 1976 began to work aggressively in efforts to connect systems. The Linked Systems Project (LSP) stemmed from the joint LC and CLR activity in 1980. As characterized by Avram (Avram and Wiggins, 1988a) "the goal of LSP was to make possible the linking of the dissimilar computer systems of LC, the Research Libraries Group . . . and WLN. In 1984 OCLC joined this group as a fourth partner" (p. 3). The project provided the aegis for technical development of standards and applications that would enable the exchange of library records based on the Open Systems Interconnection (OSI) protocol. The Authorities Implementation became operational between LC and RLIN and between LC and OCLC in 1987. However, there is currently no progress on an LSP implementation between LC and the utilities for bibliographic records. This is due in part to the amount of work still remaining to complete OSI implementation and differing views between LC and the utilities on the value of undertaking this work.

At the same time that development of links between utilities and LC is stagnating, libraries' local systems are playing a larger role in the database environment, as more and more institutions shift cataloging activity to local systems and rely on utilities as a record source rather than a cataloging system. As noted in Section I, concerns have been voiced that this trend has the potential to reduce contribution to central databases. On the positive side, recent trends and developments in networking and telecommunications, including the extensive use of Internet by libraries and academic institutions and the widespread use of campus local area networks, also indicate a change in approach for intersystem communication. Applications of ANSI/NISO Z39.50 (Information Retrieval Service Definition and Protocol Specifications for Library Applications) running over TCP/IP, a networking protocol commonly used on academic campuses, are emerging and point to a trend toward linking a variety of local systems to each other as well as to bibliographic utilities, rather than the utilities to each other. This is a less centralized, monolithic approach to linking and possibly (but not necessarily) one that is less politically divisive. Given research libraries' needs for cataloging from a range of sources, links between local systems cannot feasibly substitute for links to utilities, except perhaps for some specialized projects. But the prospect of links between local systems and utilities can help insure the continued contribution of records to a large, central databases even in a local system-oriented environment.

Linking or, perhaps more accurately, the absence of linked utilities and utility links to LC, has been a factor in the conception, design, and relative success of almost every cooperative cataloging effort that has been undertaken since the late 1970s. The notable exceptions, of course, are the cooperative building of the RLIN and OCLC databases themselves. In some cases, cooperative projects have been designed specifically to get around the problem (e.g., record exchanges); in others, projects have been conceived with deliberate optimism that LSP would be fully implemented (e.g., the National Coordinated Cataloging Project). In most cases, cooperative efforts have simply worked around a less than optimal situation, sometimes with less than optimal results. In analyzing and understanding models of cooperative cataloging, factors that interact with the realities of the distributed database environment play a significant role.

IV. Lessons Learned from Key Projects

A. CONSER (Cooperative ONline SERials)

Joseph Howard (1986) has described CONSER as the "catapult that launched all other cooperative bibliographic projects." In his words, "bibliographic cooperation among libraries of the United States and Canada took a quantum leap with the CONSER . . . project. Planned in 1973 largely as a retrospective conversion effort (CONversion of SERials), CONSER today is an ongoing program to maintain an authoritative database and promote improved serials management (Cooperative ONline SERials). An important aspect of CONSER is its truly cooperative roots. It was first conceived in an Ad Hoc Discussion Group on Serials Databases that met informally during the June 1973 ALA conference. Participants in the group then brought their ideas to CLR, which agreed to fund the work of a widely representative steering committee including members from LC, the National Library of Canada (NLC), OCLC, and a variety of groups promoting work in serials union listing. Perhaps the most striking feature of CONSER is its evolutionary quality, an effort, as characterized by Bartley (Bartley and Reynolds, 1988), "which has survived by means of successful adaptations and which has emerged stronger from its periodic challenges" (p. 48).

Bartley delineates the development of CONSER in phases. The first encompasses the period from CONSER's conception through 1977, the initial period of database building, sometimes referred to as "CONSER I." Phase two, 1977–1983, is a long transition period, marked by both a healthy, active set of subprojects to expand and enrich the database and struggles with challenges posed by changing cataloging standards, separation of databases, and staggering backlogs of authentication work. Bartley considers the shift to self-authentication by participants to be of such significance that it marks the beginning of a third phase in 1984. At the end of 1986, the project leaders undertook a careful reexamination of CONSER aided by an in-depth consultant's report and a planning retreat. Phase four, the current phase, emerged from this effort with new goals defined for an ongoing program to improve bibliographic management of serials. Because the history of the project has been well documented by Heynen and Blixrud (1986) and a number of thoughtful analyses of the project's development, role, challenges, and impacts are available (Bartley and Reynolds, 1988; Striedieck, 1989), this article will limit a review of CONSER to those features that may have bearing on the design of other cooperative projects.

From its beginning, CONSER planners took a goal-oriented, flexible approach to designing the project. Breaking new ground, the project forged ahead with doable incremental steps. Although planners believed that the project should be managed by LC, LC lacked the necessary network support functions for cooperative database building. The group decided to use OCLC as a "temporary solution" (Heynen and Blixrud, 1986, p. 4) because it had the capacity both for batch loading and online input of files. Another barrier to ideal implementation was the lack of recognized standards for machine-readable serials records, and the great burden of work necessary to upgrade existing files. CLR's representative on the planning group, Lawrence Livingston (quoted in Heynen and Blixrud, 1986) recognized that "a project like CONSER cannot succeed without a high degree of consistency and standardization in serials cataloging in many libraries, but something very much like CONSER is required before that degree of consistency and standardization can be attained" (p. 3). The solution to this conundrum was a flexible approach to the standards for initial input, a minimal set of required data elements that Striedieck (1989) describes as "a marvel of pragmatism" (p. 93).

The approach to database building necessitated a multistep process to bring records up to the authoritative standard desired. The initial database was built by batch loading existing machine-readable serials union lists into OCLC. These records were then edited and upgraded online by CONSER participants, working from their own currently received titles. Participants would also input titles they did not find in the database. Work was initially divided among the participants by assigning sections of the alphabet to each. As Rather noted at the time (1984), "the use of the online capabilities of the OCLC system contributed immensely to the success of the project. Participants were able to streamline their procedures and records were made available for use quickly."

A final step was "authentication," whereby NLC (for Canadian imprints) and LC (for all others) would review records, comparing them with photocopies of title pages and other bibliographic sources sent by the participants and assuring that all records contained key data elements such as the International Standard Serial Number (ISSN). Once authenticated, records were "locked" so that only LC or NLC could make further adjustments and revisions. Because serials records require ongoing maintenance, this effectively delegated all maintenance activities to the national libraries. The authentication process not only marked the record as meeting CONSER standards, it triggered the release of the records into LC's and NLC's MARC distribution services.

The difficulties with the CONSER authentication process are well known. The project's successful growth rate created an unmanageable backlog of surrogates at LC compounded by problems engendered by the adoption of AACR2. The backlog affected the maintenance of records as well, and as Bartley notes, "the backlog of surrogates and the inability of participants to make even minor changes to an authenticated, locked record contradicted the tenet of the CONSER Program that emphasizes an accurate and up-to-date bibliographic record" (p. 56). To combat the problem, the CONSER staff and participants developed the practice of self-authentication. Several elements converged to make this a workable practice by 1984. First, OCLC developed an "enhance" capability, enabling authorized libraries to modify already authorized records. Second, the NACO project (see Section IV.B) made it possible to coordinate entry establishment for serials, so that headings on self-authenticated participant records could be made available in a national authority file. Finally, enough experience in shared online cataloging had been gained that libraries felt able to rely on each other's interpretations of standards. The development of the *CONSER Editing Guide*, first published in 1986, provided a relatively compact, authoritative manual that enabled participants to follow a set of agreed-on practices. In fact, CONSER standards as promulgated through the highly regarded *Guide* are followed by many libraries that are not CONSER members—a clear indication that there is wide acceptance of CONSER standards.

Another problem that beset CONSER during the 1980s has proved more difficult to resolve: the divided database environment. At the same time it was becoming clear that CONSER's residence on OCLC was not a temporary expediency but rather the best available mode of ongoing operation, RLIN emerged as a significant second "national" database. By Heynen and Blixrud's account (1986, p.13), as early as 1980 the ARL Task Force on Bibliographic Control recognized the problems created for CONSER by the divided database environment and urged efforts toward linking the databases and sharing CONSER data. The problem today remains unresolved. Although CONSER records are distributed on tape by LC and NLC, the time-lags introduced by tape loading are problematic in a serials database, which is by nature dynamic; access to the most current version of the record is usually desirable. In addition, the similarity of titles for serials creates problems for the matching algorithms used to detect duplicates during loading; OCLC has only recently announced that it is addressing long-standing problems the utility has faced in loading serials records. Several CONSER members are RLIN libraries, and no easy means for their contribution has yet been found. Because access to OCLC is generally available, even in most RLG member libraries, and because CONSER tapes are distributed by LC, the divided database environment has not inhibited CONSER from achieving its objectives. However, it has deterred participation by libraries that do not routinely use OCLC for their cataloging, such as RLIN users or libraries that catalog online into local systems. Eventually, these problems may be solved by system-linking software or electronic file transfer, buy they have been with the project for over a decade.

Despite the problems related to authentication and data sharing, the CONSER database grew rapidly during the 1980s. The original goal of 200,000 records was significantly exceeded; records input numbered well over 600,000, with more than half of these authenticated. (Note: In November 1987, the definition of a CONSER record was changed to include only authenticated records. These numbered over 560,000 by the end of 1991.) A number of ambitious projects to expand and enrich the database were undertaken, including the cooperation between the National Serials Data Program and the U.S. Post Office to promulgate the use of ISSN, the addition of New Serials Titles location information to CONSER records, the addition of notes indicating where serials titles are indexed via the CONSER A & I Coverage Project, and the cooperative cataloging of newspapers through the National Endowment for the Humanities-sponsored program to catalog and preserve U.S. newspapers. All of these efforts were successful and resulted in continuing maintenance of this serials information.

The planning and analysis effort undertaken in 1986 transformed CONSER from a cooperative cataloging project to an ongoing program. The work of database creation had been successful. A revised mission statement, promulgated through the *CONSER Editing Guide* (Library of Congress, 1990), was articulated: "To build and maintain cooperatively a comprehensive machine readable database of authoritative bibliographic publications for serial publications; to uphold standards and to exercise leadership in the serials information community" (p. A1.1). Although building the database remained a key part of the effort, such programmatic activities as standards development and database enhancement have been incorporated into CONSER's objectives. Examples of these activities include the CONSER Policy Committee's work on the Multiple-Versions problem and the extension of affiliate membership to organizations such as abstracting and indexing services that have the potential to enrich authenticated serials records with additional data. The newly adopted mission and goals statements were widely promulgated.

As described in the introductory sections of the *CONSER Editing Guide*, "In addition to setting new goals and objectives, expanding membership criteria, and restructuring the Program, the retreat participants overwhelmingly endorsed CONSER's effectiveness, its approach, and its continued importance to serial bibliographic control" (p. A1. 1). Although the *Guide* may be a biased source, by most accounts CONSER is viewed as a highly successful cooperative program. In her careful review of CONSER, Striedieck (1989) observes, "It is hardly necessary to establish or defend the importance of the CONSER database to serials librarianship. The library literature tells us of many serials-related projects, and almost all acknowledge the importance of the CONSER database as a starting point." (p. 99). The size and quality of the database itself is concrete evidence of CONSER's success. In addition, participants are consistently supportive of the program and have contributed their efforts over a long period of time. The program has been successful in recruiting affiliate members; four specialized services—Chemical Abstracts Library Services, EBSCO Subscription Services, Faxon Company, and, most recently, BIOSIS—contribute information to the database. The only counterindicator of an entirely flourishing enterprise is the relatively modest growth in the participant base. Most of CONSER's 15 full members (in addition to the four national library members) have been contributing records since the early 1980s; only three libraries joined after the program's redefinition in 1987, despite a conscious effort on the part of the program leadership to enlarge the membership. Although a partial explanation lies in the fact that a number of potential full members currently catalog in RLIN and would find CONSER contribution problematic, there are still many other candidate libraries among OCLC members. It may be that the library community at large is satisfied with CONSER's coverage of the serial literature and see little gain in adding to the membership roster.

CONSER is often referred to as a model for successful cooperation. Most recently, librarians engaged in planning and evaluating the National Coordinated Cataloging Program have looked to CONSER for elements that might improve coordination, ease contribution, and lower costs (e.g. BSSC, 1990, p. 6; Philips, 1991). A number of features can be identified as characterizing the CONSER model of cooperative cataloging:

1. CONSER governance is participatory. Libraries join as members, and all full and national members are represented on the governing committees. Operational staff from member libraries are involved in the committes.

2. CONSER members have the opportunity to participate not only in record contribution but in activities related to national serials management policy such as standards evaluation and program planning.

3. LC provides staff support for coordinating activities as well as considerable support for and participation in maintenance of the database.

4. LC distributes tapes of authenticated CONSER records through its Cataloging Distribution Service.

5. Because serials records are continually maintained, participants update, upgrade, and enrich each other's records. This differs from monographic

cooperative cataloging projects in which each participant's contribution is made independently.

6. CONSER members catalog independently and self-authenticate their records. Representatives from member libraries are initially trained at LC in CONSER conventions and procedures. Following training, all records submitted are reviewed by LC staff, usually for a period of about 6 months. As described in the *Guide* (p. A4.6.5), once an institution "demonstrates knowledge sufficient to authenticate its own records and to modify LC-authenticated records" records are not reviewed. Small samples of member work are drawn from the database for ongoing quality control monitoring.

7. Contribution of records is online into the OCLC database. For most CONSER members, this is the normal mode of operation and no additional procedures are necessary for CONSER contribution.

8. Libraries select the titles they wish to contribute to CONSER. For most libraries, normal serials cataloging activity constitutes the CONSER contribution.

9. CONSER cataloging standards are essentially the same standards that most members would elect to follow for their own operations.[5]

10. OCLC offers pricing incentives for CONSER participation, including additional cataloging credit and some discount on telecommunications.

11. Program members have a clear sense of mission and goals. Goals statements are part of CONSER documentation. Adaptability and openness to reconsideration of goals have marked the project since its inception.

Although cost studies have not been done of CONSER participation, most members (as exemplified in Philips, 1990) believe that there is little additional cost to the institution for CONSER contribution once training and review have been completed. Libraries have not usually needed to adjust procedures, workflow, or standards to contribute. Thus, in the view of most CONSER libraries, the cost benefit equation weighs in favor of membership.

B. Name Authority Cooperative

The acronym NACO today refers to a suite of cooperative cataloging programs coordinated by LC under the rubric National Coordinated Cataloging Operations. The largest of these programs is the Name Authority Cooperative, and despite the official name change in 1987 ("NACO Changes Its Name," 1987), the appellation NACO is largely used to refer to the name authorities effort. Fenly (Fenly and Irvine, 1986) describes the mission of

[5] There is one exception to the consensus on serials cataloging standards: the controversy over successive versus latest entry cataloging. However, while many U.S. libraries find that successive entry cataloging creates problems for readers trying to interpret local serials holdings, the great majority of libraries recognize a need to follow this standard.

NACO "to produce a nation-wide authority file which will support biblio-graphic cooperation with records which meet LC standards for quality and to share the cost burden of the most expensive part of the cataloging process" (p. 9).

The official history of NACO begins in October, 1977, with an agreement between LC and the U.S. Government Printing Office (GPO) to use and maintain a common name authority file, enabling LC in turn to accept GPO descriptive cataloging records without adjusting headings. At that time, there was no online access to a shared authority file, but the vision of such a service began to take shape. At a meeting sponsored by the Council on Library Resources (CLR) in September, 1979, ("An Integrated," 1980), representa-tives from the national libraries [LC, the National Library of Medicine (NLM), and the National Agricultural Library (NAL)] and the bibliographic utilities [OCLC, RLIN, Western Library Network (WLN)] agreed that it was both possible and desirable to build and maintain a shared "integrated, consistent authority file for nationwide use." CLR, under its Bibliographic Service Development Program (BSDP) took on the coordination of planning work, including developing procedures for building the file, identifying ser-vice requirements, and recommending policies. (The work is described in BSDP, 1984.) At the same time, LC worked within the existing environment to expand participation and gain experience in working with the contributions of other libraries. The Texas State Library was added in 1979; the University of Wisconsin at Madison and the University of Texas at Austin joined in early 1980. As activity increased, LC allocated a number of staff within its Descriptive Cataloging Division to the support of cooperative endeavors.

Initially contribution to NACO was cumbersome. Lacking an online file, participants had to search the NUC and the Name Authority microfiche to determine if a heading had been established. As described by Rather (1984, p. 10) worksheets for new headings were submitted to LC by mail; LC in turn searched local files and then input the record to the LC MARC database. Fortunately, the project made steady progress toward online implementation. Access to the online authority file at LC was available to participants in 1983. In subsequent years, RLIN and OCLC provided search-only access to the file, at first based on tape-loaded authority data. With the implementation of the LSP for Authorities, the RLIN and OCLC files could be updated as new records were added to the LC file, and by 1987, NACO participants could enter authorities data online to RLIN and OCLC for transmission via LSP back to LC (and out again). Thus, the three files could be synchronized and serve as a virtual central authority file.

As operations could be automated, NACO expanded. In 1988, the monthly contribution of records to LC via LSP averaged 1,300; in 1989, 2,300; in 1990, 5,200; and in 1991, 7,600. By 1991, there were 43 libraries participating (LC, 1991, p. 8); over 500,000 authority records had been added to the file by participants, with participant records accounting for 36% of the new authority records entering the database. (Figures are from *Library of Congress Information Bulletin*, Oct. 21, 1991, pp. 404–405, and *Cooperative Cataloging News* 1, p. 1.) The creation of the "national" shared name authority file is generally considered to be one of the most successful cooperative efforts that American libraries have undertaken. The reasons for its success are worth noting. First, it is the realization of the vision of an online shared file. That is, both contribution to and distribution of the file have been fully automated so that participation does not require an overlay of additional procedures for routine input. Rather (1984, p. 10) identifies another success factor as the lack of an authentication requirement—a lesson learned from the CONSER project. After a library's staff is trained by LC catalogers, the LC staff monitors the quality of the libraries' submissions; once a certain accuracy rate is achieved a library is deemed "independent" and its contributions are no longer reviewed.

However, there is still a significant procedural and administrative over-head for both LC and NACO participants. Much time is invested in training and review, and many libraries find the requirements for establishing headings for the NACO file to be more arduous than those they would impose locally. A cost study of 30 NACO participants conducted by LC in 1986 (Barry, 1987) found that most libraries invested significantly more staff time in such activities as training and revision for NACO work as opposed to authority work performed only for the local catalog. For all but seven institutions, NACO participation was an added cost. However, both the actual NACO costs and the percentage of increase for NACO work varied widely (as is typically the case for library cost data; practices are highly variable), sug-gesting that participants have considerable control over the workflows and practices they adopt for NACO and that a conscious effort to reduce and control the costs of NACO participation could be successful at many sites.

The known costs of NACO contribution do not seem to have greatly discouraged participation, as the number of NACO libraries continues to grow. A key aspect of cooperative name authority work is that the benefits of the effort are tangible and clearly understood. As Burger (1990) notes, "NACO worked . . . because it did something that was not being done before, namely it standardized authority data for which no standard had previously existed, and made this data available nationally" (p. 65). Although RLIN and OCLC could make member catalog records available to any library that needed it, the authority information, chiefly in the form of cross-refer-ences, which is a valuable part of the access provided by the record would be unobtainable without NACO. Few librarians would disagree that access to a nation-wide authority file saves local cataloging costs and, because it enables the low-cost provision of references, improves access for library users.

Other related and potentially problematic aspects of NACO are the very strong central governance role played by LC, which determines (with some consultation) the policies, standards, and procedures for the program and the imposition by the Library of high standards for researching and formulating headings, which in turn affects the costs for participating libraries. It may be that these terms and standards have not been questioned in part because no other model of cooperative contribution for authority data has ever been proposed or tested. LC leadership of this program has been central to NACO's success from the outset; OCLC and RLIN have provided technical support, in the form of LSP implementation (and only with urging from LC), but no leadership. The LC-defined standard of authority work is the only form of authority information that has been nationally distributed, and for many catalogers, the worksheets initially submitted to NACO were the first MARC-format encoded authority records they had created. While NACO libraries view their costs as worthwhile, only a small fraction of RLIN and OCLC members are providing authority records along with their catalog to a national file.

C. ARL Microform Project

The ARL Microform Project has been a highly focused exercise in cooperative cataloging, designed to address a clear and specific need. That need—bibliographic access to titles published in large microform sets—was recognized as early as 1960 when ARL commissioned its first study of the problem from Wesley Simonton (1962). Included in Simonton's recommendations, which addressed such issues as standards for microform production and cataloging records, was the need for cooperative cataloging of titles in major sets (p. 32). However, it took more than 20 years and several more studies before that recommendation was acted on. The investigations and discussions during that 20-year period are well documented, and are summarized in the report prepared for ARL (Boss, 1983) that finally initiated the ARL Microform Project. Although the issue was given much study and attention, before the ARL Project was established no one organization had taken responsibility for action to solve the problem. Describing the proceedings of an ALA committee meeting convened to address the need in 1976, Boss observes, "The consensus among the members of the subcommittee after the first meeting was that bibliographic control of microforms could not be achieved at the local level until direction, coordination, and definition were provided at the national level by such groups as ALA, LC, and the National Commission on Libraries and Information Science (NCLIS)" (p. 17). Apparently, this was not an area in which LC felt it could take a major leadership role. In summarizing the proceedings of a 1978 meeting convened to address the topic, Boss notes that Joseph Howard, then Associate Librarian for Processing Services at LC, indicated "that while LC thought that the subcommittee's work was of great importance, the Library would not be able to contribute much in the way of cataloging microforms until other priorities at LC had been accomplished" (p. 18). The problem was of sufficient concern to large research libraries that ARL agreed to take an active role in addressing it, including the allocation of staff time to the effort.

ARL obtained grant support to commission the development of "a plan of action for the cooperative creation and dissemination of bibliographic records for titles in microform collections" (ARL proposal appended to Boss, 1983, p. 73). That plan, prepared by Boss, was approved by the ARL Board in January 1981; in the summer of 1981 ARL obtained funding to implement the plan and hired a project coordinator. The key elements of the plan included:

1. Agreements on standards and standard practices for creating bibliographic records for microforms
2. Encouragement of contribution of records, both new cataloging and retrospective conversion, to bibliographic utilities by both libraries and microform publishers
3. Development of "set processing" or "profile matching" whereby a library can add its holdings symbol to all records for an entire set in one step and can obtain tapes (or, at the time, cards) of all records for a set for loading into a local catalog

Once both RLG and OCLC agreed to develop the "set processing" capability and standards issues had been resolved, the ARL Project Coordinator's efforts were largely devoted to establishing a database and clearinghouse of information regarding libraries' holdings of large microform sets. Information in the database enabled libraries to determine which sets should be given highest priority for cataloging and where cataloging partners could be found. The Coordinator also assisted in the preparation of grant proposals for cataloging. Within a very short time, the project had a noticeable impact on the availability of records for microform sets. By 1984, the last year in which ARL provided dedicated staff support for the program, the Coordinator (Heynen, 1984) wrote

> The basic goals of the project have been achieved or are well on the way to accomplishment. A surprising number of major microform cataloging projects are well underway in U.S. and Canadian libraries. For example, 41 of the 85 sets that were given highest-priority for cataloging in the Microform Project survey are already fully cataloged in machine readable form or are in the process of becoming cataloging on either . . . OCLC or . . RLIN. (p. 3)

The project evolved into an ongoing program with the assumption of planning responsibility by the ALA Committee on Bibliographic Control of Microforms in 1984. Accomplishment has been slow but consistently steady since the initial period of high activity.

As with any project, microform set cataloging has not been entirely free of problems. The divided database environment has created complications, although arrangements were made in 1986 to exchange records for sets cataloged with HEA Title II-C funding. ("OCLC and RLG Exchange," 1986, p.79.) Tape exchange is a relatively acceptable mode of operation for bibliographic control of microform sets; because these records are not needed for current cataloging and, in fact, are added to local catalogs in batch, timely access it not necessary. The situation was further complicated, however, because development of the set processing capability was slow to come in RLIN, where it was not available until 1990. Thus, the main locus of activity became the OCLC database. In fact, by the time RLIN released set processing, so few unique sets resided in the RLIN database that few orders were placed; RLIN announced it would discontinue the service in 1992. OCLC, on the other hand, has provided a modest level of ongoing support for the program. The Marketing and User Services Division maintains and disseminates information on the status of projects, and cataloging and related technical advice is provided to libraries that wish to undertake a project, along with pricing incentives to encourage contribution.

Standardized establishment of headings is an important aspect of cooperative microform set cataloging, because libraries must be able to add set records in batch to local catalogs without checking each record. Joachim (1986) observes that the authority control workload can be great, particularly for sets of literary works or pre-20th century titles (which are common). He stresses the importance of NACO participation for libraries contributing set records, because such work will greatly enrich the national authority file. Another benefit of NACO contribution, not mentioned by Joachim, would be the availability of authority records and cross references for libraries adding set records to their catalogs. Whereas few libraries would wish to identify those authority records individually for each title, libraries subscribing to batch authority processing services could match tapes and acquire accompanying cross references by doing so. However, NACO participation has not been considered a requirement for libraries cataloging microform analytics; checking headings against the NACO file to insure no conflict is the minimum need.

OCLC now lists close to 90 microform sets available in its database, and new sets continue to be added. Based on OCLC's listing alone, access is provided to over 378,000 individual titles in microform sets. OCLC (R. Van Orden, personal communication, January 1992) reports that 226 institutions have purchased at least one set each; more than 900 sets have been sold since the program began. Such wide distribution represents greatly improved access to titles in microform sets. Significant microform publishers have become persuaded of the value of providing bibliographic data in this manner to accompany newly marketed sets. University Microfilms International routinely provides machine-readable cataloging for its sets (entered online to OCLC and also available via tape); Chadwyck Healey and Research Publications have also used this approach. Some large sets, such as *American Fiction* have been cataloged or converted by joint projects in which the titles within the set are divided up among a number of libraries. However, this method has a cost in overhead for coordinating the individual project. A simpler procedure is for one institution to assume responsibility for an entire set. This approach still falls under the definition of cooperative cataloging, as the library assumes responsibility for cataloging the set to accepted standards and works with OCLC to include a "set symbol" in each record and to include the set in OCLC's Major Microforms List. Many of the earlier projects and some recent ones have been supported by grant funds. Publishers have also encouraged libraries to catalog their sets, providing incentives such as funding support or free copies of the set in question; such vendor/library cooperation is one of the beneficial results of the Project. Other records have been supplied as a result of cataloging that a library chose to perform as a local priority. This latter method has worked because very little additional effort or adjustment to routine workflow is required for a library to contribute set records. Ease of contribution may help to explain why sets continue to be added to the OCLC database.

The ARL Microform Project and its successor in the OCLC Major Microforms Service represent a relatively uncomplex model of cooperative cataloging. The well-defined nature of sets makes assignment of responsibility clear cut, so that little overhead is required for coordination. Libraries have continued to contribute sets, albeit at a much slower pace, even after ARL discontinued dedicated staff for the program. Whereas external grant support played a significant role in adding many large important sets to the database retrospectively, new sets continue to be added without special funding. With the exception of adding a set symbol, cataloging and workflow routines need not differ from those a library would use for full-level standard cataloging online to a utility. It is perhaps worth noting that, once initial standards for set cataloging were agreed on, there has been relatively little discussion of the quality of microform set records, and centralized training and documentation have not been seen as pressing needs for the program. Most libraries add these records to their catalogs in batch and do not routinely review the cataloging record-by-record; this is certainly one plausible explanation for the low level of criticism of microform set records. Because the records are analytics, they are viewed more as a means of catalog enrichment, rather than as a source of copy cataloging, and are accepted in catalogs on a "no-conflict" basis. Perhaps there is a lesson here for other models of shared cataloging as well.

D. ARL Retrospective Conversion Project

In the spring of 1983, CLR "initiated an assessment of the current level of retrospective conversion and an exploration of the primary issues needing attention if libraries are to convert their bibliographic files to machine-readable form effectively and economically." (Objective as quoted in the report of the study, Reed-Scott, Gregor, and Payne, 1984, p.1.) The Council study was issued in 1984 and served as the basis for an invitational conference that same year (Gregor, 1984) "to determine whether or not it was desirable to develop a strategy for the creation and standardization of a national database and, if so, to suggest the steps necessary for achieving that end" (p. 1). As noted in the conference report (Gregor, 1984), the study had identified the current situation to be one of "database anarchy" in which a decentralized approach to recon had resulted in wasteful duplication of records and a lack of consistency in applying standards. Individual libraries were striving to convert records at the lowest cost possible, and short term considerations were overtaking the larger need to support scholarship and research with an "openly accessible, consistent, logical national database of bibliographic records reflecting the nation's library resources." After reviewing various options and issues, meeting participants agreed that research libraries should participate in a coordinated program to convert research collections in a cooperative mode using a subject-based approach. They recommended that ARL assume program definition and management oversight responsibilities.

During 1985, ARL undertook a planning study (Reed-Scott, 1985) and subsequently initiated a 2-year pilot project to begin implementation of "a North American Program . . . . to coordinate the systematic conversion of 6-7 million bibliographic records for monographs" (Reed-Scott, 1985, p. 13). Key elements of the plan included

1. *Record distribution.* Agreements were reached for RLG to distribute records for designated projects via LC and for OCLC to distribute project records to RLIN and other not-for-profit organizations.

2. *Cataloging standards.* Guidelines addressing authority work and fullness of records were adopted. Authority checking was a vexing problem because many libraries chose to do batch, postinput authority processing on files of retrospective conversion records. Some libraries interpreted the guidelines to include postinput verification as long as processed records were loaded into national files.

3. *Governance and coordination.* The ARL governance structure provided policy oversight of the project and a full-time coordinator was hired.

4. *Determining subject projects.* Projects were to be developed based on LC classification and subjects, with institutions' contributions based on collection strength.

5. *Funding strategies.* Increasing the external funding available for retrospective conversion was a key element of the plan. Unlike current cataloging, retrospective conversion was not already budgeted into most libraries' operational expenditures. Given the added costs of coordination and of raising standards, and the goal of increasing the level of recon activity to improve database coverage, subsidies to participating libraries were necessary.

The ARL Recon Project operated actively through June 1987; at the spring 1987 meeting (ARL, 1987, p. 51) the association elected not to continue the staffing support for coordination beyond the 2-year pilot period. Although several successful coordinated conversion projects have been completed, only one or two—a long-running series of projects to convert Latin American titles is the only clear cut example—can point directly to origins in the ARL pilot. In its report on the pilot, the Association's Committee on Bibliographic Control (1987) noted that:

> The overall results of the project are mixed. On the positive side, coordinated projects have been planned, guidelines for record creation have been established, record sharing agreements have been adopted, interest in recon has been stimulated, OCLC special credits have been provided and a substantial number of records have been converted. On the negative side, little funding has been attracted, the development of projects has been slow, the agreement to distribute records is more restrictive than was envisioned and record distribution has been too slow for effective coordination. (p. C5)

From its inception, the ARL Retrospective Conversion Project grappled with the issue of whether coordination of retrospective conversion efforts provided significant added value to the conversion work that libraries were doing on their own. The ARL Plan (Reed-Scott, 1985) noted, "that the research library community is not united in its assessment of the need for the program" (p. 10). Perceived disadvantages of a coordinated approach over individual projects included increase in complexity and costs of projects, delays in organizing projects, and competition for funding with projects that individual libraries would consider higher priority. To understand the successes and failures of the ARL project, it is useful to consider the situation that prevailed for retrospective conversion work before the ARL pilot in comparison with the standard "utility-based model" that was operating for current cataloging.

As described earlier, the desire for a coordinated recon program stemmed from the sense of "database anarchy" in the area of retrospective conversion. The economics of retrospective conversion had worked against the adoption of some of the important norms, conventions, and agreements that were in effect for current original cataloging. For example, the split database environment was potentially a more vexing problem for retrospective conversion than for current cataloging. That is, because of the great expense of performing original cataloging, many libraries were willing to search more than one database for copy before duplicating another library's effort. Thus, although the split database environment creates additional expense for searching, it need not engender wasteful duplicative cataloging work. The economics of recon are different, however, because avoiding the costs of inputting an existing record may not merit investing in the expense of dual searching (unless the hit rate in the second database searched is still very high) or the expense of using a second utility. As a result, there was a concern that considerable duplicative input was occurring. As described in the ARL evaluation, the pilot project had only limited success in addressing this situation.

The most striking difference between retrospective and current cataloging work at the time was the lack of agreed-on standards for input of retrospective records. Because the cost of new original cataloging is high and because original cataloging is a relatively small percentage of most libraries' total cataloging workload, the profession had arrived at general agreement that the additional costs of meeting national standards for original cataloging were worth the investment. That is, commonly accepted national standards, including checking the NACO authority file, could be built into the ongoing original cataloging workload at relatively little, if any, additional cost to routine operations and had considerable payoff in savings to copy cataloging. This model did not necessarily apply to retrospective conversion work, work that in and of itself was a new expense to a library's budget. Older manual records often did not meet standards currently in effect, and libraries were reluctant to upgrade them. Each library was struggling to define an acceptable conversion standard for its own catalog. Wide adoption of the ARL guidelines, although with some compromises regarding postinput authority work, was a major achievement in ensuring that libraries would create recon records that would be economical for other libraries' use.

Once standards had been agreed on and the split database environment brought to the best level of equilibrium that could be achieved, the model for recon activity could be compared with that for current cataloging. At that point, the added value of coordination must be given careful scrutiny. In the scope of the ARL project, the real value of coordination would be to improve and increase subject coverage of the database(s). Although this is a worthy goal, the ARL project was unable to attract significant external funding to aid libraries in meeting that goal. With libraries hard pressed to find internal funds to cover the cost of recon for the highest local priorities, systematic database coverage—as opposed to the coverage built from a natural accumulation of individual projects—was not a compelling reason for libraries to bear the added costs of cooperation. In hindsight, and taking a lesson from the success of the ARL Microform Project, the overhead of cooperation might have been made low enough to bear. That is, once priorities and needs for coverage in the national database were identified, subject coverage could be achieved through a series of loosely coordinated individual projects. In a manner similar to cataloging a particular microform set, each library could determine its own area of responsibility, provide information about that scope to other libraries, and meet agreed-on standards in its conversion project. This could avoid the elaborate arrangements needed for a group of libraries to share conversion in the same subject field and to develop a coordinated plan of work. To some extent, that situation prevails now, except that there is no overall review of lacunae in the database or determination of priorities. The current "model" of retrospective conversion activity does not include explicit cooperative effort to address overarching priorities to improve database coverage.

E. National Coordinated Cataloging Program (NCCP)

Planning for NCCP began at a meeting organized by LC in May, 1986, and attended by representatives of LC, RLG Board of Directors, and the Research Libraries Advisory Committee (RLAC) of OCLC. As described by Avram and Wiggins (1988b), the group's aim was to improve on the standard model of shared cataloging in a bibliographic utility, by building "a national database in which all the records are of quality high enough to be accepted into a local database or library without any modification." The program would allow different libraries to catalog into a "single database into which the records they contribute will be integrated in a consistent manner." As reflected in the minutes of the organizational meeting (Avram, 1986), the essential features distinguishing "coordinated" cataloging from routine shared cataloging would be: agreement to follow LC procedures and rule interpretations, submission of new names and subjects for inclusion in the national name and subject authority files, operation via LSP, distribution of records by LC, and maintenance of records in LC's files. Four objectives were articulated (Avram and Wiggins, 1988b, p. 112) for the program:

1. To increase the timeliness of cataloging copy
2. To extend cataloging coverage
3. To reduce duplicative effort
4. To produce cataloging of national-level quality

Participants agreed to move forward with a relatively small pilot project consisting of eight university libraries (Harvard, Indiana, Yale, Chicago, California at Berkeley, Illinois at Urbana-Champaign, Michigan, and Texas at Austin) working with the Library of Congress. A steering committee was formed, with its core membership the directors of the eight participating libraries, along with an operations planning group of the technical services heads of the pilot institutions.

The following year was devoted to planning, as participants considered such issues as cost control, areas of cataloging responsibility, training, and logistics. The last consideration was particularly problematic because LSP for bibliographic record transfer between the utilities and LC was not operational, and arrangements had to be made for an effective direct telecommunications link between LC and each participating library. Although it was recognized that the lack of an LSP link would add significant cost and administrative overhead to the project, participants expected the link to be available soon and agreed that, because so much could be learned in the other aspects of the program, it was important to move forward with a pilot.

Planning efforts were aided by the experience of two of the NCCP libraries; Harvard and Chicago had been engaged in a cooperative cataloging effort with LC for several years and were already experienced in cataloging online to LC and in meeting LC standards. Representatives from these institutions were able to raise questions that they knew would be encountered when the pilot began operations (e.g., Nadler, 1987). Minutes of the planning meetings reflect that considerable attention was given to the need during the pilot to control and monitor the additional costs that the program was likely to create for participants. This included consideration of possible means to reimburse participants, as their efforts were intended to result in savings for LC and other libraries that would use their national-level cataloging. Another set of discussions centered on the question of how best to assign cataloging responsibilities. It is cost-effective for libraries to be guided largely by local priorities in selecting material for timely original cataloging; this is one of the attractive features of the general "utility model" of shared cataloging. However, in the case of a coordinated program, training and communication would be easier if each library restricted its contribution to a special language or subject, so that only one or two staff members in each library need be trained at the outset and LC could make best use of its staff assigned to work with NCCP libraries. Another consideration was database coverage. On the one hand was a general desire by some planners to improve the overall coverage of the national database for scholarly materials. On the other hand, providing records for other libraries to use cost-effectively was the central objective of the program, so assignments needed to reflect areas where collections—and thus need for records—overlapped. A sensible compromise was reached. LC coverage was already adequate for American imprints, and LC staff had considerable skills in lesser known languages. The areas in which copy was most needed by and from other research libraries were current imprints in Western European languages and scholarly materials in

English not covered by the CIP program. Within that broad range, each participant agreed to a fairly loose area of responsibility that essentially corresponded to the expertise and routine assignment of the cataloger(s) who would be trained for NCCP participation.

All of the planners recognized that no matter how carefully operational costs were controlled, the start-up costs for organization and training would be considerable. In addition, the pilot period would be subjected to the high telecommunications costs of equipment and line charges to link each library to LC. CLR provided a grant to LC to cover travel and partial telecommunications costs for a 2-year pilot period. LC assumed responsibility for assigning staff to training, consultation, and ongoing record evaluation. The Council shared the planners' view that careful evaluation of the pilot experiences was an essential feature of the effort. Not only was it important to test operational questions, but to understand better the factors that contribute to the underlying assumption that the coordinated cataloging model was of great value in extending the use of bibliographic products. The Council, with the agreement and advice of the steering committee, asked its BSSC [6] to conduct an evaluation of the pilot that would supplement the operational examination undertaken by pilot participants and LC. Thus from the outset, the NCCP pilot became a self-conscious laboratory for testing assumptions and models of cooperative cataloging activity.

The pilot operation, which got underway in the spring of 1988, included the following elements:

1. *LC leadership.* The project was led by and coordinated by LC. Combining the program administratively with NACO, LC provided staff for training and coordination.

2. *LC training and revision.* NCCP catalogers were provided considerable training and documentation by LC. Participants' records then underwent thorough revision until records met strict standards for accuracy as defined by LC staff. Once these standards were met, participants were then considered to be "independent," with records reviewed only on a sample basis.

3. *LC standards.* NCCP participants were asked to catalog strictly to LC-defined standards and practices. It was understood that once libraries had mastered those, the LC standards would be subjected to review by the participants in an effort to reach mutually agreed-on standards.

4. *Consistency with LC bibliographic file.* Participating catalogers were expected to search all new headings against the LC bibliographic file to assure consistency with that file. (Not all headings in the LC file are yet included in

---

[6] The author was chair of BSSC during the NCCP evaluation. Other members were Dorothy Gregor and Martin Runkle. Paul Kantor served as consultant to the Committee, and Warren Haas met regularly with the group.

the NACO file.) New headings and subjects would be established in accordance with NACO and LC practice.

5. *Online input to LC*. Participants input their records online into the LC bibliographic file. (For most participants, this duplicated or replaced input into a bibliographic utility or local system; for all, it was an exceptional practice.)

6. *LC record distribution*. LC distributed the records via its MARC tape distribution.

In May of 1990, a joint meeting of the steering and the operations committees was held to evaluate the program. At that point, some 10,000 records had been contributed via the project. Start-up had been slow in some libraries, because of telecommunications problems or staffing turnover or both. Therefore, not all libraries had yet reached "independent" status, that is, the status whereby only a small sample of records are reviewed for quality control rather than a full revision of each record by LC staff. Five of the libraries were fully independent; three were still undergoing revision in some aspects of their work. The project was only just beginning to move from "start-up" to "operational" mode. Because the pilot had not operated in the LSP mode, several of NCCP's initial objectives could not be tested. That is, increasing timeliness of cataloging, extending cataloging coverage, and reducing duplication of effort would presumably have been achieved by LC's distribution of NCCP records to an audience greater than an individual participant's bibliographic utility. Evaluations centered on the core NCCP goal, the effort to produce more cataloging of "national-level" quality.

Discussions at the 1990 meeting included the BSSC evaluation, subsequently published in August 1990 (BSSC, 1990), and assessments by the participants and LC. The BSSC report focused on the complex relationships between the added costs engendered by the NCCP model in relation to the benefits, defined as cost savings, to LC and other libraries for using the "national-level" records created. The analysis looked at the interplay of costs and savings between three groups: NCCP participants, LC, and other ARL libraries. Costs and savings for LC and participants could be directly measured. Benefits to other ARL libraries were projected from a study comparing the costs of LC copy cataloging (and presumably, therefore, NCCP copy cataloging—an assumption of similarity that could not be tested during the pilot period) with the costs of member copy cataloging in a sample of ARL libraries. That study found a median savings of 37% when a library had LC copy available. (Kantor, 1990, p. 22) The BSSC analysis also compared costs during different phases of the pilot project and in a post-LSP future: before libraries achieved independence, when they were newly independent (and still interacting frequently with LC), when libraries reached mature independence (based on Harvard and Chicago), and pre- and post-LSP. It was clear, and not surprising, that before libraries reached mature independence and until telecommunications costs could be brought down, costs would heavily outweigh benefits. Even in a fully operational, post-LSP environment, the cost/benefit picture would be complex. At best, LC savings would outweigh participants costs, and additionally, each library that used the records would benefit, so that the overall model could be cost-beneficial. However, without some direct compensation from LC or, even less likely, from other libraries using the records, there would be no way for participants themselves to recoup their significant costs. (Although participants, like other ARL libraries would achieve some savings in copy cataloging when they used other NCCP library records, studies of collection overlap indicated that their use would not be frequent enough to equal their investment.)

BSSC (BSSC, 1990, pp. 3–7) suggested several areas to explore to improve the balance and effectiveness of the NCCP model.

1. Costs of telecommunications should be lowered. If LSP did not become operational, direct input to the participant's utility (as in CONSER) should be considered. This in turn would require further investigation of the relative importance of searching LC's files before cataloging.

2. Participants needed to move to independence more quickly. This implied not only consideration of a participating library's ability, but also the requirements of independence.

3. LC and the participants did not yet share a common view of the standards and practices that define "national-level" cataloging. Participants' costs could be lowered if LC brought its practices more in line with those of participants.

4. Cataloging assignments and selection of future participants should aim for contribution of high-use records, so that the maximum benefit of the investment in "national-level" cataloging could be gained. During the pilot phase this had worked well, as the average use of an NCCP record for copy cataloging by an ARL library was considerably higher than the use of ARL member copy generally in OCLC.

Participants' evaluations also reflected a desire to lower the investment required for contribution. At the meeting, many indicated that during the pilot, the costs of NCCP contribution had translated into somewhat lower production of original cataloging. They expressed concern about LC's too-rigorous evaluation of their records and especially disagreed with the standards by which their subject cataloging had been reviewed. (One cannot help but note the similarity of their criticisms to those made by the 1940 committee evaluating LC's earlier Cooperative Cataloging and Classification Service.) However, they also highly valued the close working relationship their catalogers had developed with LC staff, the advantages of access to LC's bibliographic file as a resource tool in cataloging work, and, perhaps most important, the opportunity to work with LC to shape cataloging standards. LC, in turn, noted the great potential savings for its operations of continuing NCCP and equally valued the opportunity to work with other research libraries to seek ways to optimize cataloging standards. It was clear to all that a great deal was being learned from the pilot effort and that there was considerable opportunity for improvement and continued development. Although LSP bibliographic record transfer was not yet available, all agreed that a 1-year extension of the pilot was desirable as long as participants did not need to bear the direct cost of telecommunications. The pilot was extended through October of 1991.

At the end of the pilot's third year, in November 1991, another joint meeting of the steering and operations groups was held to determine next steps (NCCP Steering Committee, 1992). Attendees frankly acknowledged that although LC was realizing savings from the use of NCCP records, costs to participants of NCCP cataloging continued to be a problem. It was also apparent that LSP would not become operational for bibliographic records in the immediate future, so that participants could not expect to gain savings by inputting to LC via a utility or their local system. To confront these problems, LC proposed a new model for NCCP operation. While libraries would continue to input records directly to LC, many of the other exceptional routines required by NCCP would be removed. The key change in the new model was, to use CONSER terminology, essentially a shift to full self-authentication. As described in the summary distributed to NACO participants ("Alternative Model for NCCP Pilot—Year 4," dated December 24, 1991; see "Alternative Model," 1992), "Record quality/accuracy will be the responsibility of each participant. LC will cease sample checking for quality control purposes. Record level/completeness will adhere to the full-level record requirements as defined by the utility of choice for each participant." Participants were also invited to extend their contributions to any subject and language areas they wished, once competence was demonstrated in one area. Another major change agreed to for Year 4 was to open participation to additional NACO member libraries. Training for new libraries could be on-site either at the library or at LC, followed by full review and feedback for a period of only 3 months. Conscious of the importance of assessing their approach to coordinated cataloging, the group agreed to track costs to participants and savings to LC, and to conduct a formal evaluation at the end of 1 year.

Throughout the design and evaluation effort for the pilot, planners have carefully considered the elements of the model and have often used comparisons with CONSER to help focus on relevant features. (Comparisons with CONSER are included, e.g., in Welsh, 1987; Philips, 1991; NCCP Steering

Committee, 1992). The new NCCP model more closely aligns the models of training, revision, evaluation and "self-authentication" for the two programs. Also, NCCP participants are now free to contribute records in any subject they handle in their routine cataloging, as do CONSER members. However, there are still some significant differences, and these may prove instructive at the point of NCCP's fourth-year evaluation (and in CONSER's ongoing planning):

1. *Participation and governance.* Although both NCCP and CONSER are coordinated through LC, CONSER functions more in the manner of a membership organization, with participants taking a more equal and active role in determining policies and activities than they do in NCCP. This style has evolved as a function of CONSER's history; NCCP is more similar to NACO in the centrality of LC's founding leadership.

2. *Program goals.* CONSER's programmatic goals are broader than database contribution and include an explicit effort to play a leadership role in improving serials librarianship. Although NCCP discussions have in fact led to national efforts such as cataloging simplification and a conference to streamline LCSH (LC subject headings) subdivision practice, it is not a stated goal of NCCP to serve as program to address general issues related to cataloging. For example, CONSER members form task forces to address particular issues and problems; NCCP has not functioned in this mode to date.

3. *Agreement on standards.* There is wide agreement among CONSER members on cataloging standards as represented by the editing guide. NCCP is striving to reach such agreement on standards, but has not yet achieved this.

4. *Consistency with NACO versus LC file.* Although both NCCP and CONSER catalogers perform authority work against the NACO file, NCCP members search the LC bibliographic file online before cataloging to insure that their records are consistent with the LC file; CONSER members search the CONSER file on OCLC. NCCP members incur added costs for searching the LC file; LC (NCCP Steering Committee, 1992, p. 2) indicates that it incurs added costs for modifying CONSER records when it uses them for cataloging.

5. *Online input to LC versus OCLC.* CONSER members input records online to OCLC; for those libraries that are OCLC members, this does not represent any additional workload or costs in routine. Although NCCP was originally designed for contributors to input records into their utility and then send them to LC via LSP, the reality for the foreseeable future is that NCCP contributors will continue to input records online to LC; for most libraries this represents a duplicative or nonstandard input stream.

The last two elements are likely to undergo the greatest scrutiny as the NCCP model evolves. LC has been unwilling to relinquish the requirement that contributors search the LC bibliographic file, maintaining that this search is what insures "national-level" quality. Others maintain that consistency against the NACO file is the appropriate "national-level" standard; the additional search of the LC file saves local cataloging costs at LC but places undue burden on the overall system of cooperative cataloging. Unfortunately, the BSSC study of member versus LC copy cataloging costs did not address this issue but simply assumed that NCCP cataloging would be the same as LC's. There are no empirical data comparing the costs to ARL libraries of using records with "NACO-consistent" versus "LC-consistent" headings. The requirement for online input to LC is a matter of technical limitations on tape loading at the Library. If a search of the LC file online is desirable, then the matter of input is just a small additional overhead. However, if searching the LC file is not deemed worth the cost, an alternate means of sharing records with the Library will need to be found.

The invitation extended to a wider group of libraries to join NCCP has opened up the discussion about the value of the NCCP model to a larger audience. As noted previously, the pilot has served quite explicitly as a laboratory for testing assumptions about coordinated cataloging. And, in addition to the concerns expressed by BSSC and by participants about cataloging standards and costs, there have been other criticisms. OCLC members (Racine, 1989) have noted the potential for losses to the OCLC database as a result of the distribution of member cataloging by LC. Burger (1990) has cautioned against the potential harmful effects of the "vague goal" of "national level quality" that can negatively affect the nation's overall original cataloging production by increasing the cataloging costs of NCCP participants. These concerns highlight the complexity of designing an effective cooperative cataloging program within the already complex, and largely effective, shared database environment.

V. Aligning Models and Goals of Cooperative Cataloging

A. What Can Cooperation Achieve?

Burger's caution against "vague goals" is apt in the realm of cooperative cataloging, for it has frequently been a problem. When NCCP was in very preliminary planning stages, an optimistic editorial in *Journal of Academic Librarianship* (Dougherty, 1986) proposed, "What do we have to gain from such an effort? Lower costs, higher productivity, a richer database, and better served users." Although the overall system of cooperative cataloging on shared databases has achieved this promise, it is not evident that any more highly coordinated program can provide all of these benefits to all of the participants. Certainly NCCP libraries have not achieved this. For a cooperative project to be successful, it must be carefully designed so as to achieve its precise objectives and to insure that the benefits forecast by those objectives will outweigh the inevitable overhead costs of coordination. To some, this caution may seem counterintuitive. Cooperative cataloging on the bibliographic utilities has been so highly beneficial that it should be possible to improve the system further by even greater cooperation. Two principles from the field of operations research may help to illuminate why this is not necessarily the case.[7]

The first principle relates to the familiar circumstance of suboptimization that can occur when individual sectors of an organization each strive to maximize their separate gain, rather then trying to optimize the operation of the organization as a whole. This has often been observed in libraries when one department develops a short-cut procedure that creates an additional workload for another department. It is possible to view the creation of the national database as a unified enterprise and, thus, strive to design programs and procedures that optimize that enterprise. However, the overarching optimization process often requires one department to lose and another to gain. For example, one department takes on a workload because it is more efficient to locate the work there while another department is freed of the effort. Because libraries cataloging into utilities are separate entities, the balance of gains and losses cannot always operate effectively when the loser is not compensated. This was a problem faced by the NCCP participants. When the units of a larger system are in themselves independent entities with separate funding, local service requirements, and different constituencies, any effort that aims at coordinating these individual units to try to optimize the overall system must also address any negative effects on individual units.

A second relevant principle is that it is not possible to improve a system by adding resource constraints, including constraints on the way resources are allocated. At best, adding constraints will make no difference; at worst they will have a negative effect. For example, if a cook has $100 to spend on the ingredients for a dinner party, the outcome of the meal cannot be improved by imposing constraints on how the money is to be spent. That is, a cook instructed to spend, say, 50% of the money on meat, 20% on vegetables, 20% on dessert, etc., will not shop more wisely or prepare a better meal than one who is allowed to respond to bargains in the marketplace and use recipes flexibly.[8] This can also be shown in a library operations example. If staff is asked to design the speediest workflow, adding a constraint to its effort—such

---

[7] The author acknowledges and thanks Paul Kantor for suggesting the applicability of these principles to the problem at hand.

[8] Illustration suggested by Carol Kantor.

as the requirement of specific equipment—cannot improve the outcome. That is, lifting the constraint and allowing them free choice of equipment may improve, and cannot diminish, the quality of their design, whereas restricting the choice of equipment could engender a less than optimal workflow. Although constraints may be necessary, they do not improve a system. Thus, if a library is already performing original cataloging to its best advantage on a utility, adding constraints such as limiting choice of subject to contribute or changing local priorities to conform to a cooperative agreement will not improve its operations. Therefore, cooperative programs that place constraints on participants' normal operations should be given careful scrutiny. Such programs may be desirable to enrich the database or ensure coverage of a certain type of material, but they will not improve the effectiveness of participants' cataloging operations. At best, they will not have a negative effect while at the same time achieving an "external" objective. This is the mode of operation that should be aimed for in a cooperative project.

B. Enhancing the Database versus Improving Cataloging

With these cautions in mind, it is useful to analyze the objectives that cooperative programs have set out to achieve, and consider how these goals can best be facilitated. The goals of most cooperative programs fall into two categories: database enhancement and improvement in cataloging operations. Some projects hope to achieve both, but often that cannot be the case. That is, although database enhancement can improve operations in the long run for the "national cataloging enterprise," the effort of enhancement will be a cost in some way to those engaged in the program, whether this cost is an additional workload required for enhancement or just the costs of coordination. Many of the most successful cooperative projects have been those aimed at database enhancement. These include: (1) retrospective conversion projects such as the early phase of CONSER and the ARL Latin American cooperative conversion project; (2) database enrichment projects such as the CONSER A & I Coverage Project and the new cooperative effort to add subject headings to fiction titles in OCLC; and (3) projects to increase database coverage in targeted areas such as the U.S. Newspaper Project and the ARL Microform Project. Each of these projects has had a positive impact on the national database and on the libraries that use and will use the records created or enriched. At the same time, participation in these projects did not reduce costs or improve cataloging operations for the contributors. The projects were successful for contributors either because costs were supported by external funding, costs were those that participants would have expended anyway in their normal operations, or participants bore some additional cost or constraint without detriment to their normal operation.

Projects aimed at database enhancement need to be clear in their goals. Database enhancement and cataloging efficiency should be understood as two separate, separable—and sometimes mutually exclusive—objectives. Grover (1991) points out the different and sometimes conflicting views on cooperative projects between bibliographers, who strive for access to titles uniquely held by different institutions, and catalogers, who wish to share records, that is, whose work capitalizes on collection overlap rather than collection differences. He describes the failure of subject-based cooperative cataloging projects, illustrating unsuccessful agreements made to catalog Latin American materials made by bibliographers whose objectives conflicted with local cataloging priorities. Grover postulates (p. 414) that the key to success for such projects would be administrative commitment. However, the real explanation for the failure of many subject-based cooperative projects is in fact "vague goals," which allow different participants to interpret project goals differently.

The goals of cooperative projects aimed at improving cataloging operations are also subject to lack of clarity. For a project or program to "improve" cataloging, its objectives must focus on how that improvement will be achieved. There are several means to this end:

1. Facilitating the creation of more records that will be available for libraries to use.

2. Improving the quality of records so that they are easier, that is, less expensive, for libraries to use. (This should be distinguised from efforts aimed to enrich records for other purposes, such as access. In some cases, these efforts may be viewed as overlapping, as with an effort to upgrade headings. But they are not always the same, e.g., the CONSER A & I enrichment, and the distinctions may be key to the design and evaluation of the success of a project.)

3. Facilitating the timely availability of records for current imprints, as these are the focus of most libraries' cataloging operations.

4. Making best use of scarce expertise.

Even these are very broad objectives, and none is easy to achieve. The following sections will consider the nature of project design that would be aimed at these objectives.

1. More Records

Increasing the number of unique bibliographic records available in the national database not only improves access to materials but enhances cataloging operations by making more records available for use in copy cataloging. There are a number of avenues for expanding the size of the database, including: (1) increasing the resources available for original cataloging; (2) increasing the productivity of original catalogers; (3) maximizing the contribution of original records to the national database; and (4) minimizing duplicative original cataloging effort. The first avenue is perhaps the most difficult to achieve, particularly as libraries face shrinking budgets and are forced to cut back on staffing. However, cooperative efforts have played a positive role in expanding resources by attracting funding for well-defined, well-focused projects with demonstrable benefits. The U.S. Newspaper Program and the ARL Microform Project are two good examples of efforts that have attracted external funding to add original cataloging records to shared databases.

Cooperative programs have had less success in the area of streamlining the functions of original cataloging; as noted earlier, such projects may even add some element of overhead or additional workload to the original cataloging process. To the extent that NACO makes available headings used in original cataloging, it can be said to have contributed to the objective of increasing original cataloging productivity. However, NACO participation can also slow cataloging when new headings must be established and contributed. NACO participants have not published studies that weigh these costs and savings to the original cataloging process. (Note: NACO costs are all in the area of original cataloging; however, the greatest NACO benefits are to subsequent use of the records.) Programs of cooperative cataloging per se will not increase original catalogers' productivity unless they are specifically geared to strive toward new methods of cataloging, streamlined standards, or development of new or improved tools. Although they would be desirable, such programs have not yet been designed.

Contribution of records to a nationally available database has been an element in almost all cooperative projects and is central to the overall system of shared cataloging in place today. Although the benefits of contribution are well understood, there are factors that work against it. A survey of projected cataloging trends in 25 large research libraries by Lowell (1990) indicates a growing reliance on local systems, likelihood of more frequent creation of less-than-full cataloging records, and the probability that many of these records will reside only on the local database or, if contributed, will not be sent to the utilities in a timely manner. Wetherbee (1991) surveyed libraries participating in local systems and found that

> most local shared systems have a strong interest in the concept of a national database but it is secondary to the development of the local system database. Local systems will continue to post holdings to the NBD [national bibliographic database] if they can do it as an integral part of local catalog maintenance and if it is cost effective (p. 35)

She anticipates that "local system libraries will demand more efficient uploading and downloading to and from the utilities" (p. 37). Lowry (1990) believes that the current system of pricing incentives for original cataloging contribution needs to be improved if the system is to be maintained effectively. He argues that "libraries are supplying piece-work cataloging to the utilities at a sweat labor price which is resold to other libraries for a tidy sum" (p. 15). Individual cooperative cataloging programs, such as NCCP and CONSER, can ensure that records created as part of the program are widely available. To achieve maximum contribution, however, it may be more important to design programs that focus on keeping the current system of shared databases from deteriorating. Such programs would focus on the cataloging standards, economic incentives, and technology needed to maintain and increase current levels of contribution.

Avoidance of duplicative cataloging is another potential means of increasing the number of unique records available. The disadvantages and causes of duplicative original cataloging are well understood. Mandel and Rhee (1986) analyzed the causes of such duplication and identified two as meriting the most concern: duplication of records among the bibliographic utilities and duplication by LC of other libraries' cataloging. This first cause of duplication is probably of somewhat less concern today, as many libraries catalog on local systems and tend to search more than one utility as a source of cataloging copy. Lowell's survey (p.5) indicates a trend toward greater flexibility in choosing record sources. Although the split database environment continues to be a problem, the cost is largely in duplicative searching rather than in duplicative cataloging. The second problem, that of duplicative effort by LC, is also being addressed somewhat as LC begins to use other libraries' copy for its arrearage cataloging and to make use of NCCP contributed copy when cataloging current imprints. However, there is still more that LC could be doing to take advantage of external cataloging copy and to allocate the savings gained by copy cataloging to the creation of additional records for current imprints. LC views expansion of NCCP as a step in this direction, but the optimal balance between the Library's perceived requirements for its use of external copy and the demands placed on NCCP participants, which in turn lower their output of original cataloging, is still being sought.

2. Records That Are More Cost Effective to Use

Nadler (1987) indentifies a third significant source of duplication: "partial duplication, when an existing record is reviewed and possibly modified to make it conform to local policies of the institution that is using the record. . ." (p. 6). Cooperative programs have made a significant contribution to reducing this form of duplication by promulgating a shared understanding and implementation of standards among participants. NACO and the availability of a cooperative authority file has had a major impact by enabling libraries to accept the headings used on each others' records without local modification or duplicative creation of cross references. The CONSER editing guide has provided libraries with a valuable tool for standardizing serials cataloging practice and, thereby, sharing serials records. Although few ARL cooperative recon projects were implemented, the ARL recon guidelines for inputting converted records, however, are widely followed and have enhanced libraries' ability to use each others' recon records.

Despite this significant achievement, however, there may still be more that could be accomplished to reduce the costs for libraries to make use of cataloging copy. As previously cited, the BSSC study of copy cataloging demonstrated that most libraries are able to perform copy cataloging at lower cost when using LC copy than when using member-contributed original cataloging. Based, in part, on that premise, NCCP has been designed to create more "national-level" records that can be used in the same manner as LC cataloging. However, as Nadler (1987, pp. 7–9) has observed, there can be any number of definitions of a "national-level" record, and the NCCP experience has subjected the initial definition to some scrutiny. It may not be necessary to meet current LC standards to achieve cost-effective use of records. Further, it is likely that not all of the adjustments that libraries make either to LC or member copy records are really necessary or desirable. The BSSC (Kantor, Cherikh, and Rich, 1990) analyzed a general survey of library copy-cataloging practices in an effort to determine gross patterns of treatment, but found little similarity among ARL libraries. A cooperative project designed to focus expressly on participants' *acceptance* of each other's records, for example, including analysis of changes made to records and a commitment to develop the minimum standards that would be mutually acceptable, could enhance libraries' ability to create more records that are more cost-effective to use.

3. Records Available More Quickly

There are essentially two different, but interrelated, problems involving the timely availability of records: time lags between the creation and distribution of records and redundant searching effort and delays in access caused by libraries' common practice to see whether copy will become available before electing to perform original cataloging. The first problem exacerbates the second. Delays in record distribution lead to duplicative cataloging or to increased overhead in processing as libraries wait for records. The delays are essentially a function of the distributed database environment in which records are created in one system and must be transferred to another to become widely available. When LSP was conceived, this delay was largely a problem of timely access to LC records via utilities. Now, as libraries create records on local systems and send records to utilities on tape, it is an even greater concern. Lowell's survey (1990) indicated that turn-around processing times for tape transfer would be a month or more, with a potential negative impact on the timely availability of cataloging data. Cooperative cataloging programs cannot solve this problem, but it is important to design projects that do not exacerbate it. For example, in the absence of LSP, records from NCCP libraries that input directly to LC instead of to a utility will be available more slowly, although more widely, because the records must await LC tape distribution. (In practice, some NCCP participants perform dual inputting so that records reach utilities at the same rate as in the past.) Efforts aimed directly at improving the transfer and distribution of records will improve the overall system of cooperative cataloging.

A question yet to be answered is whether a cooperative cataloging program can be designed to combat the second problem, that is, to alleviate the overhead caused by searching, re-searching, and waiting for copy. The notion often expressed is that if cataloging responsibility were divided up so as to achieve predictability in the availability of copy, libraries could better organize their processing efforts and cataloging decisions. For example, LC found a cooperative Slavic cataloging program with the University of Illinois library to be beneficial (J. Heynen, personal communication, January 1992). Illinois took responsibility for cataloging all titles from selected publishers, enabling LC to await Illinois cataloging for these titles. However, there are significant differences between LC practice and the normal practice in most libraries. LC does not routinely search for other libraries' copy; most libraries search a utility database to determine whether copy is available before performing original cataloging. Thus, predictability is far more important to LC. It could be argued that such predictability would allow libraries to make searching/re-searching more efficient, but that is unlikely. It would still be necessary to search, and sometimes re-search, to discover when copy was available; despite a cooperative partner's best intentions to provide timely copy, a library cannot completely control the timely receipt, or even processing, of a publication, and the library assigned to provide cataloging will not necessarily be the first to receive the title or to need to catalog it. The next argument made in favor of this form of cooperative is that, although libraries would still need to search and possibly re-search for copy, coverage of certain needed titles would be assured. Further, libraries would catalog titles in their area of responsibility, thus saving re-searching on at least these titles. This view is reasonable in the context of coverage for a national database, but it does not take into account local cataloging priorities. That is, if the current system were one in which libraries selected books to catalog on a random basis or on a first-in-first-out basis, then it would be desirable to provide some overall priority system governing which titles reached the national database most quickly. However, most libraries select items for original cataloging according to local priority; when a book is needed at a particular site it is cataloged and copy is supplied to the national database.

To the extent that each library is devoting its cataloging resources to titles most needed by local clientele (and therefore by a known segment of the "national clientele"), any constraint on that process, such as a commitment to catalog a specific series or imprint, has the potential to divert resources to less needed materials. Assumption of responsibility could assure more timely database coverage for certain categories of materials, because libraries would catalog their assigned titles rather than put them aside to wait for copy. However, the benefit would only be worth the investment if (1) a library did not need to compromise its local priorities to meet the commitment and (2) other libraries in fact needed copy for materials that would otherwise be cataloged first. It is possible that the overall system achieves the optimal distribution of timely cataloging on a title-by-title basis rather than on a category-by-category basis. To date, the potential benefits of a cooperative program based on strict categories have yet to be tested. One program by RLG libraries to share responsibility for selected monographic series was disbanded after 3-years uneven participation when it became apparent that LC copy would eventually become available for most of the titles and libraries were electing to wait for this copy rather than invest effort that would be duplicated. If a category-based cooperative program were attempted, it would need to include LC.

4. Making Best Use of Scarce Expertise

Another problem that reduces the overall effectiveness of original cataloging output is the limited availability of expertise required to handle the full range of materials held by libraries, particularly materials in lesser known languages. Mandel and Rhee (1986) observe that many research libraries lack personnel with the cataloging expertise needed to handle a special area of the collections. A corollary to this problem is that even when special expertise exists within a library, it can often only be partially dedicated to special materials. "Whenever special expertise is diverted to the processing of more standard materials, the potential total national cataloging output of records for special materials is reduced" (p. 35). Obviously, this is a situation that would benefit from cooperation and sharing of personnel. A number of libraries have developed arrangements for sending items or surrogates (e.g., photocopies of selected pages) to other sites where the necessary cataloging expertise is available. These arrangements may operate on an exchange basis such as a recent cooperative venture in which the University of Washington provides Arabic cataloging for the University of Minnesota, which in turn provides cataloging of Swedish titles. Another alternative for operations is a more standard contract with libraries providing this service for each other on a fee basis. Writing in 1986, Mandel and Rhee cautioned that lack of access to local files could pose a problem for such arrangements between libraries; today this concern is largely obviated, at least for most research libraries, by the availability and extent of the shared NACO authority file and by Internet access to remote library catalogs. With the process for exchange of contract cataloging becoming increasingly feasible, such arrangements could be further facilitated by a clearinghouse that maintained a survey of available expertise and directed requests for assistance; this would follow the successful model of the initial stages of the ARL Microform Project. Although it is possible to envision more elaborate models of cooperation such as a central service based at LC or a clearinghouse that contracted and subcontracted for service, a low-overhead investment in facilitating library-to-library cooperation is likely to produce a more favorable ratio of benefit to cost.

VI. Future Prospects for Cooperative Cataloging

As seen from the preceding review, the environment in which cooperative cataloging operates today is highly complex, a system with many participants, many agendas, and a complicated interplay between contributors and beneficiaries. It is also a dynamic environment, sensitive to technological and economic change. Factors that affect the success of cooperative programs include: the extent of agreement on cataloging standards and practices; support of (or compensating factors for) the inevitable costs of cooperation; reconciliation of the inherent inequities between costs borne by contributors and benefits gained by others; surmounting the barriers engendered by the distributed nature of the "national database;" resolving competing—and sometimes conflicting—interests in database coverage of unique items versus the benefits of adding high-use records; accommodating competing—and sometimes conflicting—local versus national priorities; and, most important, the clarity of program goals and extent to which design of program elements advance those goals.

The programs reviewed in this article illustrate many of the issues that should be addressed to improve the overall system of cooperative cataloging and to advance the goals of specific projects. The following summary highlights the broadest of these.

1. *Maintaining an adequate supply of original cataloging*. Original cataloging is a relatively scarce and expensive resource. Programs to make it less costly (e.g., by developing tools and streamlining practices) are needed. LC, as the largest supplier of original cataloging, can work cooperatively with others to achieve this objective. For example, just as CONSER has an explicit programmatic goal to take leadership in serials librarianship, NCCP (or, more likely, a successor program with a more cooperative governance structure) could broaden its role and mode of operation to encompass the objectives

of less costly original cataloging and increased productivity of the original cataloging enterprise at LC and other ARL libraries.

2. *Optimizing national cataloging standards.* Although there has been considerable achievement in gaining wide acceptance of national standards, there are still outstanding issues and areas of disagreement. As pressures on library budgets increase, more libraries are turning to less-than-standard cataloging. Rather than allow the sharing of standards to erode, it would be better to revisit standards cooperatively and revise them as needed. It is also important to arrive at clear agreement regarding the standards for a "national-level" record. A key question has been raised by NCCP: that is, is the most cost-beneficial record one with headings that are consistent with the NACO file, or is searching in the LC bibliographic file for headings not found in the NACO file worth the additional cost? Empirical data could be collected (e.g., by searching a sample of headings against NACO, LC, and various libraries' files) to answer this question.

3. *Increasing acceptance of copy.* Related to defining the critical elements of the "national-level" record is understanding the barriers to cost-effective use of cataloging copy. Although to some extent this needs to be an internal investigation in each library using copy, a cooperative program aimed explicitly at maximizing acceptance of copy (e.g., sharing analyses, coordinating policies) could inform the participants' internal practices. There is still considerable room for improvement in this aspect of the efficiency of the overall system of cooperative cataloging.

4. *Maintaining the extent and timeliness of contribution to large shared databases.* As studies have demonstrated, a relatively large base of contributors is necessary to satisfy the copy-cataloging needs of research libraries. Potential trends toward fragmentation in record sources and delays in contribution must be avoided if the effectiveness of the current system is to be maintained. Providing smooth mechanisms for record transfer is the most promising route for addressing this problem.

5. *Increasing the resources available to extend the national database.* Cooperative programs have been successful in attracting funding to endeavors that expand database coverage or enrich the content of records. Even without significant overhead in coordinated cataloging projects, cooperative planning could also achieve this end by identifying national priorities, capturing the attention of funding agencies interested in these priorities, and stimulating appropriate projects. There are still large, valuable collections of uncataloged materials and unconverted records that would enhance the national database. Coverage of foreign language materials continues to be a problem; could the success of the NPAC initiative for Congressional funding be replicated?

6. *Sharing specialized expertise.* Although libraries are beginning to effect agreements to provide specialized foreign language cataloging for each other,

such activities could be expanded if assisted by a clearinghouse or a central contracting service.

Much has changed since 1965 when Skipper (1966) observed that "the mechanics of cooperative cataloging generate too much friction and produce inordinate time delays, all of which seriously reduce the theoretical potential . . . " (p. 64). Since the development of shared online databases, cooperative cataloging has become a staple of library operations. In addition, a number of highly successful cooperative projects have greatly expanded and enriched the national bibliographic database and have transformed cataloging operations. Although the success of cooperative cataloging has been enormous and the benefits great, the environment in which it functions is not stable, and possibly not secure, and there are still significant unanswered questions and unresolved problems. Cooperative cataloging has been a great achievement, but the "theoretical potential" is still greater.

References

Alternative Model for NCCP. (1992). *Cooperative Cataloging News* **1(1)**, 1.

American Library Association (ALA), (1983). *The ALA Glossary of Library and Information Science.* ALA, Chicago.

Association of Research Libraries (ARL), (1979). *National Planning for Bibliographic Control: Minutes of the 94th Meeting, May 10–11, 1979.* ARL, Washington, D.C.

Association of Research Libraries (ARL), (1987). *Government Information in Electronic Form: Minutes of the 110th Meeting, May 7–8, 1987.* ARL, Washington, D.C.

Association of Research Libraries (ARL), Committee on Bibliographic Control, (1987). ARL Recon report. In *Government Information in Electronic Form: Minutes of the 110th Meeting of the ARL*, pp. C1–C9. ARL, Washington, D.C.

Avram, H. D. (1968). *The MARC Pilot Project: Final Report on a Project Sponsored by the Council on Library Resources.* LC, Washington, D.C.

Avram, H. D. (1984). The barriers: Knowing and facing the problems. In *The Sum of the Parts: Sharing The Responsibility for Bibliographic Control: Minutes of the 103rd Meeting, Association of Research Libraries (ARL)*, pp. 17–24. ARL, Washington, D.C.

Avram, H. D. (1986) *Coordinated Cataloging Project Meeting: Minutes of the Meeting, May 14, 1986.* Photocopy. LC, Washington, D.C.

Avram, H. D., Knapp, John F., and Rather L. J. (1968). *The MARC II Format: A Communications Format for Bibliographic Data.* LC, Washington, D.C.

Avram, H. A., and Wiggins, B. (1988a). The linked systems project: Introduction and background. In *The Linked Systems Project: A Networking Tool for Libraries* (J. G. Fenly and B. Wiggins, eds.), pp. 1–6. OCLC, Dublin, Ohio.

Avram, H. D., and Wiggins, B. (1988b). The national coordinated cataloging program. *Library Resources & Technical Services* **32(2)**, 111–115.

Barry, R. K. (1987). Report of the 1986 NACO cost survey. Unpublished. LC, National Coordinated Cataloging Operations, Washington, D.C.

Bartley, L. K., and Reynolds, R. R. (1988). CONSER: Revolution and evolution. *Cataloging & Classification Quarterly* **8**, 47–66.

Bibliographic Service Development Program (BSDP), Task Force on a Name Authority File Service. (1984). *The Name Authority Cooperative/Name Authority File Service.* Council on Library Resources, Washington, D.C.

Bibliographic Services Study Committee (BSSC), (1990). *The National Coordinated Cataloging Program: An Assessment of the Pilot Project*. Council on Library Resources, Washington, D.C.

Boss, R. (1983). *Cataloging Titles in Microform Sets: Report of a Study Conducted in 1980 for the Association of Research Libraries*. ARL, Washington, D.C.

Buckland, L. F., and Basinski, W. L. (1978). *The Role of the Library of Congress in the Evolving National Network*. LC, Washington, D.C.

Burger, R. H. (1990). NCCP as a national information policy: An evaluation. *Technical Services Quarterly* **8(2)**, 55–65.

Crawford, W. (1984). *MARC for Library Use: Understanding the USMARC Formats*. Knowledge Industry Publications, White Plains, New York.

Crowe, W. J. (1981). Cataloging contributed to OCLC: A look one year later. *Library Resources & Technical Services* **25(1)**, 56–62.

Dougherty, R. M. (1986). Coordinated cataloging: The prospects for a nationwide program. *Journal of Academic Librarianship*. **12**, 67.

Fenly, J. G., and Irvine, S. D. (1986). The name authority co-op (NACO) project at the Library of Congress: Present and future. *Cataloging & Classification Quarterly*, **7(2)**, 7–18.

Gregor, D. (1984). *Retrospective Conversion: Report of a Meeting Sponsored by the Council on Library Resources*. CLR, Bibliographic Service Development Program, Washington, D.C.

Gregor, D., and Mandel, C. A. (1991). Cataloging must change! *Library Journal* **116(6)**, 42–47.

Grover, M. L. (1991). Cooperative cataloging of Latin American books: The unfulfilled promise. *Library Resources & Technical Services* **35(4)**, 406–415.

Hanson, E. R., and Daily, J. E. (1970) Catalogs and cataloging. In *Encyclopedia of Library and Information Science 4*, pp. 242–305. M. Dekker, New York.

Heynen, J. (1984). *Microfilm Sets in U.S. and Canadian Libraries: Report of a Survey on the Bibliographic Control of Microform Sets conducted by the Association of Research Libraries Microform Project*. ARL, Washington, D.C.

Heynen, J., and Blixrud, J. C. (1986). *The CONSER Project: Recommendations for the Future* (Network Planning Paper Number 14). LC, Washington, D.C.

Houbeck, R., Marko, L., and Richards, T. (1985). *Overlap Study [of Shelflist Sample Drawn from University of California, Berkeley, Columbia University, Cornell University, the University of Michigan, the University of Pennsylvania and Yale University]*. Ann Arbor, Michigan. Photocopy.

Howard, J. (1986). Guest editorial. *Cataloging and Classification Quarterly*, **7(2)**, 5–6.

Immroth, J. P. (1976). National union catalog. In *Encyclopedia of Library and Information Science 19*, pp. 182–186. M. Dekker, New York.

An Integrated Consistent Authority File Service for Nationwide Use (1980). *Library of Congress Information Bulletin* **39(28)**, 244–248.

Ishimoto, C. F. (1973). The national program for acquisitions and cataloging: Its impact on university libraries. *College and Research Libraries* **34(2)**, 126–136.

Joachim, M. D. (1986). Recent developments in the bibliographic control of microforms. *Microform Review* **15(2)**, 74–86.

Jones, J. F. (1986). Online catalog access to the titles in major microform sets. In *Advances in Library Automation and Networking 3*, pp. 123–144. JAI Press, Greenwich, Connecticut.

Kantor, P. B. (1990). Economic Aspects of the NCCP pilot project: Report prepared for the Bibliographic Services Study Committee. In *The National Coordinated Cataloging Program: An Assessment of the Pilot Project*, pp. 9–32. Council on Library Resources, Washington, D.C.

Kantor, P. B., Cherikh, M., and Rich, S. I. (1990). A survey of copy cataloging practices at ARL libraries. In *The National Coordinated Cataloging Program: An Assessment of the Pilot Project*, pp. 49–59. Council on Library Resources, Washington, D.C.

Kaplan, L. (1975). Library cooperation in the United States. In *Encyclopedia of Library and Information Science 15*, pp. 247–264. M. Dekker, New York.

Library of Congress (LC). (1991). *Cooperative Cataloging and the Library of Congress: A Report Submitted to the Joint Committee on the Library and the Senate and House Committees on Appropriations.* LC, Washington, D.C.

Library of Congress (LC). Serial Record Division. (1990). *CONSER Editing Guide.* LC, Washington, D.C.

Lowell, G. R. (1990). Local systems and bibliographic utilities in 1992: A large research library perspective. *Journal of Academic Librarianship* **16**, 140–144.

Lowry, C. B. (1990). Resource sharing or cost shifting? The unequal burden of cooperative cataloging and ILL in network. *College and Research Libraries* **51(1)**, 11–19.

Mandel, C. A., and Rhee, S. F. (1986). Shared cataloging: Some remaining issues. *Cataloging & Classification Quarterly* **7(2)**, 29–38.

NACO Changes Its Name. (1987). *Library of Congress Information Bulletin* **46**, 44.

Nadler, J. (1987). *The National Coordinated Cataloging Program: A Discussion of Some of the Issues.* Photocopy. Chicago.

National Coordinated Cataloging Program Steering Committee. (1992). *Minutes of Meeting November 12, 1991.* Photocopy. LC, Washington, D.C.

OCLC and RLG Exchange of Preservation and Microform Set Records (1986). *Technical Services Quarterly* **4(2)**, 79.

Philips, S. (1991). *UT Austin's Perspective on Cooperative Cataloging Projects.* Photocopy. Austin, Texas.

RLG and OCLC Part Company. (1991). *Library Journal* **116(3)**, 23.

Racine, D. (1989). *Memo to OCLC Users Council, January 17, 1989.* Photocopy. OCLC, Dublin, Ohio.

Rather, L. J. (1984) The keystone: The role of the Library of Congress. In *The Sum of the Parts: Sharing the Responsibility for Bibliographic Control: Minutes of the 103rd Meeting of the Association of Research Libraries (ARL),* pp. 9–16. ARL, Washington, D.C.

Reed-Scott, J. (1985). *Plan for a North American Program for Coordinated Retrospective Conversion: Report of a Study Conducted by the Association of Research Libraries.* ARL, Washington, D.C.

Reed-Scott, J., George, D., and Payne, C. (1984). *Issues in Retrospective Conversion: Report of a Study Conducted for the Council on Library Resources.* CLR, Bibliographic Service Development Program, Washington, D.C.

Reid, M. T. (1990). Is there a crisis in copy cataloging? No relevant indicator yet found. *ALCTS Newsletter* **1**, 11–13.

Simonton, W. (1962). The bibliographic control of microforms. *Library Resources & Technical Services* **6(1)**, 29–41.

Skipper, J. E. (1966). The characteristics of cataloging in research libraries. In *Minutes of the 68th Meeting of the Association of Research Libraries (ARL),* pp. 55–85, ARL, Washington, D.C.

Smalley, D. A., Griffith, W. G., Walker, A. M., and Wessells, M.B. (1980). *Technical Report on Linking the Bibliographic Utilities: Benefits and Costs: Submitted to the Council on Library Resources.* Battelle Columbus Laboratories, Columbus, Ohio.

Striedieck, S. (1989). CONSER and the national database. In *Advances in Serials Management 3,* pp. 81–109. JAI Press, Greenwich, Connecticut.

Welsh, W. J. (1987). Letter to Sidney Verba, March 4, 1987, copied to members of the NCCP Steering Committee. Photocopy. LC, Washington, D.C.

Wetherbee, L. V. (1991). *The Impact of Local Shared Automated Library Systems on the Development of a Comprehensive Nationwide Bibliographic Database: A Report to the Library of Congress Network Advisory Committee on a Study of Representative Local Shared Automated Library Systems.* Photocopy. Prepared under contract to the Library of Congress, Washington, D.C.

Yee, M. M. (1987). Attempts to deal with the "crisis in cataloging" at the Library of Congress in the 1940s. *Library Quarterly* **57(1)**, 1–31.

The MARC Format: Private Road or Public Highway?

Patricia B. Culkin
CARL Systems, Inc.
Denver, Colorado 80210

I. Introduction

The concept of the MARC (machine-readable cataloging) record structure has been so completely subsumed into the culture of librarianship and information science that it is easy to forget that MARC is only 30 years old and that use of MARC in production environments has been commonplace for fewer than 10 years. Given MARC's relative youth, it is surprising that the original concepts underpinning its invention have become blurred. MARC was intended originally as a means to an end; it has become, instead, an end (and a business) unto itself.

II. MARC: A Capsule History

A. Objectives

It may be time to both revisit the simple objectives dictating the invention of MARC and determine if they can be recycled to support current information requirements in a more cost-effective manner. MARC was invented to accomplish the following objectives:

1. Standardization of data communication and transfer
2. Labor and production cost recover from one-time descriptive cataloging effort
3. Standardization of intellectual description conventions to ensure consistent, precise description of materials

B. Pre-MARC Processing Scenario

Before the mid-1970s, the cost and effort of cataloging materials acquired by a library fell to the library itself. Libraries maintained technical-service

ADVANCES IN LIBRARIANSHIP, VOL. 16

83

departments staffed by professional catalogers and clerical employees whose collective job was to describe and file into the public catalog information about all material acquired. The redundancy and duplication of effort, if measured by modern industrial standards, was staggering. It was not uncommon for 10 or more individual (acquisitions, cataloging, filing, and preparation) staff members to be involved in getting a book to the library shelf.

C. New Technologies

The rising prevalence of reproduction and computer technologies in the early 1960s made it clear to the profession that these tools should be incorporated into the technical services effort. It took almost 20 years from this realization to actual incorporation of these technologies into production routines. The delay served the profession well in some ways, but the magnitude of the delay allowed for the invention of routines for sharing and distributing MARC records that today are arguably more expensive than those they replaced.

D. Design Process

Most of these 20 years were spent in the design, testing, and promulgation of the national standard for communicating bibliographic data. This standard became known as MARC. The Library of Congress (LC) and the Council on Library Resources (CLR), in concert with several "partner" library institutions, were instrumental in managing this design and the resulting MARC format specifications. There were two CLR-sponsored studies conducted before 1963; LC, CLR, and the Committee of Automation of the Association of Research Libraries (ALR) cosponsored two conferences in 1965 to consider these studies, and the MARC Pilot Project was born (Avram, 1968). The project resulted in a format and data base for partner libraries to review. After review, the project was judged a success and spawned MARC II (1968–1974) (Avram *et al.*, 1968).

E. Design Results

MARC I and MARC II formats differ substantially, but the structure of MARC II has remained stable since the original draft was issued in January 1968. MARC II includes the separate directory, subfield codes, and structured tags that did not exist in MARC I.

> The structure of MARC II has remained essentially fixed since the original draft was issued in 1968, and has proven flexible and valuable, handling a range and volume of materials far greater than that of any similar development. The structure has survived for two decades with no substantial changes, while content designators and content continue to evolve. (Crawford, 1989, p. 207)

Some percentage of this development time was justified in that it resulted in a durable, flexible, and expandable instrument in service of the original objectives. Its utility has been further proved in that MARC has become both the world-wide standard for the dissemination of traditional bibliographic data and the accepted standard for nonbibliographic information data bases.

III. MARC: First Implementations

A. Utilities and Consortium Use

Becoming the standard, however, involved another investment of time. Once the basic format was established, there were several library automation projects that were established to take advantage of the capability. These were not centered in the single institution, but in either major university/university-consortium environments or newly formed bibliographic utilities. The utilities included OCLC, Stanford-BALLOTS (now RLIN), the Washington Library Network (WLN), and the University of Toronto Library Automation System (Utlas).

Because the MARC formats are complex and because a MARC database can become very large very quickly, the utilities invented for themselves a crucial role in redistribution of MARC cataloging to single institutions. In fact, from 1972 until the mid-1980s, much of the redistribution was not in machine-readable records, but in card or list products generated from the local library's editing of the record in the utility database.

An agency or institution would subscribe to the utility services, access the consolidated MARC file, add its "ownership" symbol to the master file, edit the record to local specification, and receive back a series of products based on the editing session. These products usually included the edited MARC record on a tape subscription and, more important for many sites (at least through the mid-1980s), also included a card set that contained the edited bibliographic data and local holdings and format data that were automatically printed on the cards from a profile of local data conventions submitted by the library. Most local card-production technologies were abandoned, and because cards describing newly arrived materials arrived weekly, presorted by catalog, much of the card-management activity was also eliminated.

B. Local Library Use

A further leap was made when local computer-based catalogs became more prevalent in the 1980s. As commercially vended and home-grown local systems proliferated and as better software was generated to load, manipulate, and retrieve data from public access catalogs, it became more the norm that the machine-based records were directly loaded into the local computer-based catalogs and that card production was dropped.

It seemed as if the golden age of automation had dawned, and if cost were ignored, in many ways it had. Henriette Avram ends her *MARC, Its History and Implications* with the following paragraph:

> The benefits that accrue to a library and its clients from the establishment of and the conformity to standards are many. Products from different sources will mesh. Records from different libraries will be interchanged. Machine systems will be more easily developed and shared. Union catalogs will be possible without costly editing for consistency, thus facilitating interlibrary loan. Cost of local changes to catalog records will be minimized. It will be advantageous to vendors to manufacture hardware to handle the requirements of libraries. The process of ordering, cataloging, etc. will be more uniform. Therefore, less searching and bibliographic verification will be necessary and duplication of effort will be avoided. Networking will be facilitated. Various data bases will be accessible through the use of standard protocol. Service to the user will be improved and that is really what MARC is all about. (Avram, 1975)

These contentions are all accurate and defensible, yet by objective economic measure, unfortunately still not fully realized.

IV. Demystifying the Quest for MARC

A. Distribution Mechanisms

An unfortunate effect of the lengthy transition from invention of the MARC format to effective and innovative local library use of MARC records is that the concept of middleman redistribution became completely institutionalized. This process has had two very unfortunate effects: one, the cost savings realized by eliminating the local cataloging, card production, and filing efforts were just reconstituted in the invention of paraprofessional class of staff and per-use charges payable directly to the utilities, and two, that many of the smaller institutions were shut out of the redistribution link.

Unfortunately for the economics of information management, the beautifully conceived and remarkably well-executed effort to utilize computer technologies in representing materials in local catalogs has stalled in the redistribution module. One could argue that we have not begun to exploit the MARC product in the service of one of its primary original objectives: elimination of redundancy in the descriptive effort.

B. MARC: Current Development Front

Clearly, development effort on the MARC front has not completely stalled. The research and development conducted in the MARC communication formats has been rich and varied. There are two major groups who propose, advise, and recommend continued development of the formats. These are MARBI, and ALA committee whose full name is "Committee on Representation in Machine Readable Form of Bibliographic Information," and the USMARC Advisory Group, which is an informal combination of an LC network agency and MARBI.

In general, the effort has been marked by refining and expanding the scope of existing formats, creating the linked-record technique to support analytics, inventing the archival, manuscripts, and computer files formats, the holdings format, and techniques to support non-Roman data (Crawford, 1989, p. 213).

The most highly profiled current activity is the concept of format integration, and content designators and content continue to evolve. Some of the profession's heaviest hitters have worked with the development of the MARC format over the past two decades, and its flexible, durable structure reflects the breadth of that talent.

However, much of this is inner-directed effort, and we must not let the MARBI effort constitute the entire substance of thinking about how to benefit from MARC in contemporary information environments. We, as a profession, cannot afford to move at the development pace set in the past three decades.

C. Economic Realities

The economic reality of using MARC-based cataloging in current production falls far short of expectation. The most conservative estimates of what it costs to put a book on the library shelf is between $15 and $20, more in some cases that the cost of the book itself.

Harris (1989) looked at the history of cataloging costs and other economic trends and found that cataloging is becoming more complex and that most libraries (69.2%) are unable to state their cataloging costs. Quick arithmetic calculations of obvious cost factors (labor, annual utility fees, transactions charges, etc.) might lead one to surmise that the numbers are so big, nobody wants to know.

Saffady (1989) compared the costs of cataloging using a variety of middlemen MARC redistribution services: the utilities, the on-line information services, the CD–ROM products, and the microfiche-printed catalogs. Reporting in 1989 dollars, he finds a per-unit-cataloged range of cost between $13.48 and $27 for the utilities, with the average at $16.63. The range for on-line information services and CD–ROM services is less wide, with the average cost being $11.84 and $8.50, respectively. The microfiche and printed cataloging tools are $8.92.

These costs are high enough on first examination, but when the fact that Saffady's labor costs were computed at $6 per hour, it becomes obvious that many institutions' costs are probably much higher. Paraprofessional labor tends to be compensated at the high end of pay scales. In many institutions, these positions are viewed as desirable and challenging: staff starts at a high classification level, remains stable, and makes high demand on the clerical salaries budget as merit, cost-of-living, and benefits-package increases cumulate. The bottom line is that the primary and most obvious benefit that the invention of a standardized communications format was supposed to address has not been realized.

V. MARC: Changing the Paradigm

A. Interactive versus Automatic

The crux of the issue is redistribution techniques and the economies thereof. In many cases, the cost of acquiring cataloging for a single title equals or betters the purchase price of the title. Middleman redistribution costs for annual service and transaction processing are extremely high. They in turn support and encourage the local library practice of searching, selecting, and editing the MARC copy. They reinforce the myth that the local library has to make copy-cataloging decisions in a labor intensive, item-by-item basis.

Libraries, being under severe pressure to defend and preserve their annual buying power, need to reexamine the dependence on the interactive nature of the MARC redistribution practice and on the local clerical effort that it requires. MARC redistribution must be reconceived as automatic rather than iterative.

B. Library of Congress Role

Clearly the biggest and most expensive component of the effort is already being underwritten by the federal government: LC's effort to catalog current publication and its catalog-distribution service have committed to preparation and delivery of the base record. There is also contribution to the universal MARC cataloging pool from the National Cooperative Cataloging Project (NCCP).

The records generated by LC and its partners are distributed from the Library of Congress Cataloging Distribution Service (CDS) to subscribers in both the public and private sector and to for-profit and not-for-profit agencies in the United States and abroad. A full list, or even good categorization of MARC subscription service partakers, proved difficult to obtain, but the breadth and diversity of MARC subscription service became clear by the protest registered when, in July 1989, James Billington, Librarian of Congress, announced that LC would require MARC subscribers to sign a licensing agreement and provide lists of those to whom they redistributed any MARC Distribution Service projects.

C. Defending the Status Quo

K. Wayne Smith, OCLC president and chief executive officer, was first to protest Billington's announcement, and OCLC spearheaded an organized protest by librarians all over the country. JoAnn Segal (Segal, 1990 p. 27) recounts that

> Armed with information supplied by OCLC (Lighthill, 1989), librarians wrote letters to Congress, to the American Library Association and to the Librarian of Congress. Statements such as that of the Association of Research Libraries (ARL) (ARL Newsletter, December 27, 1989) found their way into the library press (Advanced Technology/ Libraries, December, 1989). ARL's statement was based on its earlier "Statement on the Unlimited Use and Exchange of Bibliographic Records (Association of Research Libraries, 1989). OCLC's Users Council has also advocated opposition, urging OCLC member libraries to a letter writing campaign (Library Hi Tech News, November, 1989).

Billington took a strong stand initially. As Segal further relates (p. 28),

> Billington's responses initially indicated his determination to continue with the licensing plan on the grounds that "the Library of Congress . . . has greatly subsidized the development of bibliographic control worldwide and has supported libraries and library vendors" and that "those who benefit most from the value of the library's data . . . are being asked to return some benefit to the library" (Library Hotline, October 9, 1989) He elaborated further that those who would be hardest hit would be "some secondary vending institutions [that] obtain the Library's data [and that] have amassed millions of dollars in assets . . . in large part from the salability of high quality cataloging produced through public funds" (Computers in Libraries, November, 1989).

D. Rethinking the Status Quo

Whereas the preservation of an inexpensive means to share and exchange records is an objective worthy of focused attention, librarians who participated in protesting LC's licensing proposal may have acted in haste. Billington's proposal makes some sense in the grander scheme of things: revenues generated by LC's effort should be returned to fuel and support that effort and not be siphoned off by middlemen who provide no added value.

One could argue that libraries are paying for these records two and three times. They pay first as citizens to finance the initial LC effort. They sometimes pay again through projects such as NCCP in labor and materials. They pay a third time to get the record into the local system, and they pay in time in the production cycle waiting for the MARC record to be delivered locally.

The distribution model should, instead, be much more fully automated. LC should establish its licensing program at a fair and reasonable cost to the world at large. Publishers, vendors, and other businesses who sell information to libraries should afford the automatic supply of descriptive cataloging as a minimal add-on charge. This scenario would meet two of the original objectives of the MARC project—to eliminate redundancy of effort and to standardize descriptive practice. A MARC record with a purchased book should be as natural an expectation of librarians as a pencil with lead.

This model has tremendous potential for the economics of technical services as well as for the economics of information supply in general. Book and journal vendors are desperately competitive and extremely interested in preserving their library market share. Although it is easy to disparage them, one cannot ignore the crucial savings and service they supply to libraries in their bulk supply and discount packages. Those who could guarantee a MARC record with every title purchased, either on shipment of the title or in a reasonable time frame, would ensure their survival in the market. They are a natural to assume responsibility for MARC redistribution services. The models for this are two: (1) vendors can license LC CDS subscription products and develop local software to associate books with appropriate MARC cataloging, and/or (2) they contract with the utilities to ship appropriate copy to ordering libraries using control-number based (i.e., accurate and cheap) record identifiers. If they cannot supply or if they are a small enough vendor or publisher, they give the customer credit in one of the utilities to get cataloging as available.

Utilities don't disappear in this scenario. They redefine themselves as retrospective conversion shops and concentrate more on maintaining national holdings lists and providing direct public access services. They do purvey current cataloging and encourage contributed cataloging, but serve in a fallback role for difficult-to-obtain-copy instead of as first line of supply. They add software to their search and retrieval package that responds to batch-supplied, record identifiers, that is, publisher ABC requests that the following MARC records be shipped to institution XYZ, thus allowing smaller vendors and publishers the opportunity to compete in supplying cataloging without investing in local software development.

Libraries save in several ways: once the book is identified for purchase, most subsequent clerical and cataloging operations are eliminated; the book comes; the MARC record comes and is filed into the local system; local-system profiles generate local fields; some editing can be performed, but as a policy is discouraged. The public catalog knows about the acquisition immediately.

VI. Libraries: Influencing Their Own Destiny

Some vendors have already announced MARC-redistribution projects. Librarians should look at these projects and encourage their development as an alternative to the status quo. Too often, the paradigm for library management is to defend the status quo until a third-party enterprise steps into the void—usually at a cost that is more than it needs to be.

In this instance, libraries have the leverage in terms of both their expertise (they know how MARC records are created and distributed) and their buying power to force change in the distribution paradigm that will expedite local processing and free funds for direct procurement of materials.

References

ARL statement of licensing agreement. (December 27, 1989). *ARL Newsletter*, no. 148, pp. 4–5.

ARL, OCLC, others issue statements. (December 1989). *Advanced Technology/Libraries* **18,** 12 1, 8–9.

Association of Research Libraries (ARL). (1989). *ARL Reaffirms Statement on Unlimited Use and Exchange of Bibliographic Records.* ARL, Washington, D.C.

Avram, Henriette. (1968). *The MARC Pilot Project.* Library of Congress, Washington D.C.

Avram, Henriette. (1975). *MARC: Its History and Implications.* Library of Congress, Washington, D.C.

Avram, Henriette, Knapp, John F., and Rather, Lucia J. (1968). *The MARC II Format: A Communications Format for Bibliographic* Data. Library of Congress, Washington D.C.

Crawford, Walt. (1989). *MARC for Library Use,* 2nd ed. G.K. Hall, Boston.

Harris, George. (1989). Historic cataloging costs, issues and trends. *The Library Quarterly,* **59,** **(1),** 1–21.

Librarian of Congress Statement on Licensing of MARC Data. (October 9, 1989). *Library Hotline,* p.1.

Lighthill, David P. (September 26, 1989). *Memorandum to Users Council Delegates.* OCLC, Dublin, Ohio.

OCLC Users Council Urges Opposition. (November 1989). *Library Hi Tech News* **65,** 13.

Saffady, William. (1989). The cost of automated cataloging support: An analysis and comparison of selected products and services. *Library Technology Reports* **25(4),** 461–584.

Segal, JoAnn. (1990). Library networking and cooperation in 1989. In *Bowker Annual Library and Book Trade Almanac,* 35th ed., 1990/1991. R. D. Bowker, New York.

Strategic Quality Management in Libraries

Donald E. Riggs
University Library
University of Michigan
Ann Arbor, Michigan 48109

I. Introduction

Strategic planning became an important management process in the corporate world during the 1960s. This type of planning is not something that is separate and distinct from the process of management; strategic planning is inextricably interwoven into the entire fabric of management. Not-for-profit organizations and service institutions began adopting strategic planning during the 1980s. It has proved to be the best type of planning available because it touches every aspect of the institution/organization. Several libraries and the American Library Association (ALA) have become very involved with strategic planning.

In the 1980s, a new way of looking at the management of corporations surfaced in the United States. Total quality management (TQM), having been used by the Japanese since the 1950s, began catching the attention of American businesses. W. Edwards Deming tried to get the U.S. businesses to use TQM in the 1950s, but was ignored in his own country. He was welcomed in Japan and became instrumental in turning the Japanese industry into an economic world power that still has many U.S. organizations reeling. The Japanese embraced Deming's program for managing productivity and quality, which gave them a 30-year head start on the United States. Strategic planning and TQM share many of the same management principles. They both emphasize forward thinking, teamwork, the human dimension, a culture change, enhanced productivity, and strategies for improving quality. In a sense, they go together like hand-in-glove. It would be counterproductive for a library to implement TQM without already having a planning process in place, and if this planning activity is to be effective, it must include the components of strategic planning.

ADVANCES IN LIBRARIANSHIP, VOL. 16

II. Preliminary Steps

A. Strategic Vision

Libraries are undergoing one of the most difficult times in their history. For example, services are expanding while the size of the library staff is remaining stable or decreasing. Greater productivity is expected with fewer resources. The gigantic increase in new information and knowledge resources places greater stress on the staff and compounds the situation of "doing more with less." In recent years, more prognosticators are predicting the demise of libraries as they are currently configurated.

Library managers are positioned to take the leadership in creating the future of libraries. Their strategic vision is crucial if libraries are to be better understood and treated more favorably by funding sources. The strategic vision sets forth the direction the library will be going in the next decade. It is written in an abstract manner; however, the strategic vision's simulation of the future will likely be on target. The vision will include the library's potential for following various alternative courses. Although identification of the "right" course of action is far more significant than generating numbers of alternatives, the fact that more alternatives are brought forth for review may produce ideas that a lesser effort would not (Steiner, 1979). The successful implementation of the principles of TQM will depend, to a large extent, on how carefully crafted the visison statement is.

B. Mission

The library's mission statement is based on the vision statement. And the mission statement is also written in the abstract; it does, however, address the current as well as the future state of the library. A stated mission should never be considered "carved in stone." It should encourage creative growth via strategic planning and TQM, and the mission statement should also give the library legitimacy in the construct of its parent institution. The importance of the library's mission statement is not to be discounted, since all goals, objectives, strategies, and policies are predetermined by the organization's mission. Following is an example of a mission statement the author (Riggs, 1982, p. 2) coordinated the creation of:

> The primary responsibility of the Arizona State University Libraries is the support of the current and anticipated instructional, research, and service programs of the University. This responsibility entails the procurement, organization, preservation, and availability of library resources necessary for these programs.

C. Goals

Goals follow the mission statement in the strategic plan. They are broad general statements or desired or intended accomplishments. Goals are normally long-term in nature (e.g., 2 to 5 years). Goals play a prominent role in the implementation of TQM; the writing of the library goals should evolve from the team work that is advocated by TQM. Goals should never be written in isolation or by one person, nor should they extend beyond the realm of reality. Moreover, goals must be capable of being converted into specific, measurable objectives.

D. Objectives

Objectives begin to bring more focus to the library's intentions. They are stated in more specific terms than goals, and they are more internally focused. They are purposeful, short-term, consistent with goals, linked to other objectives, precise, measurable, and understandable.

While formulating objectives for a nonprofit organization such as a library, Hardy (1972, p. 65) recommends that the following questions be asked:

1. Is the objective designed to contribute directly to the achievement of one or more goals?
2. Is the objective feasible in the light of internal/external constraints?
3. Is the objective measurable? Are the results observable?
4. Were those who are accountable for achievement involved in setting the objectives?
5. Does the objective have a challenging quality?

After all objectives are written for the respective goals, they should be placed in priority order. The ranking of the objectives should be based on reality. Are they achievable within the designated time period? The success of strategic planning and TQM depends on realistic projections, not on fantasies and unachievable dreams.

III. Strategies

After the vision statement, mission, goals, and objectives of the library have been established, the next step is to formulate program strategies. Through strategies, all goals and objectives of strategic planning and TQM will be realized. There is no more important part in the strategic planning/TQM process than actually dealing with strategies (Riggs, 1984). And one must not forget that strategies directly involve the human dimension in their formulation and implementation. Strategies are the specific major courses of actions or patterns of action for achieving goals and objectives. They are normally well conceived and well planned, but they can emerge from ad hoc situations. A strategy entails an explanation of what means will be used to achieve goals/objectives. There are many types of strategies; they include

1. Organizational strategies
2. Personnel strategies
3. Growth strategies
4. Opportunistic strategies
5. Innovation strategies
6. Financial strategies
7. Retrenchment strategies

Strategies will vary according to the circumstances. Their effectiveness depends on how well they are linked to the goals and objectives. After each year, and sometimes during the course of the year, the strategies have to be assessed to see if they are getting expected results. It is not uncommon to merge strategies, create substrategies, and even dissolve some of them. The author (Riggs, 1984, pp. 46–47) has determined that the effectiveness of strategies can be gauged by the following six criteria:

1. Internal consistency
2. Consistency with external environment
3. Appropriateness in view of resources
4. Acceptable degree of risk
5. Appropriate timetable
6. Workability

IV. The Next Moves: Implementing TQM Principles

A. Focus on Quality

After the strategic plan is in place, the principles of TQM are to be given high emphasis. Quality is the alpha and omega of TQM. Quality improvement becomes a way of life in the library. Coupling the principles of strategic planning with those of TQM creates a powerful management tool for the library. Strategic quality management coalesces new and old ideas; greater attention is given to systematic thinking, statistical process control, theories of human behavior, and transformational leadership. All of these emphases come together to form a new culture for the library.

Three prominent gurus of TQM have been recognized throughout management literature. They are Philip Crosby, W. Edwards Deming, and Joseph Juran. Juran followed Deming to Japan and also worked with Japanese industries on the improvement of quality. He first coined the term "fitness for use or purpose" and distinguished it from the definition of quality often used, "conformance to specifications." In Juran's view, less than 20% of quality problems are due to workers, with the remainder caused by management (compared with Deming's 94%). Juran is adamant that top management needs to be involved in TQM because he believes that all major quality problems are interdepartmental. Juran's 10 steps to quality improvement (Oakland, 1989, p. 289) are

1. Build awareness of the need and opportunity for improvement
2. Set goals for improvement
3. Organize to reach the goals (e.g., establish a quality council, design team, teams with the library, designate trainers)
4. Provide training
5. Carry out projects to solve problems
6. Report progress
7. Give recognition
8. Communicate results
9. Keep score
10. Maintain momentum by making annual improvement part of the organization's regular systems and processes

Crosby is best known for the concept of "zero defects" that he developed during the early 1960s while in charge of quality for different missile projects. Like the other TQM gurus, Crosby is a strong believer that top management has to have a visible commitment to quality. He observes that committed management can obtain a 40% reduction in error rates very quickly from a committed workforce. Crosby believes that many companies compound quality problems by "hassling" their employees and demotivating them by using "thoughtless, irritating, unconcerned" ways of dealing with people (Oakland, 1989, p. 282). The main strength of Crosby's program is the attention it gives to transforming quality culture. His program involves everyone in the organization by stressing individual conformance to requirements. Because of his focus on first changing the management culture, Crosby's approach is clearly a top–down process. He is best known for defining the new management culture with his four "absolutes" of quality management (Lowe and Mazzeo, 1986, p. 24):

1. Definition of quality: Conformance to requirements
2. System: Prevention
3. Performance standard: Zero defects
4. Measurement: Cost of quality

The above "absolutes" are self-explanatory and they give management a very explicit plan for managing the transition to quality improvement.

W. Edwards Deming is often referred to as the "father" of TQM. He earned this recognition by being one of the very first people to preach the attributes of TQM. When he visits American businesses, he excoriates them for their cheap, shoddy goods; he tells them that an emphasis on quality will reap lasting benefits in market share and profitability; and he lays out principles for making quality a strategic advantage. This article, or any serious piece on TQM, would be remiss without delineating Deming's 14 points for management to follow in quality improvement. Entire books (e.g., Miller, 1991) have been written with their focus on Deming's 14 points.

1. Maintain consistency of purpose for the improvement of product and service.

2. Adopt the new philosophy of refusing to allow defects.

3. Cease the dependence on mass inspection and rely only on statistical control.

4. End the practice of awarding business on price tag alone (provide statistical evidence of quality).

5. Improve the system of production and service.

6. Institute training.

7. Institute leadership, giving all employees the proper tools to do the job right.

8. Drive out fear; encourage communication and productivity.

9. Encourage different departments to work together on problem solving.

10. Eliminate posters and slogans that do not teach specific improvement methods.

11. Use statistical methods to continuously improve quality and productivity; eliminate numerical quotas.

12. Eliminate all barriers to pride in workmanship.

13. Provide ongoing training to keep apace with changing products, methods, services, etc.; institute a vigorous program of education and retraining.

14. Clearly define top management's permanent commitment to quality; take action to accomplish the transformation.

From the foregoing descriptions of the gurus' philosophies on quality improvement, one can readily extract their difference in some concepts. For example, one of Crosby's slogans calls for zero deficits in a product, whereas Deming's 10th point is to "eliminate slogans, exhortations, and targets for work force." Deming's 8th point warns managers to "drive out fear" so that employees can do their jobs, while Juran believes, "fear can bring out the best in people."

The differences among Crosby, Deming, and Juran are small when compared with their many similarities. Each of these three gurus, along with most other authorities in TQM, agrees that to have a TQM program an organization has to

1. Have a "total" commitment to quality
2. Be customer (user) driven
3. Eliminate rework
4. Place emphasis on teamwork
5. Give high priority to training
6. Show respect for all people in the organization, and empower people throughout the organization
7. Create an ongoing appreciation for quality

The remainder of this article will focus on the above seven areas and their application in libraries.

B. Total Commitment

The word "total" in TQM has special significance. If the library intends to implement TQM, it most certainly should not plan on doing so without total commitment. The library director must be fully committed to making the principles of TQM work. And this commitment has to be evident throughout the library. Ideally, the library's parent institution will be engaged in TQM. Deming believes that having a firm commitment from the top is the most important step in implementing TQM (Petersen and Hillkirk, 1991). Failure on the part of top management to be deeply involved with strategic planning and TQM will give good cause for other library staff members not to be fully committed. Resources will have to allocate to the strategic quality management (SQM) program. All services and products provided by the library should come under the scrutiny of TQM. The coupling of strategic planning and TQM serves as a safety measure in assuring that the entire library will be involved in SQM. The system, rather than the employee, should come under the microscope. All of the work procedures/processes in the library should be studied to seek out problems that prevent quality. A common language should prevail throughout the library about SQM. Enthusiasm and accountability are good features to display early in the implementation stage. Early success stories will help to make believers and encourage other successful endeavors. Peters and Austin (1985) believe that quality is a hands-on proposition.

The total commitment to SQM has to be reflected in the library's vision statement, mission, goals, and objectives. Strategies will also reenforce the commitment. Effective communication of the philosophy, expectations, and benefits of SQM is a must. The library director has to take the initiative in preparing the first few documents on the SQM; these communiques should be delivered to the entire library staff and its advisory boards/councils.

C. Customer (User) Driven Service

The proponents of TQM believe that the "quality of an organization is determined by the customer/user satisfaction level. When one thinks of the satisfaction of library users, it becomes quite clear that libraries are natural beneficiaries of TQM. Libraries are one of society's best service organizations. Librarians have exercised a strong service philosophy for the past century or more. Nevertheless, there is always room for improvement in the quality of services. After many years of providing excellent service to users, librarians have fallen short in their understanding of how their patrons actually learn. Library schools have been remiss in not focusing a course or two on the theories of learning. Librarians should have a better grasp of, for example, the theory of cognitive learning. The recent arrival of the online public access catalog has reaffirmed the need for a better understanding of the patron's learning patterns. Interaction between the human and the machine is a complex endeavor and one that requires more research. Library users normally have a more sophisticated understanding of computers than librarians believe. Also, their expectations are higher than may be anticipated. For example, users are beginning to ask questions such as, "Why does the library have so many terminals to access various databases?" "Why does one have to use an OCLC terminal to access the OCLC database, why not have one terminal that will access all databases?" "Why aren't the CD–ROM databases in the online public access catalog?" These are all good, logical questions; the users deserve to know that the local library does not have control over which terminals can access the various databases, if that is indeed the case.

Libraries exist for the people for whom they serve, and not for the people who work in them. This truism carries much meaning. However, sometimes the library staff tends to forget the reason for the library's existence. The people who work in the library are the library's most important resource. And the services delivered to the users will come essentially from the work of the library staff. SQM places a high premium on both the users and the library staff.

As part of the strategic planning process, the library should conduct an environmental scan. This study should include a survey of the users' satisfaction level. To make the study more objective, the library should employ an independent person or firm to conduct the survey. The library would work with the person/firm in establishing areas that should be surveyed [e.g., collections, reference assistance, help screens on OPACs (online public assistance catalogs)]; after the areas have been identified, the library would cease its involvment in the study. Space should be available on the survey form that would encourage the user to list areas where the library could be more helpful, recommendations for improving service (e.g., establishing a telephone renewal service for checked-out books), and some of the things that the library does that the patron does not find useful.

SQM will provide a new mind-set regarding the user. Some long-held assumptions will be challenged. Services will be examined more carefully and analyzed in a quantitative manner (Coffey, Eisenberg, Gaucher, and Kratochwill, 1991). Pilot projects will be necessary before long-term commitments are made to full-fledged endeavors.

D. Eliminate Rework

One of the obvious principles of SQM is that of doing one's job better and providing the user a value-added quality product/service. The library staff members should understand that their work is in direct relation to the user's needs. Questions like "Are we doing the right things for our users?" and "If not, how can we improve our work processes?" should be occasionally posed. It is human nature to continue doing things the way they have always been done without pausing to ask, "Why am I doing this work, and who will it benefit?" Libraries have made some signal improvements in work processes in recent years. Some of these improvements have resulted from the use of technology. A few years ago, libraries would direct the staff to write specific information (e.g., vendor, price) on the verso of the title page and stamp the "secret" page. Such work has been eliminated in many libraries.

Because much of library work is task oriented and labor intensive, all levels of library employees eventually do some of all types of work; therefore, it is easy for the professional staff to get bogged down in the mundane tasks that can be performed by others. Due to staffing shortages, some of this type of work may not be avoided in the smaller libraries. Nevertheless, it is almost criminal for professional staff to fulfill their day's work doing these mundane tasks. They must be involved with the more intellectually demanding work, be creative in offering more refined services for users, and take the initiative in solving workflow problems.

SQM stresses that the library should simplify, standardize, and get the work done right the first time. The time spent fixing earlier mistakes, in useless work that has to be redone, and in extra steps that add little or no value to the product or service result in a huge amount of unproductive time and generally bring little benefit to the library user. One of the first steps necessary in improving workflow is to conduct a work sampling. Various types of sampling techniques are available to assist in detecting errors in current work activities (Fuller, 1985).

E. Teamwork

Little or no progress will be made in implementing the principles of SQM without teamwork. From the library director's office to the mail room, within departments and among them, quality issues are attacked in teams. One should not confuse teams with the typical library committees. Teams are better characterized as "self-directed work groups." Teams bring together most or all library staff who work in an area to improve the respective area's quality. All persons on the SQM team will share responsibility and will benefit from "team learning." Developing a strategic plan for reference service is an example where the team approach will function well. Teams can comprise either persons from a respective department/unit or there can be cross-departmental teams.

The focus of SQM can be on many dimensions of the library. For example, a team could zero in on how to improve a particular library service area by studying how to improve the way the work gets done (the methods) rather than simply assessing what is done (the results). Scholtes in his *The Team Handbook* (1988, pp. 5–68) states that

> The main difference between projects under previous styles of management and those run under quality improvement is summed up in one word: planning. Teams must spend time in the early stages of their projects planning how the project will unfold. Planning is the heart of using a scientific approach to quality improvement. Only then can teams study the correct problems, gather data that will prove useful, and learn from experience.

F. Training

Implementation of SQM in libraries cannot be done without additional costs. Wide-range training is essential. Leadership training, library-wide training, specific program training, and department/unit level training are some examples of necessary human resource investments to get the SQM process off the ground. If library leaders think they can implement the principles of strategic planning and TQM without any additional costs, then they should get their heads out of the sand. Without the training sessions, SQM will be a colossal failure. The right hand must know what the left hand is doing.

When the trainers are being trained, they will glean a better understanding about the importance of improving service for the user—this thrust will be the cornerstone for all SQM activities. One of the goals for the training program should be that of developing the skills and abilities of the library staff so that they will ultimately be able to bring about improvement in users' services. Furthermore, the training program should encourage creativity and innovative potential of each library employee.

Proper training will provide the cadre of library staff to teach others how to implement SQM in their respective areas. Teaching the proper use of

SQM tools and techniques will repay the library huge dividends. Excellence in library service is a constantly moving target. Training can create the framework and structure to help guide the library toward the pursuit of quality improvement.

G. Empowering and Respecting People

One of the many attributes of SQM is the change of culture within the library. Decisions will be pushed down to the lowest level. Many of today's large libraries continue to function as bureaucracies. Most decisions come up to and are made in the director's office. Staff members in these bureaucratic libraries are treated with little respect.

Most of the gurus of TQM believe that most of an organization's problems are traceable to the process itself and few problems can be attributed to the staff. They advocate that administrators should stop attacking people and look more critically at the processes/systems. TQM is known for empowering people. People generally want to do the right thing and they want pride in their work. Whenever surveys are conducted on why librarians chose librarianship as their profession, most of the respondents indicate that they went into the field because they like providing service to others and they enjoy working with information and knowledge resources. With a strong desire to provide service to others, librarians are already geared for SQM. Now what they need is the "empowerment" to do their work as effectively as possible. Library managers bear the responsibility of removing barriers that prevent their staff from functioning fully. Giving the people who actually do the work (those who are closest to the processes) empowerment to change things that are obviously done wrong and deter service for users is a wise step in the SQM direction.

Many of the morale problems in libraries are created and perpetuated by library managers. They may lack good people skills, be poor communicators, or simply not understand basic principles of humanistic management. SQM, through team work, training, and empowerment, will raise the respect for all of the employees in the library. Invisible walls between the professional and nonprofessional staff will disappear when the library has developed teams to work on strategies for achieving goals and objectives. Self-respect will also be garnered when the empowerment of the staff allows full contribution and satisfaction.

Empowering the library staff and showing necessary respect for them will be one of the best things achieved in any library. Most of the actual work in libraries is done by the rank and file. This valuable group of employees is at the "moment of truth" everyday in dealing with the users. It only follows logic that if they are treated well, empowered, and respected, the library will be a much better place for the user.

H. Ongoing Process

SQM is not a one-time deal. It should not be set in place only in bad financial times. And it should not be purported as a panacea for all library problems. In a sense, it should not be described as a "change of things," but as a "way of life." Continuous improvement in the library's services and products is the chief rationale for using SQM.

Unlike traditional planning, strategic planning is an ongoing planning process. SQM, like its strategic planning component, should be recognized as a management process that is going to be part of the library for a long, long time.

V. Conclusion

Inventing the future and strategic directions for the library and making them happen are awesome responsibilities. Library managers need as much help as possible with this endeavor. Combining the principles of strategic planning and TQM is an approach that is difficult to quibble with when one considers the various management processes. SQM will produce many refined, value-added services/products for library users. The total library staff will be more productive and will significantly enjoy their work more. Work will be simplified and streamlined; some procedures/processes will be eliminated. There will be many frustrations associated with implementing SQM. Some staff will initially resist it; some will wonder why the library is asking the already overstressed staff to take on this additional responsibility. Training will be expensive and it will evolve slower than one desires. Teams will express dissatisfaction about the amount of time it takes to bring about "a new way of doing things." And there will be some disagreements about the new way(s) things should be done (Chaffee, 1990).

In a nutshell, despite various frustrations, SQM, when fully implemented, will result in a significant improvement for library users. Tangible enhancements will be evident in workflow throughout the library. One of the more important benefits to the library will be the culture change that SQM has created in how the library staff has become involved in assessing the various operations, participating in determining strategic directions for the library, and functioning as a team. Strategic quality improvement is a phenomenon that offers an opportunity to dramatically transform some areas of the library, implement quality-driven programs, focus more on the users, and provide the library with a healthy "gust of fresh air."

Opportunity rarely knocks on your door,
Knock rather on opportunity's door if you ardently wish to enter.

B.C. Forbes

References

Chaffee, E. E. (1990). Quality: Key to the future. *American Journal of Pharmaceutical Education* **54**, 349–352.

Coffey, R. J., Eisenberg, M., Gaucher, E. M., and Kratochwill, E. W. (1991). Total quality progress at the University of Michigan Medical Center. *Journal of Quality and Production* **17**, 22–33.

Fuller, F. T. (1985). Eliminating complexity from work: Improving productivity by enchancing quality. *National Productivity Review* **4**, 337–344.

Hardy, J. M. (1972). *Corporate Planning for Nonprofit Organizations.* Associated Press, New York.

Lowe, T. A., and Mazzeo, J. M. (1986). Three preachers, one religion. *Quality* **9**, 22–25.

Miller, R. I. (1991). *Applying the Deming Method to Higher Education.* College and University Personnel Association, Washington, D.C.

Oakland, J. S. (1989). *Total Quality Management.* Heinemann Professional Publishing, Ltd., Oxford.

Peters, T., and Austin, N. (1985). *A Passion for Excellence: The Leadership Difference.* Random House, New York.

Petersen, D. E., and Hillkirk, J. (1991). *A Better Idea: Redefining the Way Americans Work.* Houghton Mifflin, Boston.

Riggs, D. E. (1982). *Arizona State University Libraries' Annual Report.* Arizona State University, Tempe.

Riggs, D. E. (1984). *Strategic Planning for Library Managers.* Oryx Press, Phoenix.

Scholtes, P. R. (1988). *The Team Handbook.* Joiner Associates, Inc., Madison, Wisconsin

Steiner, G. A. (1979). *Strategic Planning: What Every Manager Must Know.* Free Press, New York.

Digital Technology: Implications for Library Planning

Karen Horny
Northwestern University Library
Evanston, Illinois 60208

I. Introduction

By the end of the 1980s, advances in technology presented a new possibility
to librarians: image digitization of printed materials as a viable option for both
preservation and communication of information currently stored in library
collections. One of the most critical factors focusing attention on this option
is the high priority challenge of preserving documents on rapidly deteriorating
acidic and brittle paper. Another influential factor is escalating construction
costs for new facilities for overcrowded and steadily growing library collections. With the substantial increase in the rate of publication and the resulting
increase in the rate of library acquisitions over the past several decades, many
libraries are nearing the capacity of buildings that were constructed some 20
or 25 years ago. Prospects for substantial expansion of these facilities are not
promising in the economic conditions of the 1990s.

Does digital computer technology offer likely amelioration for these pressing problems? Although the answer is not a simple "yes," media conversion
is certainly an avenue that demands exploration by librarians involved in
planning to best meet the service challenges of the future. Digital technology
includes many aspects, with applications varying from digitized images
through digitized alphanumeric text files. All have a potential impact on
library planning.

This article identifies some of the complex aspects of this developing
technology including costs and quality of conversion, longevity of digitally
stored data, potential technological obsolescence and its impact on retrieval,
methods of access and communication, copyright implications, and the potential impact on space planning and other considerations for collection storage
facilities. Although there is an obvious relation between the issues involved
with digitization of documents originally produced in print-on-paper format

ADVANCES IN LIBRARIANSHIP, VOL. 16

and the challenges facing libraries in dealing with materials initially produced in electronic form, this article focuses primarily on the former.

Anyone interested in in-depth exploration of the potential of digitization might usefully begin by consulting "Preservation and Access Technology: The Relationship Between Digital and Other Media Conversion Processes: A Structured Glossary of Technical Terms," by M. Stuart Lynn and the Technology Assessment Advisory Committee to the Commission on Preservation and Access (1990). This excellent glossary places the terminology in an enlightening and thought-provoking structured context. More good background material appears in another report that was submitted to the Commission on Preservation and Access, Michael Lesk's "Image Formats for Preservation and Access" (1990).

The technology for digitization of library materials is rapidly evolving and the contextual environment and implications for library planning are likewise changing. New studies are frequently being launched and completed, providing additional information that will need to be consulted by planners. The following discussion provides some starting points for further investigation.

II. Costs and Quality of Conversion and Storage

Scanning of documents has become a technically reliable option for conversion of text to digital form. Digital conversion captures print images in the standard electronic form of bits (a sequence of numerals 0 and 1) for storage on magnetic or optical media. The image of the text itself is preserved for on-demand facsimile reproduction or review at a computer workstation. This process, however, is not yet fully capable of accurate optical character recognition to provide for further electronic interpretation and manipulation of the text content. Therefore, conversion of documents to digital form does not provide the increased opportunities for access and retrieval that are possible through keyword searching of text, although further conversion to alphanumeric representation may become an option in the future.

One recent effort in this area is Project ADAPT (Automated Document Architecture Processing and Tagging), as described in the *Annual Review of OCLC Research July 1990–June 1991*

> For three years, Project ADAPT has investigated methods that must be developed to support economical conversion of information into electronic information systems—not just symbol recognition but document recognition. ADAPT system software provides a prototype methodology for hands-off conversion of document images to a tagged, structured document database. ADAPT also includes pilot efforts to increase optical character recogni-

tion (OCR) accuracy and to increase automated structure analysis capabilities of systems-document format recognition. (1991, p. 2)

Although the project has revealed interesting potential, constraints of inaccuracies in OCR conversion and need for further development in document structure recognition techniques have demonstrated that further technological advances will be required to permit significant progress. Despite these limitations, at present, scanning can preserve a page image by converting the scanned text into electronic image information at reasonably high levels of resolution. In fact, one potential benefit of electronic imaging is the possibility that the image quality of some deteriorating materials may be enhanced in conversion to minimize problems of low or variable contrast.

An important technological and cost factor is accommodation of gray scale and color. Image resolution and fidelity may be negatively affected by choice of compression techniques that are used to limit space required to maximize storage economy. Media such as optical laser disks, which have excellent capability for color images, may have access speed constraints. In addition, despite efforts such as those to establish the "High Sierra" or ISO/DIS 9660 Standard for CD–ROM (ISO, 1988), there are still significant variations in the access software required by various manufacturers. The fact that even such a widely available technology as CD–ROM has unresolved difficulties in standardization does not bode well for likely consistency in workstation technology for other digital conversion, storage, and retrieval processes in the near future.

Another major obstacle to large-scale document conversion is the high staff cost of identifying and handling materials to be processed. A page-by-page scanning operation is obviously not a highly economical means of converting documents to digital form. At present, a major barrier to high-volume conversion of documents to microfilm, the current prevalent choice for preservation purposes, is the cost of the necessary page-by-page manual processing required. Preservation demands, however, are already requiring many libraries to obtain financial support for the kinds of labor-intensive activities essential to convert deteriorating paper to other media. The recent success experienced by libraries in obtaining funding for preservation microfilming projects, especially those carried out cooperatively, suggests that if a convincing case can be made for conversion of older paper materials to digital format, financial support may be forthcoming. Even if digital preservation technologies become the accepted norm, however, page handling will still be required.

Unfortunately, some of the methods that might potentially speed handling of materials for conversion and thereby lower costs have not yet proved sufficiently reliable for large-scale use. One of the findings of the ADAPT

Project was that "ironically, sheet-feeding technology may be a major constraint on productivity for such systems; present systems result in excessive numbers of double feeds and skewing of the page image. Scanning of bound material requires destruction of the binding or time-consuming human handling, further complicating the skewing issue" (*Annual Review*, 1991, p. 3).

A. Current Projects: Research Institutions

1. Cornell University

Recent attempts to create economically attractive conversion arrangements that can produce high-quality on-demand output at reasonable cost include a joint digital book preservation study sponsored by Cornell University, the Commission on Preservation and Access, and the Xerox Corporation. As announced in the August 1990 "Newsletter" of the Commission on Preservation and Access, this 18-month study centers on the scanning of 1000 volumes from Cornell's collections to investigate the technical feasibility and cost-effectiveness of the conversion, storage and retrieval process. An "Update on Digital Techniques," by Kenney and Personius, reported on the project's progress in the November–December 1991 issue of the Commission's "Newsletter," indicating some promising results. They note that

> some preliminary findings of the Cornell/Xerox Project suggest that the use of scanning technology represents an affordable alternative to microfilming for reformatting brittle material. The time spent in actual scanning is comparable with microfilming production rates if all of the post-processing testing and quality control required of microfilming services bureaus are taken into account. In the Cornell/Xerox Project, scanning rates over 1500 images per day have been attained for sustained periods as long as three weeks or more. ("Newsletter Insert," p. 1)

A detailed cost study is expected to be released at the end of the project.

Among other preliminary findings, the paper output produced from converted documents is very high, with legible, sharp-contrast reproductions. High-quality microfilm is also being produced from the digital files as a part of the project. Because the scanning function is conducted in a library that is a half mile distant from the computer center where printed output is produced and storage can be separated from output workstations, the project demonstrates a clear potential for networking and remote retrieval of digital format documents. Kenney and Personius report that

> during this last year, Xerox, with the involvement of Cornell, has designed and is in the process of developing the architecture that provides the means for creating, organizing, storing, printing, and accessing digital images in a network environment. The CLASS system is composed of a software application that controls the scanning workstation, a flexible document structure architecture, a storage system, and a user interface designed for the public, all connected by a network to the DocuTech printer. (p. 3)

Cornell plans to maintain a digital image storage facility in the computer center with an optical disk jukebox and associated image server accessible over the university network and allowing researchers to review documents on a workstation screen or request production of prints on demand. The intent is to develop a server that will eventually permit access to digital images from anywhere on the high-speed, high-capacity National Research and Education Network now in development, using any of a selection of common workstations of various makes and models. Beyond the formation of the network itself, one of the important challenges in establishing such information access is the need for standardized document structure information to maintain the correlation between the digital images and the page numbering of the paper text. Ensuring continued ability to utilize content retrieval mechanisms such as the table of contents and index of the original text is another significant challenge.

2. Yale University

Another interesting effort, the "Open Book Project" being conducted by Yale University, is a study of the potential costs and benefits of converting materials already preserved in microfilm into digital images. Given the general lack of user appeal of microforms, this possibility has immediate attractions. The initial planning for a targeted larger project is reported by Waters in "From Microfilm to Digital Imagery. On the Feasibility of a Project to Study the Means, Costs and Benefits of Converting Large Quantities of Preserved Library Materials from Microfilm to Digital Images" (1991). This substantial report begins by detailing the context, in particular reviewing recent studies on the ways scholars work to create and disseminate knowledge and how aspects of a library's organization, especially in regard to preservation efforts, affect access to needed information. It then focuses on identifying both the functional choices that will determine adoption of digitization as a preservation process and the technical requirements for system architecture. In seeking to demonstrate the viability of scanning preserved materials from microfilm, the report concludes by proposing "a plan of work to develop the architecture and to generate the information that libraries will need to make prudent choices about the costs and benefits of image technology" (p. 12).

3. National Library of Medicine

Major governmental organizations, including the Library of Congress, the National Agricultural Library, and the National Archives and Records Administration, have also been involved in a variety of research projects investigating scanning technology and system architecture. Waters (1991) cites several of these studies. In particular, the National Library of Medicine (NLM) has turned its attention to cost studies and development of suitable facilities for converting and storing documents. In 1989, Thoma, Gill, Hauser, and Walker reported on an NLM project that emphasized that costs are most influenced by the labor component of conversion, the factor universal to any preservation reformatting. Using a prototype facility established by the Lister Hill National Center for Biomedical Communications to derive preliminary performance and cost estimates, the project produced a Document Conversion System consisting of three workstations: one for document capture, a second for quality control, and a third for archiving. The next step was development of "an Image Retrieval Workstation capable of retrieving document images from both a local as well as a remotely located optical disk drive, in conjunction with a MEDLINE or CATLINE search via Grateful Med" (p. 3). The research program also produced a detailed hardware design and a complete control software package.

Among its findings, the project determined that "for a representative sample of bound volumes in the NLM collection, the average conversion time per page is 50 seconds. This is the time taken for all the stages in the conversion process, including document preparation, capture, quality control and archiving the page images on optical disk" (p. 11). Because costs are primarily sensitive to labor time, ways of decreasing conversion time can substantially reduce costs. Estimates for per page conversion cost ranged from a high of 28 cents to a low of 12.5 cents, depending on factors such as the fragility of the materials being handled. Project conclusions also observed that capture of documents in image form offers tremendous potential advantages in access and storage space considerations: "It allows the creation of vast machine-readable text/image databases in very compact space (the equivalent of 350,000 to 400,000 document pages on a single 2 GB optical WORM disk, or about 50 million pages on a 128-disk jukebox)" (p. 20). In considering this observation, it is useful to turn to cost figures identified by Lesk in his report, "Image Formats for Preservation and Access," where he indicates that for optical WORM (write-once-read-many) disks "a typical drive costs $10,000 to $20,000 and holds two to six gigabytes per removable cartridge. The cartridge is bulky; typically 12-inch diameter platters are used, mounted in housings roughly an inch thick. They can be dismounted, cost about $200 and are reasonably permanent, with 30-to-100-year lifetimes quoted by manufacturers" (1990, p. 305).

4. American Memory

Another project that has received considerable attention recently is American Memory. Developed by the Library of Congress, this project produces electronic copies, with accompanying bibliographic records, of such diverse types of materials as photographs, sound recordings, motion pictures, and manuscripts as well as books. Copies of these archival collections are being distributed to a group of pilot study libraries for use on special workstations equipped with a high-powered microcomputer with two peripheral optical disk players: one accommodating CD–ROMs containing digital information and the second for television videodisks with analog signals. As described in the February 26, 1990 and July 16, 1990 *Library of Congress Information Bulletin*, this software and hardware prototype system will be used to evaluate and establish standardized formats for the conversion, storage, and retrieval of images.

B. Current Projects: Commercial

One of the commercially available current options for reproduction of documents is the Xerox DocuTech system. Used primarily in larger universities for production of such materials as academic course packs, newsletters, and other short-run publications, the DocuTech workstation incorporates scanning and printing capabilities. Although currently economically viable only for relatively large-scale copying operations, such installations offer possibilities for future preservation and on-demand printing activities. This equipment is being used by Cornell in its conversion study project mentioned earlier.

A necessary factor in any calculation of cost-benefits of digital conversion is the overall cost of maintaining the converted records in appropriate storage with suitable ease of access. Computer-based storage options have been decreasing steadily in cost as they increase dramatically in capacity. Although such storage and related equipment costs are declining rapidly, the initial capital investment in necessary equipment remains so high as to deter most libraries from investing in digital image systems for any large-scale use at present. Even when digitization, storage, and retrieval equipment become more widely available, it is unlikely that libraries will rapidly be able to afford the immense total cost of conversion, storage, maintenance, and access for the vast quantities of print materials now in their collections.

Selection of which documents should have priority for scanning will be a complex issue. Collection management professionals must lead the way in planning for joint resource sharing projects to provide funding and consistent access policies for centrally stored digital libraries of the future. Although shared resources efforts to cooperatively build collections that will supplement each other and be readily accessible through interlibrary loans have made some progress in recent years, independent decision making regarding local collecting policies and practices has tended to remain the norm. Cooperative projects for preservation microfilming have achieved somewhat greater success and may be useful models for future efforts in digital imaging.

III. Durability of Digital Media

A crucial consideration in evaluating the potential of electronic digitization as a large-scale storage solution for library collections is the durability of the medium. There is as yet little long-term data in this area. It is, however, notable that fresh digital copies without the loss of resolution common to repeated copying in other media can be readily produced. The affects of length of storage on record content in magnetic or optical form will need close scrutiny before libraries can safely rely on these methods of maintaining collections. Potential long-term use of such storage devices to maintain master copies of library materials requires special attention to the causes of degradation or destruction of data in such media. Will more stringent environmental controls be required to maintain the quality of digitally stored records? What kinds of disaster preparedness will be necessary for reliable storage of these records? Is the potential of damage due to sabotage a possibility that might require stringent and perhaps costly countermeasures in the future?

One of the most prevalent forms of image storage and retrieval in current use by libraries is CD–ROM. Compact disk technology represents only one of the storage possibilities and its relative appeal must be measured in terms of both longevity and ease of access. Although compact disks are now commonplace, the life span of records in CD–ROM format is still a matter for testing and debate. Assuming that the useful life of this medium is acceptable for large-scale storage, limitations in access speed and convenience must be weighed. Because of storage compression features, CD–ROM is especially attractive for graphic materials.

The useful life of the several digital electronic storage media is variably projected based on current laboratory testing. Will data need to be recopied every few years or merely at intervals of decades to preserve integrity? Perhaps even riskier than loss of converted data due to deterioration in storage is the prospect that whatever storage medium is chosen today may soon be as obsolete as LP phonograph records are on the verge of becoming now. It seems to have become virtually axiomatic that microcomputers are outdated to the point of limited useability in little more than 5 years. What analogy should librarians draw when considering electronic digital conversion and storage of documents?

Will libraries need to attempt to maintain no longer commercially available models of equipment for access and retrieval of digitized materials in the future? If preserved documents are available to users only via a slow and complex process that may require queuing for downloading or facsimile reproduction, libraries will face problems similar to those many have dealt with for obtaining prints from microcards or for scheduling access to single workstations for CD–ROM products now in heavy demand. As long as subsequent copying of stored digital materials to whatever newly predominant technologies will appear remains relatively easy and economical, there may be little cause for concern. There are, however, no guarantees, and the burden for this subsequent conversion may fall to libraries as a matter of institutional responsibility.

IV. Access, Retrieval, and Communication

In an article discussing copyright law changes for electronic publishing, Garcia aptly observed

> In an era of digital, electronic technology, intellectual works are simultaneously available to many individuals who may access them from a central store of works, or "database." With the new technologies, intellectual works are, moreover, reproducible at very fast speeds and very low costs. And now perfect copies can be made from copies. The technology is also extremely versatile; the media are very high in capacity, and many different types of works can be stored and communicated digitally. In addition, now almost anyone can reproduce a work, as highly capable machines become ubiquitous in homes and offices. These machines can also be linked by switched telephone circuits so that intellectual works can be transferred in much greater quantity and with impunity. Furthermore, the new technologies are dynamic, in that they are interactive and constantly evolving. (1991, p. 3)

This cogent statement presents a number of the key opportunities and challenges that face librarians in approaching digital conversion of documents as a viable option.

A. The Role of Standards

As mentioned in Section II, access and retrieval methodologies for digital document systems are not yet subject to fully established industry standardization. The field is evolving so rapidly that new developments are virtually constant. Morrow's 1990 review of the considerable range of standards applicable to CD–ROM retrieval illustrates the complexity of this area. Crawford (1989) also provides an interesting discussion of the evolution of standards related to optical media, pointing out that "when you work with almost any technological field, you will find many things labeled 'standards.' Labeling something a standard does not make it so, and more particularly does not establish it as a formal consensus technical standard" (p. 31). He identifies "industry standards" as types that represents gravitation toward an accepted definition by informal consensus rather than accreditation by bodies such as the American National Standards Institute. Crawford also discusses progress in the area of formal standards and emphasizes the potential of developments such as Common Command Language (Z39.58) for interactive retrieval systems using optical media.

Authors such as Saffady (1990) have issued state-of-the-art reviews that can be useful sources of timely information and can also suggest directions for further exploration. Walter and Fisher (1990) have discussed the role of standards development in advancing optical disk-based document management systems (OD/DMS). They note that of the four groups of standards for this area, computer systems standards and communication standards have received the greatest attention to date, whereas application standards and test and measurement standards are just becoming the focus of much needed attention. Various document content architectures and compression standards have been developed by major computer corporations and these proprietary standards are now being openly offered and promoted in hopes of becoming de facto industry standards. As Walter and Fisher emphasize, "By far the most important standards to the future of OD/DMS applications are those that cover document content and interchange. Document content standards are those that allow for both the exchange of revisable documents and/or the exchange of documents that the sender does not wish to be altered" (p. 25).

B. Document Usage and Corruptibility

Once in a user's hands, paper materials have always been vulnerable to defacement or removal of pages. A similar concern facing both librarians and the public is the possibility of content alteration of documents in electronic form. While, except in cases of rare materials, other copies of paper format materials are likely to exist elsewhere, a digital master record might be the only accessible copy of a document in existence. Will one archival copy of each document in its original format need to be preserved for the future? Will an archival digital master record library need to be stored in some secure vault in a way similar to how certain archival microfilm masters are safeguarded today? Although digital image records are probably somewhat more secure than alphanumeric electronic documents, the prospect of users being able to alter a record must be taken into consideration for preservation of data integrity when access, retrieval, and communication methods are determined.

Direct facsimile reproduction in paper form or downloading of an image record before any further manipulation is permitted will provide the best security for master copies of digitally stored documents. Depending on the sophistication of user workstations, further use of the supplied downloaded copies of the records, however, may permit alterations that would make second-generation documents inaccurate. Preserving an uncorrupted original record for subsequent verification of data content will be one of the most vital responsibilities for librarians as digital format documents become integral parts of our collections. This need will become even more crucial as direct user repackaging of data gains in popularity.

Although colleges and universities have long been aware of the tendency of faculty members to devise course packets containing copies of various articles and portions of texts, recent trends include publisher-sponsored text customization. As reported by Watkins in the November 6, 1991 *Chronicle of Higher Education*, McGraw-Hill and the University of California at San Diego have reached an agreement that permits faculty members to design their own course textbooks, which are promptly produced via electronic publishing at the campus bookstore. McGraw-Hill provides a database, called Primis, with an online catalog that can be accessed at the bookstore and used to select articles, chapters, et cetera, to be compiled, printed, and bound within 48 hours. The average cost of such a text is reported to be approximately $20. Although the size and content of the database is still quite limited, the potential is apparent.

C. Document Content Searching Capabilities

A current difficulty blocking optimal use of scanned digitally stored data is their lack of accessibility by keyword searching within the text. Reasonable prospects, however, are developing for eventual conversion of documents currently preserved in digital image format to alphanumeric form. If such a technique becomes both reliable and economical enough for wide-spread use, it will be possible to greatly expand content identification and retrieval capabilities. At present, access information for users must be provided through standard cataloging and indexing techniques. The type and amount of additional cataloging that is required for proper retrieval of preservation microfilms is likewise essential for materials converted to digital image format, necessitating a not inconsequential addition to conversion costs. Ideally, especially because digitally stored documents are not as self-evidently and readily browsable as books grouped by classification numbers on a shelf easily "to hand" for the prospective user, additional cataloging and indexing access points should be provided.

One area of concern that does not yet have confirmed solutions is the potential problem of slow response time for users querying vast data files. Recent experience with local loading of massive files of indexing information has often resulted in less than advantageous response time for these online catalog systems. It is essential to ensure that the process of identifying relevant materials in the "electronic library" of the future does not present frustrations of this type.

D. Document Delivery: Networks, Transmission, and Reproduction

Lynch and Brownrigg (1986a) noted that the advent of online catalogs with their direct accessibility from home or office leads naturally to a demand for electronic delivery of the material thus identified. It is clear that the addition of indexing and abstracting databases to the online catalog service intensifies such interest. It is likely that, as user computer sophistication continues to grow, libraries will experience ever-increasing demands to provide new delivery mechanisms. This scenario suggests that early targets for digitization should be the most heavily used and therefore generally the more current materials rather than older, less frequently requested items. Such conversion efforts would, by definition, focus on a group of materials not now targeted for conversion because of preservation concerns. Assuming that libraries will experience and wish to respond to increasing demands for electronic delivery service, a number of challenges must be met to fulfill the potential without significant disadvantages.

Among the most exciting prospects for the future is the possibility of linking online indexing and abstracting services and international bibliographic databases with files of digitized texts to allow rapid retrieval and transmission of an identified document directly to a user's workstation via a short- or long-distance network connection such as the INTERNET. Development of the extensive high speed transmission capabilities planned for the National Research and Education Network (NREN) will further enhance these prospects. Such current experiments in full-text transmission as those developed by Ohio State University in its FAX (facsimile transmission) workstation for libraries of the Committee on Institutional Cooperation: The "Big Ten" plus the University of Chicago and Pennsylvania State University (CIC) and the Research Libraries Group (RLG) in its Ariel Project suggest that communication of documents maintained in digital form will be relatively easy in the near future. FAX relies on use of a digital image scanner for its current operation. The speed of transmission has been improving significantly as FAX technology advances and this speed can be expected to continue to accelerate. The wide-spread distribution and acceptance of FAX technology demonstrates the attractiveness of rapid document delivery. User demand is likely to continue to increase markedly. The RLG Ariel Project, which relies on direct transmission of scanned documents for reproduction on a laser printer at the receiving library, goes beyond current transmission speed limitations of the present FAX technology.

As resource sharing cooperation becomes more essential to library service in these days of economic constraints on purchasing for each collection, the ability to rapidly provide a document that the potential user's library does not own becomes an even more significant measure of a library's success. The steep escalation in interlibrary loan activity is a clear indication of these growing service needs. Aside from the pressures to preserve documents currently at risk because of paper deterioration, resource sharing agreements demand that a library be able to make materials available beyond its local user community. There is a growing perception in preservation activities that producing a readily shareable master copy has dual advantages. The master image may be retained by the library that owned the paper original while copes are transmitted and reproduced on-demand for use at other locations.

E. Cost Coverage and Copyright Issues

Along with the prospects for direct and immediate user access to digitally stored documents and other electronic sources will come the challenges of covering the related costs. Although a number of libraries now require users to pay the charges levied by some other libraries to provide items via interlibrary loan, most access to library materials is offered free to the user community. If a potential user of a digital image document will be expected to pay a fee for a copy, that user must be able to determine the cost in advance to judge if the price of the order is acceptable. The day is already here when a person at home or in an office can search a catalog/index and place a request directly from the local workstation for a desired document, paying for the copy with a credit card. Perhaps a regular user of an electronic library will be billed for retrieval of online texts in a way similar to that by which long-distance phone calls are currently charged.

All of the aspects of access mentioned above have implications related to copyright. Most of the current experiments with conversion of documents to digital form are focused on materials no longer under copyright regulation. The need to obtain explicit permission from copyright owners for conversion of and provision of access to each document whose usage is legally protected presents a major barrier to building the electronic library of the future. There will undoubtedly be standard forms of agreement and methodology for obtaining proper permission, but only at substantial cost.

Fortunately, many of the items now in greatest need of reformatting for preservation purposes are already exempt from copyright strictures. The attention on digital image conversion that is likely to focus in the preservation area for some time may prompt analysis of and decisions about copyright-related issues before libraries are ready to proceed to convert copyrighted materials extensively. Efforts to address licensing issues, such as the Coalition for Networked Information's READI (Rights for Electronic Access to and Delivery of Information) Program, are already being launched. The Corporation for National Research Initiatives is also currently preparing a report examining four possible scenarios for digital libraries, with a special focus on copyright issues.

F. Initiatives in Developing the Electronic Library

Despite the variety of legal issues that are yet to be resolved, there is a growing optimism about the future of the "electronic library." In a 1992 article, Smith asserts that this development will break the bonds of "The Print Prison." He projects the

> solution of the print era's information problems: the scattered, incomplete, highly redundant collections and complex, incomplete bibliographic apparatus that have been characteristic of this period. . . . Correction of these problems requires the gathering of a single comprehensive collection, including all extant current, past, and future scholarly publication. Such a collection is possible in the electronic era. Furthermore, just as scattered and incomplete collections have frustrated the creation of a single complete, consistent, and comprehensive bibliographic apparatus, it is precisely such an apparatus that can and must be established to maintain and control a single unified collection. (p. 50–51)

Although considerations such a telecommunication costs will be determining factors in the degree of centralization or dispersed duplication of electronic collections, there is little doubt that such libraries are beginning to develop. Witness the expansion of periodical article indexing and delivery services.

It is now apparent that the nascent "electronic library" will continue to grow both through expansion of electronic publishing and through text conversion efforts such as Project Gutenberg, the National Clearinghouse for Machine Readable Texts. This is one of a growing number of cooperative efforts throughout the world to convert to electronic form a core of important texts. Project Gutenberg, begun in 1971 at the University of Illinois, is one of the oldest initiatives in this area and aims by the year 2000, through use of a nationwide group of volunteers, to create an ASCII format collection of some 10,000 English language public domain works in heavy use. The Project Director, Michael S. Hart, has stated the intent of reducing "the effective costs to the user to a price of approximately one cent per book, plus the cost of media and shipping and handling. Thus we hope the entire cost of libraries of this nature will be about $100 plus the price of the disks and CD–ROMs and mailing" (1990, p. 6). Hart also mentions the prospect of widely used hand-held electronic text readers produced by companies such as Sony as of particular interest and promise.

Among other electronic text projects, a cooperative effort of Rutgers and Princeton Universities, the Center for Electronic Texts in the Humanities, is inventorying available texts, pursuing the development of appropriate standards for production, and investigating policy issues covering the whole range of creation, access, and distribution activities. The Center is planned to serve as a node in an international network of similar projects. It is gratifying to librarians to note that administration of the Center is headquartered at Rutgers' Alexander Library. Hockey (1992) has provided a concise summary of the Center's plans.

A related effort, the Text Encoding Initiative, jointly sponsored by the Association for Computers and the Humanities, the Association for Computational Linguistics, and the Association for Literary and Linguistic Computing, is attempting to establish format conventions for encoding electronic texts, beginning with the Association of American Publishers' Standard Generalized Markup Language (SGML) and extending to conventions for electronic title pages. It is now likely that large libraries of electronic texts will require the SGML standards to ensure the utility of their collections.

Along with all of these rapid developments, the concept of the "virtual library" is receiving ever broader attention. Although exactly what will constitute a "virtual library" remains a subject of some debate, there is a general view that such a library, housed electronically, will provide direct, immediate remote access to catalog, index, and abstract information along with full-text and image materials. In attempting some provocative predictions about the future of libraries, Seiler and Surprenant have wondered, "When we get the libraries we want, will we want the libraries we get?" (1991). In this article, they speculate that

> Society will totally convert to digital information and with society, so will libraries. . . .the many libraries we now have will be replaced by far fewer electronic ones. A heavy investment in communications hardware will substitute for the small and large libraries that are now geographically dispersed. General-purpose libraries, each like a Library of Congress but holding more information, will be located regionally. Such regional libraries might be sold as turnkey systems with a common hardware platform and bundled with identical collections of information and software." (p. 29–30)

As technology allows increased speed of multiple-user access to electronic documents, will only a single master copy of a text in a single library become the norm?

Seiler and Surprenant also project that direct accessibility of document databases to users outside the library will have a major impact on the future of librarianship, resulting in a situation where "librarians will be cast out of the electronic library building to assume new roles in an information-rich society" (p. 31). Is the profession ready for such a change? If users of electronic libraries are charged for document access, as for some current interlibrary loans, the line will blur between library services and other free-based agencies. Will for-profit information vendors supplant librarians? Will only a few library buildings remain with a small staff designated to help users too poor to afford direct at-home access? Before decisions that will determine the future of the profession are made, it is essential to take a close look at the positive and negative factors and shape the choices to maximize the potential benefits. Librarians must be sure to play a deciding role rather than stand by as observers while their future is set.

V. Library Space Implications

As current library buildings have been reaching capacity, librarians involved with space planning have been facing prospects that often include off-site storage facilities for bound volumes. In 1986, Lynch and Brownrigg cited the University of California's annual need for some 12 new linear miles of shelf space to house its new acquisitions and the resulting necessity to build regional warehouses for older or less-used materials. They pointed out that

> Two problems are implicit in the current state of affairs. First, maintaining the regional storage facilities, while less costly than building new libraries, is still expensive. In the future, continued expansion of the facilities will be required on a periodic basis due to the inexorable requirements for ever more shelf space. Second, the lower-cost regional storage facilities have substantially reduced access to the portion of the collection stored there. The long-range solution is to digitize this material . . . and to deliver the material over telecommunication links. (1986b, pp. 100–101)

Lynch and Brownrigg have admitted, however, that one disadvantage to this particular scenario is that it would result in digitization of lower-use texts rather than the more heavily used portions of the collections.

Indicating the need for advance planning, Waters suggests that

> Digital image technology will likely have a significant, perhaps profound, effect on the ways in which the library of the future views, organizes, and values its spaces and staffs. For example, to the extent that the digital library arises as a way of renewing and replacing large stocks of paper and microfilm materials, and to the extent that the digital library is stored and accessible remotely from the library proper, the use of the central stack space of the library will almost certainly change and the balance of staff functions traditionally associated with circulating and shelving collections stored in paper will likely shift to modes of delivering documents generated on demand from electronic formats. (1991, pp. 10–11)

This prospect suggests that a radical rethinking of the library's role and, in particular, the role of librarians will be required.

Before librarians and the governing bodies that control their libraries rush to decide that no further construction or obtaining of collection shelving space will be necessary, it is essential to remember that, for all the text conversion activities now underway, the vast majority of paper format materials remain unlikely to be converted in the near future. Conversion costs, as noted earlier, are substantial. As an illustration of magnitude, using the lowest cost estimate of 12.5 cents per page projected in the NLM's study (Thoma et al., 1989), conversion of a 300-page book would cost $37.50. To convert some half million such volumes would require a minimum investment of $18,750,000. If actual costs approached the high-end estimate of 28 cents per page identified in the same study, the expenditure needed for converting half a million volumes would rise to $42,000,000.

Although certain public domain documents are slowly being scanned into digital form and most current publications are produced from electronic text, as long as research and study require ready access to the immense bound-volume collections of present-day libraries it will be necessary to continue to accomodate that physical format. Even with joint projects addressing preservation priorities, cost factors are sure to limit the quantity and rate of conversion that can be accomplished. Although some libraries may take the far-sighted view that they should invest the money that would soon need to be spent on a building addition in conversion of documents instead, it is likely that most administrations that control library budgets will opt to wait for smaller-scale efforts to produce digital replacement collections more gradually.

The book itself is generally recognized as one of the most effective and attractive inventions of all time. The durability of the standard paper volume as a format for transmission of knowledge (and entertainment) indicates the wide-spread acceptance and approval of this particular physical manifestation. It is notable that most of the current projects involving digitization of texts project that on-demand printing will be a primary means of using the digital image masters in the future. Current commentators often remark on the tendency of users of online files to print anything that they expect to continue to need. Perhaps a psychological change will come quickly and persons who grow up with microcomputers and online files will not hesitate to accept an electronic database as a definitive source of information without any need for a hardcopy record. These library users may eventually prefer electronic downloading, maintenance, and manipulation of documents to handling of paper copies (and may well want to do it all at home or in their offices rather than visit a library). At present, most users continue to demand hardcopy.

Regardless of how fast, or in precisely what direction, some of the trends in usage of electronic files develop, libraries are already faced with the need to reformat large portions of their collections that are embrittled and rapidly deteriorating. Although microfilm has been the conversion method of choice for most libraries, as has been noted in Section II, this format is unappealing for direct use and produces less than facsimile-quality paper copies. The prospect of large-scale, high-quality on-request copying as well as downloading from digital image files is already showing strong potential to better meet user demands.

Although document conversion costs are certainly not trivial, libraries have little choice but to invest in some form of preservation if texts currently in existence only on paper, which is being rapidly destroyed by its acidic content, are to remain accessible. Both microfilming and digital image conversion offer the ability to readily produce additional copies from a master record. This possibility is not directly furnished by the process of mass deacidification, the other option that is becoming a viable possibility for preserving deteriorating paper-format collections. If cooperative collection management decision making results in single deacidified copies of bound volumes remaining as the archival copies of record, resource-sharing difficulties of physical handling to photocopy or ship the item will continue to limit accessibility for prospective users. It is also necessary to consider the danger of loss intrinsic to circulating the only existing copy of a work. If that risk is not acceptable, then further duplication of the text would be required if the library is to fulfill its objective of providing the material to the prospective user.

Digital conversion and storage of text with high-quality on-demand printing or downloading features offer some very attractive opportunities in comparison with other preservation options. If this choice becomes prevalent, libraries will gradually find that deteriorating paper copies of items now available from digital masters will be discarded. Depending on the rate of discard of disintegrating materials as compared with the rate of addition of new bound volumes to the collections, libraries may find themselves gradually able to make an almost "one for one" substitution for stack shelf space. Perhaps the rate of deterioration of paper volumes that can safely be discarded because some library has already converted a copy to film or digital form will at some time in the future become so rapid that extra unoccupied space will be available for uses other than shelving. This particular projection of space savings, however, for all the reasons mentioned above and most especially because of the costs of document conversion, is surely not imminent.

Equipment for converting, storing, and accessing materials being preserved will naturally require substantial space. It is likely that more and more workstations will need to be provided and staff will be assigned to assist library users in searching and retrieving documents that will meet their needs. It seems unlikely that methods of access to materials in vast machine-readable databases will be so easy and self-evident to all users that information professionals (i.e., librarians) will be unnecessary. As long as there is a perceived need for assistance in locating and obtaining desired materials, some designated location for appropriate staff (e.g., a library) will continue to be a focal point for access services. Space in such libraries, aside from that occupied by materials that will remain in print form for the indefinite future, will need to be organizaed to meet steadily increasing demands for services related to electronic format collections. When addressing this changed environment, library planners will be facing an expanded set of challenges of many new varieties to fulfill the library's service mission.

VI. Conclusions

It is evident that library planners need to devote substantial attention to the developing opportunities and challenges offered by digital image technology. There is considerable promise in these prospects but also a number of unresolved questions and implications. It is essential to address the areas of technical acceptability for conversion and storage, copyright implications, methodologies for access, retrieval, and communication of digitized material, as well as cost factors. All these aspects need to be considered when contemplating the potential role of digitization in planning for space allocation and service focuses for the future.

As the millennium approaches, it is reasonable to wonder if it will, in fact, bring a time of great progress in providing library services. In conformity with one definition in Webster's Unabridged Dictionary, will libraries experience "freedom from familiar ills and imperfections of human existence?" In particular, will librarians of the year 2001 find that vast collections of texts in image format have revolutionized services and enabled impressive improvements in providing immediate access to relevant resources to meet user needs? Such an assumption is probably premature. Nevertheless, opportunities to make progress toward the "virtual library" of the future are developing constantly. The combined demands of computer-literate users, preservation pressures, and space constraints will make it essential for librarians to attempt to best utilitze the potential for electronic image collections. In this context, digitization offers a very promising potential for advancing the mission of libraries.

References

Commission on Preservation and Access (1990). Cornell, Xerox, and the Commission join in book preservation project. *Commission on Preservation and Access Newsletter* **26**, 3–4.

Crawford, W. (1989). Standards, innovation and optical media. *Laserdisk Professional* **2**, 31–37.

Garcia, D. L. (1991). Copyright law changes for electronic publishing, Intellectual property rights and fair use: Strengthening scholarly communication in the 1990s. *Proceedings of the Ninth Annual Conference of Research Library Directors*, pp. 1–5. OCLC Online Computer Library Center, Dublin, Ohio.

Hart, M. (1990). Project Gutenberg: Access to electronic texts. *Database* **13(6)**, 6–9.

Hockey, S. (1992). Center for electronic texts in the humanities opens its doors. *ARL: A Bimonthly Newsletter of Research Issues and Actions* **160**, 4–5.

International Organization for Standardization (ISO). (1988). *Information Processing—Volume and File Structure of CD–ROM for Information Exchange* (ISO 9660-88). ISO, Geneva, Switzerland.

Kenney, A. R., and Personius, L. K. (1991). *Update on Digital Techniques* (Commission on Preservation and Access Newsletter Insert, Nov.-Dec. 1991). Commission on Preservation and Access, Washington, D.C.

Lesk, M. (1990). Image formats for preservation and access. *Information Technology and Libraries* **9**, 300–308.

Library of Congress (LC). (1990a). The American Memory Project: Technology transmits collections to the nation. *Library of Congress Information Bulletin* **49**, 83–87.

Library of Congress (LC). (1990b). Eight sites chosen for American Memory study. *Library of Congress Information Bulletin* **49**, 265.

Lynch, C. A., and Brownrigg, E. B. (1986a). Conservation, preservation and digitization. *College & Research Libraries* **47**, 379–382.

Lynch, C. A., and Brownrigg, E. B. (1986b). Library applications of electronic imaging technology. *Information Technology and Libraries* **5**, 100–105.

Lynn, M. S. and the Technology Assessment Advisory Committee to the Commission on Preservation and Access (1990). Preservation and access technology: The relationship between digital and other media conversion processes: A structured glossary of technical terms. *Information Technology and Libraries* **9**, 309–336.

Morrow, B. V. (1990). In search of a standard for CD–ROM retrieval. *CD Rom Librarian* **5(3)**, 12 +.

Online Computer Library Center (OCLC). (1991). *Annual Review of OCLC Research, July 1990-June 1991*, pp. 2–3.

Saffady, W. (1990). *Optical Storage Technology 1990–91: A State of the Art Review*. Meckler, Westport, Connecticut.

Seiler, L., and Surprenant, T. (1991). When we get the libraries we want, will we want the libraries we get? *Wilson Library Bulletin*, **65(10)**, 29–31, 152, 157.

Smith, E. (1992). The print prison. *Library Journal* **117(2)**, 48–51.

Thoma, G. R., Gill, M., Hauser, S., and Walker, F. L. (1989). *Document Preservation by Electronic Imaging, Vol. 1, Synopsis*. National Library of Medicine, Lister Hill National Center for Biomedical Communications, Bethesda, Maryland.

Walter, G., and Fisher, D. (1990). Standards help advance document management system progress. *Optical Memory News* May, 1990, 25–27.

Waters, D. J. (1991). *From Microfilm to Digital Imagery: On the Feasibility of a Project to Study the Means, Costs and Benefits of Converting Large Quantities of Preserved Library Materials from Microfilm to Digital Images* (A report of the Yale University Library to the Commission on Preservation and Access). Commission on Preservation and Access, Washington, D.C.

Watkins, B. T. (1991). San Diego campus and McGraw-Hill create custom texts. *The Chronicle of Higher Education* **XXXVIII(11)**, A25.

Buying Publishers' Trade Paperbacks versus Hardbacks: A Preventive Conservation Strategy for Research Libraries

Randy Silverman
Harold B. Lee Library
Brigham Young University
Provo, Utah 84602

Robert Speiser
Department of Mathematics
Brigham Young University
Provo, Utah 84602

I. Introduction

Since 1446, when the stationer Vespasiano da Bisticci began binding manuscript volumes for the first public library at the convent of San Marco in Florence (Ullman and Stadter, 1972, pp. 22–23), librarians have grappled with the problem of inadequate funding for shelf preparation. Once a book is acquired, attention to its readiness to provide long-term service in public use is required. Like the police department, the library's mission has long been to protect and serve. Typically, however, funding for processing and maintaining the collection diverts money from funds available for new acquisitions; hence, a historical preference exists to buy new books that are already bound. Although chaining volumes to library shelves no longer constitutes a cornerstone of library preservation activities, optimizing funds to prepare material for circulation still does.

Library shelf preparation techniques are designed to extend the durability of new acquisitions by reinforcing them before circulation. These methods have historically included (1) library binding (Bostwick, 1910, p. 223); (2) reinforcing pamphlets with "temporary," or pamphlet binders (American Library Association, 1910, p. 21); (3) paperback reinforcement of "stiffening"

ADVANCES IN LIBRARIANSHIP, VOL. 16

(Dean, 1981, pp. 81–82); and may soon include (4) mass deacidification (Boomgaarden, 1988, pp. 33–34).

The increasing number of new acquisitions published exclusively in paperback format forces research libraries to make hard decisions concerning the percentage of their preservation budgets that can be allocated to prebinding and shelf preparation. The necessity to prepare new material for the shelf, however, may compete with funding for repair, which always appears the more pressing of the two issues because damaged material is already proved to be in demand. This pattern of damage, however, is a continuum.

Today, approximately one-half of all new material purchased by research libraries requires some form of reinforcement to protect it from the rigors of circulation. If funding for shelf-preparation activities is scarce, this task may be minimized or simply skipped over, with the inevitable result that volumes destined to receive heavy use will inevitably resurface later in need of repair. At the root of this problem is the publisher's incentive to produce weak bindings; most customers are simply not willing to pay higher prices for added durability.

A. Historical Background

This trend toward economizing on the bindings of new publications is not new. Public demand for affordable books stimulated the development of inexpensive booksellers' binding styles in the sixteenth century, such as Italian limp vellum and limp paper bindings (Frost, 1979, p. 42b). In France and Germany, the Bradel trade binding developed in the last half of the eighteenth century (Rhein, 1962, p. 528), whereas binding in paper-covered "boards" came into use in England in about 1770 (Middleton, 1963, p. 292). Both of these styles were simple paper-covered bindings. Simpler still, thin books with only stitched (or "stabbed") paper covers appeared in England by the end of the sixteenth century (Foxon, 1975, p. 121). Printed paper wrappers still survive in Europe in the form of sewn books published with uncut edges known in France as *livre broché* (Feather, 1988, p. 206).

These utilitarian techniques were developed in the trade binderies to meet the public demand for reading material brought about in part by the growing popularity of the novel in the mid-eighteenth century (Feather, 1988, p. 96). These bindings were commissioned by booksellers on behalf of their clientele (Ball, 1985, p. 6), who alternatively purchased the book in signatures for custom binding (Pollard, 1956, p. 76). Editions of identical books as we know them today originated with the publisher John Newbery (Feather, 1988, p. 119) in approximately 1761 (Sadleir, 1930, p. 10). The introduction of cloth by the publisher William Pickering in 1825 (Carter, 1932, p. 21–22), followed shortly thereafter by casing and blocking (Middleton, 1963, pp. 74, 230), brought trade binderies the ability to mass produce decorative covers economically (Allen, 1979, p. 565). The ease of decorating covers inexpensively stimulated publishers to compete for visual, and consequently economic, dominance of the book-buying market, a practice that continues to shape the modern publishing industry.

B. Modern Implications

Today, whether funded as part of the library's book-processing operation or after the damage has occurred as a function of book repair, the responsibility for reinforcing its vulnerable acquisitions falls squarely on the library as a hidden cost of operations. In effect, paperbacks are once again books purchased in "temporary" paper bindings that require custom binding to meet the "collector's" specifications—in this case, usually library buckram. The cost of reinforcing the publishers' work to insure maximum return on investment is often an afterthought in library planning, but it must somehow be absorbed by shrinking budgets as more and more titles are acquired in paperback format. The problem is already worse than most librarians imagine: a recent survey disclosed that 52% of the new acquisitions purchased in 1990 by Brigham Young University (BYU), a midsized research library, were published as trade paperbacks (Silverman, 1991).

Planning a preservation response that systematically addresses the protection of new acquisitions purchased in ephemeral paperbound formats is essential to the long-term maintenance of a research library collection. This article outlines a strategy for initiating a preventive conservation program funded through a library-wide shift in ordering practice that favors the purchase of publishers' trade paperbacks over hardbacks. If we abandon the false premise that hardbacks are the more cost effective of the two formats, we can generate sufficient savings to protect *all* 52% of the library's incoming paperbound materials with at least a minimum level of shelf preparation. The cost difference between publishers' hardbacks and trade paperbacks is so significant that only a 9% switch in preference from hardbacks to trade paperbacks is required to subsidize the library's entire preventive conservation program.

Implementing this strategy can result in a long term institutional cost savings to research libraries that cannot afford to library bind all paperbacks on receipt. Reinforcing vulnerable new acquisitions before circulation will reduce the backlog of books that ultimately require repair. Additionally, reinforcing library material in relation to its projected level of future use allows resources to be allocated more equitably to protect material most likely to receive the greatest damage.

II. Definition of Terms: Mass-Market versus Trade Paperbacks

The distinction between mass-market and trade paperbacks is critical to understanding the arguments developed in this article.

A. Mass-Market Paperbacks

The concept of mass-market paperbacks began in England in 1935 when Allen Lane published the first 10 Penguin Books, offered for sale at 6d. each (Morpurgo, 1979, pp. 84–85; Schick, 1958, p. 13). The economic viability of publishing inexpensive reprints with paper covers was not original, however; it had been pioneered in the mid-nineteenth century by publishing houses catering to the leisure-reading habits of early railroad travelers. Perhaps the earliest example is Christian Bernard Tauchnitz's successful and long-running editions of Collection of British Authors began in Leipzig in 1842, followed soon after by the one shilling Parlor Library editions of Thomas Hodgson in London in 1847, the first books bound with lithographic-printed paper boards (Schmoller, 1974, pp. 288–292). Even the now-familiar physical format (180 × 111 mm), high-quality typographic layout and distinctive two-color paper covers used to denote the book's subject, was borrowed from the German Albatross editions begun in 1932 (Feather, 1988, p. 208). Lane's contribution with Penguin Books was to package these elements for a "bargain market" interested in buying extremely inexpensive reprints of popular fiction through myriad nontraditional retail outlets (Lane, 1957, p. 101). This niche, which has grown to represent a significant portion of the entire publishing industry, soon included first-time publications as well.

The term "mass-market paperback" generally describes a type of book composed of relatively cheap physical materials. These are characteristically pocket-sized, adhesive-bound books, printed on acidic groundwood paper (Dessauer, 1989, p. 108). This kind of paper is composed of between 25% to 75% mechanical wood pulp containing unpurified lignin, limiting the book's expected useful life span to approximately 25 years.

B. Trade Paperbacks

Trade paperbacks, developed by Jason Epstein of Doubleday & Co. in 1953 (Dessauer, 1989, p. 66; Bailey, 1990, p. 172), are characteristically scholarly first-time publications, produced from higher quality raw materials than their mass-market counterparts. They are typically less expensive second printings of hardbacks, aimed primarily toward the college and quality paperback markets (Bailey, 1990, p. 139), although they often constitute the first and only state of a publication.

Approximately one-fourth of modern trade paperbacks are sewn through the fold; the remainder are adhesive bound (Silverman, 1991). The typographic format and paper quality used in their manufacture are generally similar or identical to that used in hardback publishing, a point we will return to shortly.

C. Limited Paperback Editions

The term "limited paperback editions" (LPEs), coined by Abbot Friedland of Princeton University Press in 1972, refers to the simultaneous publication of scholarly trade paperbacks and hardbacks with the trade paperback prices 50–60% below the price of the hardback (or cloth-bound) edition. The pricing structure for LPEs allows the publisher to "bind 60% in cloth, 20% in LPE, and leave 20% unbound" for future binding in whatever format is required. Hardback sales to libraries were calculated to absorb the bulk of the cost of the print run, thereby subsidizing the simultaneous publication of a limited number of trade paperbacks for sale to individual professors and graduate students. Friedland anticipated that "if too many libraries switch[ed] to LPE's, the program [would be] completely undermined" (Friedland, 1974, pp. 185–186). Reporting on the program's status after 7 years, however, Friedland acknowledged that the "the program [has] indeed been successful" (Friedland, 1979, p. 275) and continues to have a significant impact on university press marketing.

III. Differences between Publishers' Hardbacks and Trade Paperbacks

Because, as we have shown, there is a major qualitative difference between publishers' mass-market and trade paperback books, we need to examine the qualitative differences between publishers' hardbacks and trade paperbacks to determine if there are any disadvantages to ordering trade paperbacks in preference to hardbacks for long-term library use.

A. Paper Permanence

At the outset, a primary concern must be whether or not trade paperbacks contain paper of an inferior quality to hardbacks, a condition that would innately affect their permanence and rule against their desirability in research library collections. Randy Butler, investigating the pH of new publications through a random survey, determined that 67.5% of all commercial American imprints acquired by BYU in 1987 (excluding government documents) were printed on alkaline paper (Butler, 1990, p. 545). This information is encouraging because, as Butler points out, it indicates a significant increase in the number of new monographs published on alkaline paper, regardless of country of origin or physical format.

Butler's study corroborates more recent estimates by Ellen McCrady that 76% of all freesheet (paper used for printing books) produced in the United States in 1992 will be alkaline (Fig. 1). These data indicate a monumental and sudden increase in domestic alkaline paper production, up from only 26% as recently as 1988 (McCrady, 1990, p. 9). These figures illustrate the prompt response by paper manufacturers to comply with requirements established by the Environmental Protection Agency, making it economically advantageous to produce alkaline paper.

Modern alkaline paper is typically produced from chemically refined wood pulp, which, when produced in accordance with ANSI standards for paper permanence, is anticipated to have a life span of several hundred years under normal library use and storage conditions (American National Standards Institute, 1984, p. 8).

The question remains; Is there any specific difference between the paper used to print hardback and that used to print trade paperback books? According to Herbert Bailey (past director of Princeton University Press), "a [trade] paperback book is simply a book with paper covers, and often clothbound and paperbound editions are identical except for the bindings" (Bailey, 1990, p. 141). Other publishers concur; the use of alkaline paper in modern book manufacture occurs equally among hardbacks and trade paperbacks because of the present availability of the raw material. This condition is influenced by a number of other economic factors that influence the publishing industry.

B. Printing and Gathering

There are no economic incentives for printing a hardback differently from a trade paperback, as there once were. When these two formats are published, they are typically printed from the same plates on the same press at the same time and subsequently folded and gathered simultaneously. Both editions are handled identically until the text is actually bound. This efficiency stems

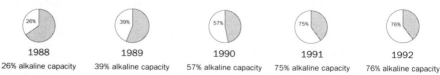

1988	1989	1990	1991	1992
26% alkaline capacity	39% alkaline capacity	57% alkaline capacity	75% alkaline capacity	76% alkaline capacity

Fig. 1.   U.S. freesheet production. Reproduced by permission of Abbey Publications.

from the smaller print runs typical of the publishing industry today. Indeed, restricting a publishers' cash flow by warehousing printed, unsold stock can spell economic disaster, so that the cost of switching paper midway through a print run or shooting two sets of plates to produce two physically different books is usually not considered cost effective.

C. Production Costs

The primary cost difference between modern publishers' hardbacks and trade paperbacks, when they are published simultaneously, occurs at the binding stage and largely involves the cover itself. Manufacturing costs to that point (royalty, editorial, design, production planning, paper, printing, and gathering) remain the same for both formats. Additionally, it should be noted that the cost of using alkaline paper for commercial book production is the same as the cost of using acidic paper of equal printing quality (Dresser, 1988).

The hardback requires rounding and backing; the paperback does not. The hardback also requires raw materials for the hardcover binding itself, which include two single-fold endpapers, one piece of spine-lining material (or mull), one piece of spine-lining paper, two pieces of binder's board, one back-lining strip for the spine of the case, and one piece of covering material ranging in quality form "C"-grade book cloth at best to impregnated paper at worst. "Luxuries" that might increase the cost of a hardback-edition binding include Smyth sewing through the fold (more expensive than adhesive binding, although this technique would probably be applied to the corresponding trade paperback edition as well), a high-quality book cloth, stain for the top edge of the text, machine-made headbands, and a four-color dust jacket as opposed to a jacket printed in only two or three colors (Dessauer, 1981, p. 96). Cover stamping, now a mere shadow of the decorative opulence once lavished on nineteenth- and early twentieth-century publishers' cloth bindings, merely adds another "penny or two" to the cost of the finished design (Edmonds, 1971, p. 59).

By contrast, the cost of the paperback's cover is primarily affected by the time expended in its design and the cost of two- versus three- or four-color offset printing. The cover is held to the spine of the book simply with the adhesive used in the adhesive-binding process or is attached with a second coat of adhesive if the book is sewn (Dessauer, 1989, p. 110).

The size of the print run directly affects the per-item cost of the edition. In 1977, for example, the average per-item cost for hardbacks ranged from $0.62 in an edition of 1,000 to $0.32 in an edition of 100,000 (Benjamin, 1977, p. 48). Although these figures are undoubtedly low by today's standards, they are useful in gaining an insight into the relatively small part the cost of the edition binding plays in the total cost of the finished book. For example, in 1976 the total manufacturing process including paper, printing, *and* binding represented only 23.1% (or $3.46) of the total retail value of a book priced to sell for $15 (Bohne, 1976, p. 143).

D. Pricing Structure

As there are no published data available concerning the cost difference between publishers' hardbacks and trade paperbacks, a random survey was conducted at BYU in 1990 to compart the two. A random selection of books received as hardbacks was searched in *Books in Print* (1948–) to determine the percentage of BYU's typical hardback acquisitions that were available in both formats. The average price difference between the publishers' hardback and the trade paperback was also determined. Because all titles searched were new BYU hardback acquisitions and the edition of *Books in Print* used was the most current CD–ROM edition, we assumed that any hardback listed together with a corresponding paperback price had to reflect simultaneous publication.

Titles available in both hardback and paperback formats were recorded, and the cost difference between the two formats compared. By the random sampling of 411 titles published simultaneously, it was determined that the average cost difference between hardbacks and trade paperbacks in 1990 was $20.25. The hardback price ranged from as much as $110.05 more than the trade paperback to as little as $4.50. Only 9% of the hardbacks searched were found to be published simultaneously as both hardbacks and trade paperbacks.

This information offers some insight into modern publishers' pricing structures. The price difference between hardbacks and trade paperbacks seems to be largely unrelated to the qualitative differences between the two formats. This situation is analogous to the difference between full-price and economy fares on commercial airlines. The business traveler, needing to travel on short notice and to hold to a rigid time schedule, is forced to pay a higher fare than passengers flying economy class seated in the same row. The aim of this price structure, in effect, is to subsidize economy-class fares through the sale of a fixed number of full-fare tickets.

Similarly, university presses (the primary publishers of LPEs) stimulate their market through the "simultaneous publication of a hardcover edition at an elevated price and a softcover edition at a much lower price, but in limited quantity" (Vandermeulen, 1980, p. 243). This practice increases the sale of trade paperbacks to the scholarly community at reduced prices, while relying on libraries to underwrite the cost of the edition through the purchase of hardbacks they assume are books of greater quality and therefore more durable.

On first examination, this dual pricing structure may appear to violate ancient guidelines of fair business dealings as set down in Deuteronomy

25:13–15, "You shall not have in your pouch alternative weights, larger and smaller. You shall not have in your house alternative measures, a larger and a smaller. You must have completely honest weights and completely honest measures" (cited in Plaut, 1981, p. 1507).

However, it may be shortsighted for the library community in its haste to shout "foul" to ignore the present economic plight of the publishing industry. The capitalist system has long endorsed the working principle "whatever the market will bear."

Publishers' price structures remain quite reasonable on the whole, given escalating manufacturing, discount, promotion, royalty, editorial, and administration costs. The burden of typing up liquid assets in unsold warehouse stock has forced publishers to print smaller editions in the hope of selling out within the first year of publication (Berry, 1980, p. 1999), and labor-intensive smaller press runs send per-item book cost spiraling. Start-up costs (such as author's royalties, editing, advertising, and publicity) are reduced or nearly eliminated by second editions, but the number of reprint editions has slowly declined in relation to new publications over the past 30 years. Of the books printed in the United States in 1958, 22% were reprints (*American Library and Book Trade Annual*, 1960, p. 45), compared with 17% in 1988 (*Bowker Annual: Library and Book Trade Almanac*, 1990, p. 480).

The total number of U.S. titles published annually (excluding mass-market paperbacks) has rocketed as well, jumping from 13,462 in 1958 (*American Library and Book Trade Annual*, 1960, p. 45) to 52,462 in 1988 (*Bowker Annual: Library and Book Trade Almanac*, 1990, p. 480). As a result, libraries, with budgets that are often fixed or dwindling, are forced to choose between an ever-expanding list of new publications. This, once again, affects the publishers' pricing structure, as sparse sales of individual titles drive the per-item price still higher.

This fiercely competitive economic environment makes it critical for research libraries to assess their current policies.

E. Durability

Many research libraries have historically avoided ordering paperbacks in an effort to acquire books durable enough to withstand the rigors of library circulation. Although hardbacks *are* more durable than paperbacks, the advantage is marginal at best. Based on a survey conducted at BYU in 1990, it was estimated that unbound trade paperbacks circulated an average of 8.5 times before they were sufficiently damaged to require rebinding, whereas publishers' hardbacks circulated 11.0 times (Silverman, 1991).

If publishers' hardbacks are 2.5 circulations more durable than trade paperbacks (recalling that the average cost difference between the two formats is \$20.25), those last 2.5 circulations cost the library slightly more than \$8 apiece. This information serves to further illustrate the historic decline in the durability of publishers' hardbacks as discussed earlier.

IV. Preventive Conservation Treatment Options

A. Implications for Preservation Funding

To recapitulate, there seems to be little physical difference today between publishers' hardbacks and trade paperbacks, except for the cover proper. Additionally, hardbacks are not signigicantly more effective than trade paperbacks at withstanding the rigors of circulation. What, then, is to prevent research libraries from buying trade paperbacks in lieu of hardbacks when a choice is available? If the library's collection-development policy is currently committed to acquiring new acquisitions in hardback format (as has historically been the case by BYU), it is possible for a number of benefits to accrue by modifying this predilection.

An immediate institutional savings would be realized through the purchase of trade paperback editions whenever possible. This savings, based on the cost difference of \$20.25 between hardbacks and trade paperbacks, will affect approximately 9% of the library's annual acquisitions (the number of titles presently published simultaneously in hardback and trade paperback formats). At BYU, based on the current acquisition level of 33,600 monographs annually, this amounts to approximately 3,024 titles per year, or \$20.25 × 3,024 = \$61,236.

In other words, \$61,236 in discretionary funds could be recyled annually back into the collection-development budget for the purchase of other new acquisitions. However, the result of this short-term gain would be to create a collection increasingly vulnerable to physical damage, thereby ultimately inflating the library's repair costs. To balance collection growth against permanent retention, this discretionary funding would be better used to support a preventive conservation strategy. This response would allow the library to expand its shelf-preparation practices in anticipation of the increasing number of new publications produced in weak or vulnerable formats, without reducing its total number of new acquisitions.

Simply planning to replace paperbacks as they wear out is not a realistic option for a research library. Because of short press runs and the limited number of second editions being produced, it is not reasonable to assume that a title will always be available for repurchase after the first copy wears out.

However, before an institution can responsibly commit the savings we have described to the preservation of its collections, one final question needs to be addressed: Will this redistribution of collection-development funding for preventive conservation really prove cost-effective in the long run? How much more effective is applying one of the aforementioned shelf-preparation treatments—library binding, the use of pamphlet binders, and stiffening—to new acquisitions before circulation than simply buying new acquisitions as hardbacks? We shall address this vital question by comparing three basic preventive-conservation treatments. The cost and circulation statistics following each technique (gathered at BYU) will be used in the example of mathematical optimization to follow.

B. Library Binding

New trade paperbacks typically require one of two standard methods of library binding as determined by the physical format of the book: double-fan adhesive binding or recasing (Library Binding Institute, 1986, p. 3).

The majority (77%) of trade paperbacks received by BYU in 1990 were adhesive bound by the publisher (Silverman, 1991), limiting the library's treatment option for books bound this way to double-fan adhesive binding. Library binders' double-fan adhesive binding differs significantly from publishers' adhesive binding. Double-fan adhesive binding relies on the durability of an internally plasticized polyvinyl acetate (PVA) adhesive that is designed to remain flexible over time. This adhesive is applied cold to the fanned leaves of the text block, insuring that $\frac{1}{64}$ in. of the binding edge of each leaf receives an adhesive coating—in effect "tipping" the entire text block together. Some library binders even notch the spine of the text to improve the adhesive's ability to bond, especially to coated papers. Publishers' adhesive bindings, on the other hand, have a greater likelihood of breaking down than double-fan adhesive bindings because most hot-melt adhesives become less flexible over time. Additionally, the adhesive is applied only to the spine edge of the text block.

Recasing is appropriate for material that has been machine sewn through the fold (or Smyth sewn) by the publisher, a condition affecting 23% of the trade paperbacks received at BYU in 1990. Recasing insures that the book's original sewing is retained, allowing the volume to open completely to the back margin when it is read or photocopied. Recasing is more labor intensive than double-fan adhesive binding and, therefore, more costly. To recase a Smyth-sewn binding, new endpapers are sewn by hand to the existing text block, followed by the sequence of rounding, backing, and lining of the spine. Even though the edges of the book may remain untrimmed, the boards must be cut by hand, and preparation of the text block requires a significant amount of time (Library Binding Institute, 1986, pp. 6–8).

With either double-fan adhesive binding or recasing, the finished library binding is covered with a durable, utilitarian-looking buckram case. From the outside, both finished products appear identical to the casual observer, although recasing requires nearly twice as much time to execute as a double-fan adhesive binding, reaffirming the cliché "you can't judge a book by its cover."

Occasionally, the physical requirements of newly published material demand library binding options beyond the two just discussed, as with a suite of single plates printed on extremely stiff paper. This type of material may require a box or some customized solution that is outside the scope of typical library binding operations. Therefore, for the sake of clarity in the discussion to follow, the two forms of library binding just described will be used to represent the universe of library binding options available.

Werner Rebsamen (Rebsamen, 1989) argues that it is cost-effective to library bind all publishers' original paperback or hardback bindings for library use. This position does not address the cost of buying publishers' hardbacks and rebinding them when the trade paperback edition is published simultaneously or the inability of most research libraries to engage in unlimited library binding. Additionally, Rebsamen's displayed data provide experimental evidence that seems to contradict his assumption that one can predict the break-even number of times a book needs to circulate before library binding becomes cost-effective.[1]

The authors of this article agree with Rebsamen and others (Walker, 1982, p. 69; Merrill-Oldham, 1984, p. 1) that the durability afforded by library binding is an excellent preventive measure for circulating collections. Budgetary constraints are far too common in research libraries, however, to avoid critically evaluating each item's individual need for physical protection and weighing that against the overall needs of the entire collection.

Based on circulation statistics at BYU, it is reasonable to expect that a library binding will survive 30 or more circulations before requiring further rebinding. BYU's present cost per-item for library binding (averaging the cost of recasing and double-fan adhesive binding) is approximately $7.50 per volume.

C. Pamphlet Binders

In an earlier study (Silverman, 1988), the requirements for a binding suited to the conservation of both rare and nonrare pamphlets was defined. Two elements of that specification are applicable to the physical and chemical performance requirements for commercially manufactured pamphlet binders as well. These are (1) the nature of the physical attachment between the pamphlet and the binder should not cause damage to the pamphlet over time, and (2) the durability and chemical stability of the materials used in the manufacture of the binder should promote the longevity of the pamphlet.

---

[1] Indeed, the displayed data on page 13 clusters in such a way as to suggest that Y_1 is probably *not* a function of PR.

1. Problems

Many commercially produced pamphlet binders do not comply with the ideal previously described. The most blatant offenders cause physical damage to the pamphlets they house with the adhesive used to attach the pamphlet to the binder. For example, a pregummed cloth flange incorporated into a pamphlet binder's design will tend to stiffen with age as the adhesive cross-links with the paper. This often results in discoloration and embrittlement to the pamphlet at the point the flange attaches to the paper. Further, the hard edge created by the flange has a tendency to break the first and last leaves of the pamphlet's title page. Additionally, this form of adhesive attachment tends to stiffen the spine of the pamphlet, needlessly restricting its openability.

Another common form of physical damage is caused by stapling the pamphlet to the binder through the pamphlet's side ("side-stitching"). This practice restricts the pamphlet's openability and forces the paper to crease and become weakened at the edge created by the staple. However, if the pamphlet was originally side-stitched, stapling it to a pamphlet binder through the side can be argued to be no more damaging than the original method of manufacture and may be required with respect to efficiency. On the other hand, attaching a pamphlet to a pamphlet binder through the fold is less damaging for any pamphlet originally sewn or stapled through the fold and is sometimes preferable for pamphlets already damaged by side-stitching.

Chemical degradation to a pamphlet can be caused or accelerated by housing it in a pamphlet binder manufactured from acidic materials. Chemical degradation is slow but relentless and can prove dramatic after decades of storage. The effects of acid migration from the binder to the pamphlet are intensified by the slim mass of the pamphlet in relation to the mass of the acidic binder surrounding it.

These forms of damage are unacceptable within the context of permanent retention of pamphlets within a research library, as they result in inevitable repair costs and irreversible damage to the collection.

2. Solutions

Pamphlets should be attached to pamphlet binders, whenever possible, by sewing or stapling through the fold. When paper strength is a concern, sewing proves less stresful over time than stapling. In the case of weaker papers, stress to the fold can be minimized by the use of a "free guard," that is, a folded piece of Japanese paper placed (without adhesive) in the center of the section before the pamphlet is sewn to the binder. The free guard acts as a physical reinforcement to prevent the tension of the sewing thread from cutting the paper (Silverman, 1988, p. 118).

If the pamphlet was previously side-stitched (with thread or staples), it can be reattached to the binder by side-stitching if the paper is strong enough to withstand the process. Although side-stitching is a time saver, it should be handled with discretion, as it can result in damage to the paper in time, as mentioned previously. Side-stitching is an ill-advised technique for pamphlets with damaged spine folds, which are better mended with Japanese paper and paste before being sewn through the fold.

Pamphlets that are adhesive bound can be successfully sewn through the spine or side-stitched if the margin width and paper flexibility will allow. No adhesive attachment between the pamphlet or the binder should be necessary in any case.

Materials used in the manufacture of commercial pamphlet binders must be chemically stable as well as rigid enough to prevent physical damage to the pamphlet. Alkaline board or archival-quality polyester should be used in the construction of the pamphlet binder. Book cloth should be of an appropriate library weight and durability. Pressure-sensitive acrylic adhesives applied to the cloth should never come into contact with the pamphlet itself and should be resistant to cold-flow to prevent problems in the future. Pockets used to contain loose parts or maps should be made from alkaline paper or other archival materials.

Many commercially produced pamphlet binders are available, but few meet the specifications just described. In purchasing pamphlet binders for a research library, the librarian should weigh the quality of materials and structural design against the long-term effects these will have on pamphlets slated for permanent retention. The ongoing cost of upkeep and repair should be factored into the original purchase price, as short-term savings may result in significantly higher repair costs in the long run.

One commercially produced pamphlet binder that does conform to the specifications listed above was developed by Barclay Ogden, Hans Wiesendanger, and Fritz James in 1987 (U.S. patent number 4,741,655) and is commercially available through the Library Binding Service (Library Binding Service Archival Products, 1987). This product will be referred to throughout the remainder of this article as a generic pamphlet binder. It will be used for cost comparisons with the other shelf-preparation techniques discussed.

This commercially produced pamphlet binder can be expected to circulate aproximately 15 times before needing replacement. The average cost for a pamphlet binder at BYU today is approximately $3 including the in-house labor to attach the pamphlet to the binder.

D. Stiffening

"Stiffening" is a term used to describe a number of methods for reinforcing the covers of paperback books to gain increased durability in use and greater stability on the shelf. Techniques for stiffening have found increased application in research libraries during the past decade because of the modern proliferation of paperback books by publishers.

John Dean (Dean, 1981, pp. 81–85) describes one method performed in-house whereby a small hinge is glued between the inside front cover of the book and the inner margin of the first leaf, followed by a thin piece of card stock laminated to the entire inside cover. The steps are repeated for the back cover as well. Although inexpensive, there are some disadvantages to Dean's technique. The glued attachment between the hinge and the first leaf of the text may result in the loss of inner margin when the stiffening is removed to facilitate rebinding. Additionally, gluing a piece of card to the inside of the paperback's cover has a tendency to "pull" (or warp) the covers when the adhesive is dried. Still, the visual aesthetic of the printed cover remains unaffected with this technique, which may contribute to increased patron use.

In an earlier study also conducted at BYU, John Christensen examined the most economical way to extend the circulating life of mass-market paperbacks in a popular reading collection, where high use and eventual discard were collection parameters. He compared three variables:

1. The cost per circulation to buy mass-market paperbacks prebound by a jobber
2. The cost per circulation to reinforce the covers of mass-market paperbacks in-house with clear polyester tape and
3. The cost per circulation to simply circulate mass-market paperbacks unprotected

Christensen found that the library's greatest economy in terms of cost per circulation was achieved by reinforcing the covers of mass-market paperbacks with clear polyester tape (at $0.07 per circulation), followed by simply circulating mass-market paperbacks unprotected (at $0.08 per circulation), and finally, the most expensive of the three options, prebinding mass-market paperbacks (at $0.18 per circulation). Greater overall circulation was also demonstrated for identical titles protected with clear polyester tape as opposed to the same title bound in buckram. This seems to indicate that patron demand is stimulated by the aesthetics of illustrated paperback covers as opposed to prebindings in a collection accessed predominantly for popular reading (Christensen, 1989, p. 65).

This study demonstrates the cost effectiveness of protecting paperbacks before use through stiffening, although the methods described by Christensen require significant modification for application to collections of permanent retention value. Further, it illustrates that the most durable reinforcement may not prove the most desirable, especially if the title's use does not warrant that level of protection. As we will show, the problem of specifying the treatment appropriate to the anticipated level use for new acquisitions is a title-by-title decision

A number of clear plastic cover protectors are commercially available that attach to the outside cover of paperbacks with pressure-sensitive adhesive (e.g., Easy Covers® from Kapco, and Adjustable Lyfguard® from Demco). These are primarily used by public libraries to extend the life of heavily circulated mass-market paperbacks. The pressure-sensitive adhesive makes them easy to apply, and the title and printed cover remain clearly visible to the patron through the plastic. Two disadvantages of using these products in a research library collection are (1) they are designed to attach to the spine of the text, an ill-advised practice because the adhesive has a tendency to stiffen with age, thereby restricting the openability of the text; and (2) the materials used in their manufacture are not archival.

One self-adhering paperback cover protector that overcomes these objections is called the Cover-Ups® (U.S. patent number 4,377,430) and is produced and distributed by Vinyl Industrial Products, Inc. This product warrants serious consideration for use in research libraries, as it is designed specifically to provide long-term durability to trade paperbacks. It is constructed from sheets of 7- or 10-mil polyester (depending on the size of the book to be stiffened), scored to allow the paper cover of the text to flex, and lined on both covers—but not across the spine—with pressure-sensitive acrylic adhesive.

The grade of polyester used in its manufacture is archival. The pressure-sensitive adhesive coating on the polyester is a high-tack acrylic adhesive, with a pH of approximately 6.0 and excellent aging properties in contact with paper or polyester. The cover is designed to remain clear and permanently bonded to the paperback and will cause no loss of text if rebinding is required (R. Bexley, personal communication May 1991).

An independent accelerated aging test verifies that the Cover-Ups® is constructed from archival-quality polyester and acrylic adhesive. The adhesive appears to remain flexible and retain its "tack" over time and will not cold-flow or offset onto the shelf. Some slight yellowing of the materials can be anticipated caused by aging or exposure to ultraviolet light (J. Druzik, personal communication, November 1991).

In use, the durability of a paperback protected by a polyester Cover-Ups® is largely dependent on the quality of the publishers' sewn or adhesive-bound text block. In tests conducted at the Rochester Institute of Technology, the Cover-Ups® survived flexing in a 120° arc 10,000 times without failing. The effectiveness of the Cover-Ups® when used on an adhesive-bound trade paperback, for example, is directly dependent on the plasticity and durability of the publishers' adhesive binding (J. Bexley, personal communication, May 1991). However, with both adhesive-bound and sewn trade paperbacks, a

Cover-Ups® will extend the service life of the book and minimize damage to the edges of the text. At such time as book protected with the Cover-Ups® becomes sufficiently worn to require rebinding, the paperback's paper cover and the Cover-Ups® are removed together without causing damage to the text block.

For the purposes of cost comparisons with other shelf-preparation techniques, Cover-Ups® will be used to represent the generic paperback stiffening throughout the remainder of this article. It is estimated that the Cover-Ups® applied to a trade paperback will provide approximately 15 circulations before the text requires rebinding. The cost for stiffening at BYU, including in-house labor, is approximately $1.50 per item.

V. Mathematical Optimization

A. A Procedure

Let us assume that it is possible to generate a heretofore untapped budget for preservation by buying publishers' trade paperbacks whenever possible as opposed to buying hardbacks: let p dollars represent this figure. How can this money be spent to achieve optimum preventive conservation for the collection, focusing specifically on the problem of shelf preparation for an estimated 52% of the annual monograph acquisitions? To be precise, we set

$$X = \text{number rebound in library bindings,}$$
$$Y = \text{number protected by stiffening,}$$
$$Z = \text{number of paperbacks left alone.}$$

Write n for the total number of books to be preserved. Then we must have

$$n = X + Y + Z.$$

Our task here is to determine X, Y, and Z so that our p dollars will produce the greatest benefit. For a given choice of X, Y, and Z, denote by Q the expected total number of circulations for all n books. For us, the greatest benefit would be to achieve the largest possible number of expected circulations Q. It turns out, perhaps surprisingly, that the greatest benefit will be achieved only when either X or Y is zero. In other words: *put all your preservation eggs in one basket*. So now the question is, which basket? Here is an effective procedure to determine the right basket. (For a mathematical justification, please see the Appendix.)

1. Record, for later use, the following numbers, in addition to p and n above.

a = expected number of circulations for a library binding
b = expected number of circulations for a stiffened paperback
c = expected number of circulations for an unbound paperback
d = cost of a library binding
e = cost of stiffening

2. Calculate a number s, according to the following formula:

$$s = a - c + (d/e)(c - b).$$

3. If s is positive, rebind your paperbacks in library bindings. If s is negative, stiffen. In the rare event that $s = 0$, both choices are equally good.

Here at BYU, a rough statistical analysis gave $a = 30$, $b = 15$, $c = 8.5$ as reasonable values, and our local costs gave $d = 7.50$, $e = 1.50$. We obtain $s = -11$, with the verdict that we should stiffen publishers' trade paperbacks.

B. Implications for Book Preservation

At BYU, ordering trade paperbacks in lieu of hardbacks is estimated to affect 9% of the library's 33,600 annual monographic acquisitions, or 3,024 titles. If the average cost difference between the hardback and trade paperback is $20.25, a $61,236 savings in purchase cost can be generated annually by buying trade paperbacks in preference to publishers' hardbacks. This money can then be used to support a preventive conservation program without reducing the number of monographs acquired annually.

Choosing to optimize this discretionary money for the preventive conservation of the library's new acquisitions will allow all of the new paperback acquisitions to be protected. At BYU, this affects approximately 52% of the library's total acquisitions, or 17,472 titles per year (including the 9% now ordered in paperback instead of hardback format).

It is clearly to the library's advantage to library bind as many materials anticipated to receive high use as possible, once it is determined that all new paperbound acquisitions can receive at least some level of preventive conservation. Library binding is appropriate for approximately 20% of the library's holdings, predicted by Richard Trueswell to receive 80% of the library's overall use (Trueswell, 1969). At BYU, this includes monographs that support course work, books that qualify as classics (i.e., retain a steady readership over time), and publications focused on topics of current or general interest. Additionally, future high-use patterns can be predicted to a large extent by titles, topics, and subject areas currently receiving repair. For this reason the library's book repair and bindery preparation staff are well situated to help identify new acquisitions on receipt that are likely to receive heavy use. In a fully automated library, current-use statistics grouped by call number ranges may be useful in determining which subject areas are likely to receive this kind of heavy future use. In whatever way the problem is addressed, pragmatic item-by-item sorting is ultimately required to identify the new trade paperback acquisitions most likely to receive the highest use, and therefore in need of library binding.

Additionally, certain physical formats are vulnerable by definition and require library binding as a function of shelf preparation, regardless of projected levels of future use. Examples of material that may require preventive conservation on receipt include books published with perforated pages or in single sheets, material published in three-ring binders or spiral bindings, and poor quality adhesive bindings where the adhesive has already cracked or the pages are falling out.

Based on the theory of optimization, the discretionary funds must be used in such a way as to allow all vulnerable new acquisitions that are not library bound to be stiffened or pamphlet bound before they have a chance to circulate. An optimal solution then, given $61,236 in discretionary funds, would be to employ two 0.5 FTE student positions at $5 per hour ($10,000 annually) to provide 2,000 hours of in-house labor for applying stiffeners and pamphlet bindings. The remaining $51,237 could then be applied to library binding 4,023 volumes at $7.50 each, stiffening 12,855 volumes at $1.50 each, and pamphlet binding 594 volumes at $3 each (Fig. 2). This addresses the preventive conservation of all 17,472 volumes received at BYU in paperback format, or 52% of the library's total annual acquisitions.

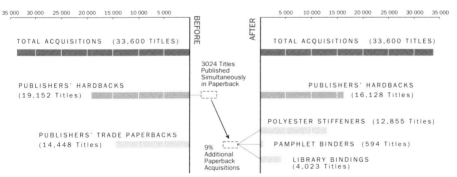

Fig. 2. Buying 9% trade paperbacks in preference to hardbacks generates $61,236 annually at BYU. Of these funds, $51,236 can be applied to preventive conservation and $10,000 to student wages.

VI. Implementation of a Preventive Conservation Plan within a Research Library

A. Obstacles with Library Book Jobbers

Implementing a plan to systematically buy publishers' trade paperbacks instead of hardbacks to fund a preventive conservation program hinges on the library's ability to systematically order books in paperback as opposed to hardback format as a part of the normal acquisition process. The greatest impact of this plan naturally falls on the library's book jobbers and is practical only in so far as the jobber can establish an ordering profile to automatically satisfy the library's requests. Within the library's ordering procedures, the purchase of trade paperbacks in preference to hardbacks must occur at three levels of the ordering process: approval orders, firm orders, and standing orders.

1. Approval Orders

With approval order plans, the library establishes a profile with its jobbers. Books falling within the parameters of that profile are automatically sent to the library for review before purchase. Coutts Library Services, Inc., (Lewistown, NY), for example, is currently able to add a librarys' preference for trade paperbacks to the institution's approval order profile and to supply titles available in paperbound format for review (J. Grantier, personal communication, October, 1991). Although customizing this aspect of the library's approval order profile is highly desirable from the library's perspective, at present Coutts seems to be unique in its ability to provide this service. This is odd in a way, according to John Grantier, vice president of Technical Services at Coutts, because the publishers' discount to jobbers allows the jobber to make an equal profit irrespective of whether they sell the hardback or trade paperback edition. For example, the hardback edition of a $20 retail book may be discounted 40% to the jobber, whereas the trade paperback, retailing at $13.50, will be discounted 60%. In either case the jobber's profit is approximately $8 (J. Grantier, personal communication, October, 1991). This demonstrates that selling either format is equally acceptable to modern publishers, making it unlikely that libraries exhibiting a preference for paperbacks will significantly impact the publishing industry, as was once feared by Abbot Friedland when he introduced the concept of Limited Paperback Editions in 1972 (Friedland, 1974, pp. 185–186).

Other library jobbers besides Coutts are not yet currently able to offer libraries the benefit of ordering trade paperbacks in preference to hardbacks when they are published simultaneously. According to Martin Warzala of

Baker & Taylor Books (Somerville, NJ), "At this time, only one format of titles available in multiple formats, usually the hard cover version, is treated [through our] approval service." In other words, were the trade paperback published simultaneously with the hardback but Baker & Taylor happened to stock only the hardback, the hardback format alone would be available to the customer. He adds, however, that the customer's option to specify the paper format is presently under discussion at Baker & Taylor Books but that

> it is our experience that the availability of information and data about simultaneous publications is capricious at best. In our future operating environment this will present a major problem: we will offer a function which provides our client users with the option of format choice, but, the data to treat multiple formats of identical titles, may not be practically available to allow control of the situation. Our ability to treat multiple formats of identical titles will be dependant upon our suppliers providing timely essential data to address this situation. (M. Warzala, personal communication, May, 1991)

2. Firm Orders

Firm orders are orders placed by the library with the jobber when the specific title requested is known. Firm orders generally include specific titles ordered from publishers' flyers and catalogs by subject specialists and bibliographers. In the case of firm orders, a library-wide policy decision to order trade paperbacks when available would consistently provide the library with books in this format, regardless of whether the title was ordered through a jobber or directly from the publisher.

3. Standing Orders

Standing orders, the last of the three purchasing agreements available through jobbers, include title standing orders and publisher standing orders. Title standing orders imply that a library would request every title published in a known series at the point of publication. Publisher standing orders indicate that a library would order all publications issued by a specific publisher (i.e., ALA). In both cases, as with approval orders, the jobber must have the capability to add a library's preference for trade paperbacks to its institutional profile before the library can be assured of consistently receiving the trade paperback in preference to the hardback when both formats of an edition are available.

It is hoped that future services provided by book jobbers will respond to the growing need for libraries to economize and, over time, provide the option to request trade paperbacks in preference to hardbacks as a normal aspect of library approval order plans.

B. Obstacles within the Library

Even if the misconception that paperbacks are generically inferior to hard-backs can be laid to rest, it must still be emphasized that longevity is assured only through the specification of *trade* paperbacks.

Also, the discretionary savings derived from buying trade paperbacks in preference to hardbacks will accumulate over time on an item-by-item basis. This means that if a library's budget is allocated to individual subject selector's accounts, tracking the savings on a title-by-title basis within these accounts will prove very labor intensive. To operate cost-effectively, the program needs to be funded independently from an item-by-item accounting system, or the loss in overall efficiency will be significant. This requires an institution-wide policy decision to buy trade paperbacks whenever possible. Then, through the mathematical calculations described in this essay, the estimated savings can be applied outright to fund the preventive conservation program.

If an institution is already buying paperbacks in preference to hardbacks, deriving discretionary funding for a preventive conservation program as sug-gested in this essay is not possible. However, the library's current use of the commercial binding budget can be reassessed with optimizing in mind, and through the use of stiffening provide at least minimal protection for all new paperback acquisitions before they circulate, if this is not already the case.

VII. Conclusion

A preservation response that systematically addresses the protection of all new acquisitions published in vulnerable paperback formats has become es-sential to the long-term maintenance of research library collections. The significant cost difference between publishers' hardback and trade paperback editions can be used to underwrite a preventive conservation strategy, if the library commits to an institutional policy to purchase trade paperbacks in preference to hardbacks whenever possible. Requesting that this preference become part of the institution's profile with its library jobbers may help stimulate progress toward automatically receiving trade paperbacks, in prefer-ence to hardbacks, as part of all library orders.

Implementing a preventive conservation strategy provides both immedi-ate and long-term savings to research libraries. Limiting the number of pub-lishers' hardbacks acquired by the library serves the long-term interests of the institution because hardbacks are inordinately expensive for their physical durability, whereas the permanence of the paper they are printed on is equal to that of trade paperbacks. Reinforcing all vulnerable new pamphlets and trade paperbacks on receipt reduces the number of books ultimately requiring repair. In addition, protecting library material relative to its projected level of future use allows scarce resources to be allocated for stiffening, pamphlet binders, and library binding, with material likely to receive the greatest amount of damage receiving the most durable reinforcement.

VIII. Mathematical Appendix

Here is the justification for our decision procedure in Section V, a standard linear-optimization. Assuming that we spend all p dollars to preserve our books, the variables X, Y, and Z will satisfy the constraints.

$$n = X + Y + Z \qquad \begin{cases} X \geq 0 \\ Y \geq 0 \\ Z \geq 0 \end{cases}$$
$$p = dX + eY$$

To rewrite our constraints in terms of X alone, we solve the second equation for Y first, then solve the first for Z and rewrite Y in terms of X. Calculating briefly, we obtain:

$$Y = p/e + (d/e)X \qquad 0 \leq X \leq p/d$$
$$Z = [n - (p/e)] + [(d/e) - 1]X$$

Hence we can write $Q = aX + bY + cZ$ as a function of X alone. Indeed, we find

$$Q = [cn + (p/e)(b - c)] + [a - c + (d/e)(c - b)]X.$$

The second expression in square brackets, by definition, is the number s defined in the main text. Because Q is a linear function of X on the closed interval $0 \leq X \leq p/d$, either Q is constant or its maximum occurs at an endpoint. Suppose first that Q is not constant. Then, for a maximum Q, we have either $X = 0$ or $X = p/d$. In the latter case, the equation $Y = p/e + (d/e)X$ gives $Y = 0$. The slope of the line given by $Q = Q(X)$ is precisely s, so we have a maximum with $Y = 0$ when s is positive, and a maximum with $X = 0$ when s is negative. If Q is constant, in other words when $s = 0$, any allowable X and Y will give the same result.

Acknowledgments

The authors express their appreciation to the members of the BYU staff who contributed to the completion of this essay: Randy Butler, John Christensen, James Fairbourn, Kathy Johansen, Kirk Russell, and Bill Slater, for data gathering; Shannon Reid for economic consultation; Linda Hunter Adams and Russ Clement for editing; and Randy Olsen (assistant university librarian for Collection Development) for supporting and implementing the concept at BYU. Appreciation is also expressed to Cecily M. Grzywacz of the Getty Conservation Institute for scientific consultation, and Jan Merrill-Oldham of the University of Connecticut Library for inspiring the concept.

References

Allen, S. (1979). Machine stamped bookbindings, 1834–1860. *Antiques* **115**, 564–572.
American Library and Book Trade Annual. (1960). R. R. Bowker Company, New York.
American Library Association (ALA). (1910). *Mending and Repair of Books*. ALA Publishing Board, Chicago.
American National Standards Institute. (1985). *Permanence of Paper for Printed Materials (ANSI Z39.48–1984)*. American National Standards Institute, Gaithersburg, Maryland.
Anstaett, H. B., ed. (1948–). *Books in Print*. R. R. Bowker Company, New York.
Bailey, H. S., Jr. (1990). *The Art and Science of Book Publishing*. Ohio University Press, Athens, Ohio.
Ball, D. (1985). *Victorian Publishers' Bindings*. Book Press, Limited, Williamsburg, Virginia.
Benjamin, C. G. (1977). *A Candid Critique of Book Publishing*. R. R. Bowker Company, New York.
Berry, J. (1980). The embattled backlist. *Library Journal* **105**, 1999.
Bohne, H. (1976). "Why are book prices so high?" *Scholarly Publishing* **7(2)**, 135–143.
Boomgaarden, W. L. (1988). Prospective preservation. In *Preservation: A Research Library Priority for the 1990s, Minutes of the 111th Meeting of the Association of Research Libraries, 22 October 1987*, pp. 26–30. The Association, Washington, D.C.
Bostwick, A. E. (1910). *The American Public Library*. D. Appleton and Company, New York.
Bowker Annual: Library and Book Trade Almanac, 35th ed. (1990). R. R. Bowker Company, New York.
Butler, R. R. (1990). "Here today. . .gone tomorrow": A pH investigation of Brigham Young University's 1987 library acquisitions. *College and Research Libraries* **51(6)**, 539–551.
Carter, J. (1932). *Binding Variants in English Publishing 1820–1900*. Constable and Company Limited, London.
Christensen, J. O. (1989). Extended life for popular paperbacks. *Library Journal* **114 (16)**, 65–66.
Dean, J. (1981). The in-house processing of paperbacks and pamphlets. *Serials Review* **7(4)**, 81–85.
Dessauer, J. P. (1981). *Book Publishing: What It Is, What It Does*, 2nd ed. R. R. Bowker Company, New York.
Dessauer, J. P. (1989). *Book Publishing: A Basic Introduction*. Continuum, New York.
Dresser, G. (1988). Major paper manufacturers' prices for acidic vs. acid-free papers in selected paper grades (as of 2/1/88, $ per CWT). *Alkaline Paper Advocate* **1(3)**, 20.
Edmonds, P. (1971). Nuts and bolts. *Scholarly Publishing* **3(1)**, 58–61.
Feather, J. (1988). *A History of British Publishing*. Croom Helm, London.
Foxon, D. (1975). Stitched books. *Book Collector* **24**, 111–124.
Friedland, A. M. (1974). Limited paperback editions. *Scholarly Publishing* **5(2)**, 183–186.
Friedland, A. M. (1979). Sales potential in limited paperback editions. *Scholarly Publishing* **10(3)**, 275–286.
Frost, G. (1979, February). Codex format bookbinding structures: A survey of historical types. *Abbey Newsletter* **2(4)**, 39–42d.
Lane, A. (1957). Paper-bound books. In *The Book World Today, a New Survey of the Making and Distribution of Books in Britain* (J. Hampden, ed.), pp. 101–105. George Allen and Unwin Limited, London.
Library Binding Institute. (1986). *Standard for Library Binding*, 8th ed. (P. Parisi and J. Merrill-Oldham, eds.), Library Binding Institute, Rochester, New York.

Library Binding Service Archival Products. (1987). *Pamphlet Binders* (promotional brochure). Library Binding Service Archival Products, Des Moines, Iowa.

McCrady, E. (1990). Alkaline penetration forecast. *Alkaline Paper Advocate* **3(1)**, 9.

Merrill-Oldham, J. (1984). Binding for research libraries. *The New Library Scene* **3(4)**, 1, 4–6.

Middleton, B. C. (1963). *A History of English Craft Bookbinding Technique.* Hafner Publishing Company, New York.

Morpurgo, J. E. (1979). *Allen Lane, King Penguin.* Hutchinson, London.

Plaut, G. W., ed. (1981). *The Torah, a Modern Commentary.* Union of American Hebrew Congregations, New York.

Pollard, G. (1956, June). Changes in the style of bookbinding, 1550–1830. *The Library*, 5th series, **11(2)**, 71–94.

Rebsamen, W. (1989). Economics of library binding. *The New Library Scene* **8(4)**, 13–18.

Rhein, A. (1962). Die frühen verlagseinbände, eine technische entwicklung, 1735–1850. *Gutenberg Jahrbuch*, 519–532.

Sadleir, M. (1930). *The Evolution of Publishers' Binding Syles 1770–1900.* Constable and Company Limited, London.

Schick, F. L. (1958). *The Paperbound Book in America: The History of Paperbacks and Their European Background.* R. R. Bowker Company, New York.

Schmoller, H. (1974). The paperback revolution. In *Essays in the History of Publishing in Celebration of the 250th Anniversary of the House of Longman 1724–1974.* (A. Briggs, ed.), pp. 283–318. Longman, London.

Silverman, R. (1988). Small, not insignificant: An examination of pamphlet binding structures. *American Institute for Conservation of Historic and Artistic Works, Book and Paper Group Annual* **6**, 111–139.

Silverman, R. (1991). *1990 Survey Comparing Cost of New Hardback vs. Paperback Acquisitions Conducted at Brigham Young University's Harold B. Lee Library.* Unpublished manuscript.

Trueswell, R. W. (1969). Some behavioral patterns of library users: The 80/20 rule. *Wilson Library Bulletin* **43**, 458–461.

Ullman, B. L., and Stadter, P. A. (1972). *The Public Library of Renaissance Florence.* Editrice Antenore, Padova, Italy.

Vandermeulen, A. (1980). Which is the cannibal—cloth or paper? *Scholarly Publishing* **11(3)**, 243–246.

Walker, G. (1982). Library binding as a conservation measure. *Collection Management* **4(1–2)**, 55–71.

The Future of Library Science in Higher Education: A Crossroads for Library Science and Librarianship

C. D. Hurt
School of Library Science
University of Arizona
Tucson, Arizona 85721

I. Introduction

The future of library science education is largely a function of its past. But nothing, even an entity as amorphous as library science education, is solely the product of its past. What is happening at the present has a great deal to do with the shape of the future. As pedestrian as some of this may sound, it is amazing that library science education and the field of librarianship seem not to grasp the basics of this concept. This is especially alarming because we are moving into a time when librarianship and libraries have a great deal to offer—even more than they have been able to offer in the past. The large question mark—and potential obstacle—is whether librarians and library science educators can see the opportunity that lays at their feet.

Librarianship and library science education have reputations for traditionalism. Whether it is Pierce Butler with his biting comment about the "simplicity of pragmatism" (Butler, 1933, xi–xii) or Will Manley in one of his columns in *Wilson Library Bulletin*, their basic point is almost always the same—traditionalism. Using the assumption that there is a traditionalist approach operating in library science education, what can be said for library science education?

Library science and librarianship have a great deal to learn from tradition provided they are not driven by tradition. We can learn, for instance, that certain practices are not workable now, though they might have been in the past. We can also examine some of the tenets of library science and the philosophy of the profession from a traditional standpoint. As long as we do so with an eye to potential change, where change is required, then a tradition

ADVANCES IN LIBRARIANSHIP, VOL. 16

is a positive aspect. Where tradition becomes an end unto itself, library science and librarianship will be the losers.

In examining the copious literature that discusses the future of librarianship, one cannot help but be struck by the rhetoric and the singular lack of action. An example is Marian Paris' dissertation on the closing of schools of library science (1986). This is a seminal work and should be required reading for any educator in library science and known by every professional librarian. Yet it is largely ignored by the very people who should be most interested in its conclusions. Library science and librarianship are not ready to hear what Paris has to say. More to the point, neither library science nor librarianship are ready to make the changes that Paris recommends.

Although the lack of attention library science and librarianship have paid to the extant literature are noted, this is not a bibliographic essay covering the literature of the topic; it is instead, an attempt to set the stage and predict the future of library science and librarianship. It makes certain assumptions, chief among them being that both library science and librarianship can and will change in the future. There is no empirical evidence that these assumptions are valid; they spring solely from the author's opinion that change is both possible and necessary. This, like all visions of the future, will suffer from myopia, tunnel vision, and a range of other vision problems. With that as a caveat, the future awaits us.

II. Definitional Problems

One of the major difficulties with writing this article has to do with definitions. On a broader scale, this is not a problem for library science only, but for librarianship as a whole. The problem is widespread enough so that it forces a virtual tabula rasa approach. In this respect, the definitional problems are the same as the problems facing librarianship—a need to reexamine and redefine what it is that we do and why we do it. It may be that the old definitions are the best, but any viable profession and discipline must take the time periodically to make an in-depth reexamination.

To begin the foray into definitions, let us start with library science. In this context it will mean an area of study, including information science, that concerns itself with the social constructs of information, information centers, and libraries. Library science is a social science. It examines why a person approaching an information entity would choose one item over another. It examines the structure of information entities to determine their social utility and "robustness." In this context, it has both qualitative and quantitative methodologic structures.

There are some assumptions built into such a definition of library science. First, it assumes that people and not objects are our focus. As innocuous as this sounds, it is a radical departure from the majority of current thought. Acceptance of this assumption has significant consequences for education and practice: The passivity that is endemic in the profession, as well as large portions of current curricula in schools of library science, would be its victim. Second, the definition assumes an external focus, that is, focus on the market-place of users and considerably less focus on the constructs of the library as the major information source. We have had the data and statistics for years to demonstrate that libraries do not serve the majority of the marketplace of users. That does not make libraries worthless, but it does place libraries in context and accomplish what White (1991) and others suggest is a necessary shift. Finally, the definition assumes that natural alliances are possible with other social sciences such as sociology and psychology. No profession or academic unit can survive without some ties to other groups. By accepting the definition, we begin defining our closest intellectual cohort.

Definitions are standardizations or normalizations of concepts. Multiple names for the same concept breed dysfunction and confusion. An example is what we call library science. The term *library education* has popular usage both internally and externally. A curious term, because there are few (and should be even fewer) academic units that educate libraries. Even if we were to stretch the meaning to suggest education about libraries, we would narrow the scope unnecessarily. The same is true of library science education. Universities and colleges do not speak of political science education or of materials science education. Why do we persist in conjoining a term that adds little or no meaning to library science? In some cases, the addition of *education* might be presumed redundant and presumptuous. Our argument to universities and to the public is that we wish acceptance. Our first step is to use or to emulate terminology already understood by our audiences.

A great deal of writing (not necessarily literature) exists about the use of the term *science* in library science. We seem to be under the illusion that if only we developed the right title we would be understood. Two examples were noted earlier, political science and materials science. Both are interesting cases, and a short examination of each will be illustrative for the definitional problems of library science.

Political science units are commonplace in most universities and colleges. They are accepted both by administrators and by their colleagues on a number of levels. These units have had ample opportunity to change their name, dropping the *science*, and have not chosen to do so. It may be illustrative to note that political science changed its name from political economy at about the same time as library science moved from library economy to library science. The point is that there is a well-understood unit on most college and university campuses also using the term *science*.

Political scientists are quick to point out that they do not educate or train politicians. This may have something to do with the relatively low opinion the general population has of politicans. Rather, political scientists define their scope of interest as an exploration of the various aspects of politics and government. This concept of an educational unit standing at a distance from a professional field will be a later theme. The points to be made are that political science is seemingly comfortable with the word *science* and that the educational aims are not necessarily oriented toward professional practice.

Materials science is a part of engineering. Its intellectual focus is to study the structure and composition of natural and synthetic materials and to combine these materials in new ways. Although not every engineering school has a separate unit with the title *materials science*, it is a commonly understood component of engineering. Unlike political science, materials science does have a heavy professional component. The applications developed in materials science units are directly transferred and licensed in industry and elsewhere. There is often a close linkage between the materials science unit and industry laboratories. The point is that engineering, a professionally oriented group of disciplines, has no difficulty with the term *science* in materials science and that there is a close connection between the academic unit and the profession of engineers in for-profit laboratories.

Both of these examples have some relevance to library science. The difference between the two is the professional versus the academic bent of the programs. A number of constraints drive the professional versus academic focus of any program, and additional time will be spent with this problem later.

Some definitional difficulty exists with the term *information*. This is a term with a wide range of meaning and nuances. It spans the range from a definable electrical and computer engineering construct to an amorphous, intangible conceptual framework. Schools of library science have spread themselves across this range and have suffered from the extension. Information science is arguably the most ill-defined term in library science in particular and in academia specifically. In some circles it has become a meaningless term, offering little enlightenment as to function or content. Some schools of library science have appended this name to indicate to administrators and the public how avant garde they are. In the rush to move into the "information game," someone forgot (with the exception of engineering) to define information.

It would be possible to define information here, but its definition would do little to elucidate the problem. The salient point is that adding *information* to library science does not accomplish very much. Mainly, it appears to have further confused both administrators and the public as to what library science actually is.

A final note on definitions concerns fields, disciplines, subjects, areas, and the myriad appellations given to library science. Partly this is an issue of semantics and partly it is an issue of grave philosophical concern to library science and librarianship. McClure and Hernon (1991) address this topic and suggest that there is no ready answer because of the lack of research initiatives and focus within library science. At present, it is sometimes difficult to envisage library science as a discipline. A discipline traditionally has a body of knowledge associated with it. A variety of features making up this body of knowledge have been suggested (Grover, 1985; Mason, 1990; Schlessinger et al., 1991; Vondran, 1990). The lack of agreement is astounding and is normally the place at which the argument rests. The underlying question is even more interesting: Is this lack of agreement common or specific to library science? There appears to be no research on this point, the investigation of which should make it excellent grist for a doctoral dissertation. In an unscientific study, ten professors of engineering were asked to delineate the body of knowledge necessary at the master's level. Except in their own specialities, they had difficulty with the question. Almost to a person they noted that the underlying body of knowledge was the province of undergraduate education. More will be said about this issue later.

Can library science be a discipline? The answer is yes, if you wish to view it as such. Is it a field, a subject, an area? Again, the answer is yes. The problem is not the name itself but how librarians view their place in the world. This is not a problem of definition. Those who identify library science as a discipline can point to an organized and coherent body of research (however small) and reasonable cohesion with the problems facing the discipline. To enable someone in the discipline to do so, however, requires a rigorous adherence to the definition of library science as a social science.

The definitions suggested above are not a panacea, but they do supply a framework into which the rest of the argument can be placed. The critical question is not whether library science and librarianship can accept the definitions, but whether library science and librarians are even willing to explore the issues. As the following will demonstrate, there is no lack of issues.

III. History

The future of library science is shaped and continues to be shaped by the past. The history of library science is over 100 years old, at least from the perspective of schools of library science. In this 100 years there are two benchmark events that still help guide library science. In extracting these two events, a selective view of history is presented. For a broader view of the history of library science within the educational framework, Richardson

(1982) has a good introduction to the Graduate Library School (GLS) at the University of Chicago.

The first benchmark event was the report to the Carnegie Corporation of New York authored by C. C. Williamson (1923). This was an illuminating look at the state of library science as it was taught at the time. Williamson was interested in bootstrapping the quality of instruction in library science and in ensuring that it held as comfortable a place in the university hierarchy as possible. What he found was the dialectic that continues, unabated, even to today; that is, the dialectic between the clerical nature of positions and the education requirements.

> A shortage of persons fitted for the higher grades of library work has been felt for some time, and it will no doubt continue to be felt until some differentiation is recognized by library administrators in the organization of library staffs between duties of clerical and routine character and those requiring professional outlook and attainments (Williamson, 1923, p. 4).

Williamson also found that schools of library science in 1923 were not in the mainstream of their respective institutions. He remarked that

> Every existing university library school is a negligible part of the institution, often unnoticed or looked down upon by the other faculties and especially by departments in which research is emphasized. The causes for this lack of prestige seem to be the smallness of the library school, the brevity of the course, the predominance of women in both faculty and student body, the preponderance of teachers having only the rank of instructor, and the total lack of anything recognized as productive scholarship. All of these conditions are remedial and will tend to disappear as the standards of the library profession are gradually raised, increasing the size and importance of the professional schools (Williamson, 1923, p. 71).

Williamson identified a range of problems within library science as it was taught in the 1920s. A selected list is illustrative to denote how far we have come since 1923.

1. *Smallness of the unit.* Library science units in most colleges and universities are still among the smallest academic units.

2. *Brevity of the course.* Except for some experimentation with 2 year and expanded programs, the course of study remains fixed at 1 year.

3. *Predominance of women.* Historically this was a problem for library science. Statistics clearly show that women are paid less than men for the vast majority of jobs, and any profession having a majority of women has historically paid less. Pay aside, the subtle and not so subtle issues of gender discrimination are readily apparent in library science both in the education side and the practice side in terms of advancement and status within the organization.

4. *Productive scholarship.* Since 1923 there is much more in print in the name of library science. Any number of authors, however, have bemoaned

the lack of quality in library science publications (McClure and Hernon, 1991). Productive, yes—scholarly, perhaps.

5. *Not a part of the university.* This was a major problem in 1923 and continues to be a major problem today. It is the criticism most often leveled at schools of library science by their administrations. It is also one of the primary reasons given for closure of schools of library science (Paris, 1986; Cole, 1990).

The second major influence in the history of library science was the founding of the GLS at the University of Chicago. This was a benchmark for two reasons. First, the faculty was composed predominantly of members who were not librarians. There was a distinct social science flair to the faculty of the original GLS. The second point of interest in the founding of the GLS was the hiring of faculty with a strong research interest and, with one exception, no library experience.

The opening of a school such as Chicago's GLS would seem to fulfill a majority of Williamson's recommendations. Interesting enough, although the school gained an excellent reputation, it also generated much controversy. Houser and Schrader (1978) argue that the GLS quickly lost the original intent and that the research focus of the school was adulterated.

The seminal issue of the scholar versus the experienced librarian continues even today. Samuel Rothstein, who helped shape academic librarianship in North America, placed the highest value on teaching in recruiting faculty, noting that a good record of publications was not really important in itself (1966, p. 68).

The questioning of the place of library science in the makeup of the research university was not confined to the University of Chicago, the Williamson Report, or even to the present day.

> Library schools are viewed by many academic administrators as independent of the core of activities in their institutions. Professional education in the research university has been questioned before. Unless it has a strong research component, an intellectual content that contributes to the corpus of knowledge vital to the academic disciplines normally considered appropriate to an institution, and is integrated with relevant academic and administrative elements of the university, it is vulnerable to elimination (Colwell, 1949).

Problems identified in the educational realm moved quickly into the practice realm. Although education's aim is twofold—the pursuit and attainment of knowledge and the preparation for productive careers—library science focuses mostly on the second. Robbins-Carter and Seavey (1986) report that employers seem to prefer graduates from a program accredited by the ALA (American Library Association) but seem not to be interested in hiring graduates with specific coursework except in school media. Further, there is good evidence that additional or specialized degrees are not rewarded by the profession in higher salary scales (White and Paris, 1985). The provision of first-day skills as opposed to education for a lifelong profession are the root of the dialectic.

The Williamson Report attempted to separate the education sphere from the professional sphere by means of a certifying examination. This suggestion has never been implemented in any meaningful way. There are states that have certification for librarianship; Virginia is an example. In Virginia, certification may be obtained by one of two means. A test is given by the State Library and, if passed, a certificate is issued valid for the practice of librarianship within the Commonwealth. The second means of obtaining certification in Virginia is to graduate from an ALA-accredited program with a master's degree in library science. Both means of certification have some value, but only one fulfills the recommendation of the Williamson Report.

This discussion calls into question the nature of the professional commitment in librarianship. Any number of writers have discoursed at length and with great feeling about the nature of professionalism in librarianship and other professions. The discourse aside, one of the major marks of any profession is that it polices itself. Librarianship has chosen to abrogate that responsibility by placing the entire burden on the educational side. Accreditation, done well, is a benefit to all concerned. Part of the problem with accreditation in library science is confusion about the aims and goals of the process. Accreditation, as practiced by ALA, is being confused with certification. This is philosophically and procedurally flawed. Resolution of this confusion does not appear likely in the near future and will only delay librarianship and library science from realizing their potential. The utter shame is that the solution is so readily apparent and has been since 1923.

The founding of the GLS at the university of Chicago was a grand experiment that ultimately failed. The seeds for the failure were sown by the reluctance of librarianship to accept a research-oriented school. Carl Milam, president of ALA when planning for the GLS was initiated, voiced his concern about the direction and focus of the GLS (Richardson, 1982). That concern about the focus of library science programs continues unabated and unresolved. On one hand, librarianship wants graduates ready to move into positions within organizations without the need to further educate or train; on the other hand, librarianship sees a positive value in having library science programs exist in the milieu of higher education. Indeed, librarians seem convinced of the necessity of holding the master's degree but seem less committed to the process of education normally required for attaining the degree. The University of Chicago experience can be interpreted in a number of ways. One interpretation is that librarianship was not ready for scholarship.

What can be carried from the past into the present? Fortunately and unfortunately, a great deal. Librarianship and library science are products of the past and must work within the framework given them. Working within a framework does not necessarily mean that the framework cannot be mutated. As we work within historical context, the future of librarianship and library science should be our focus. The shaping of the present had a great deal to do with the two events discussed above. The present and the future will be characterized by how far we can move from these two events.

IV. Current Issues

Just as two major items dominated the historical underpinnings of library science, two major forces are at work shaping the current outline of library science. The accreditation issue and the institutional context within which library science must operate are the major forces that are shaping library science today. Admittedly, there are a range of other issues that may be considered, but the two chosen have philosophical and emotional depth other issues lack.

The holding of accreditation for a program leading to the first professional degree in library science is an important plateau for most programs. It allows the program to attract and recruit the best students interested in library science. Accreditation also has the benefit of allowing the program to recruit and attract quality faculty members for the program. In this regard, accreditation is a useful tool.

The concept behind accreditation is that it exists, "to protect the public interest and to provide guidance for library educators" (American Library Association, 1972, p. 5). The unacknowledged outcome of the accreditation process is that schools of library science are driven by the process and only rarely draw benefits other than the two noted above. The root of the problem is serious confusion about what accreditation is supposed to accomplish.

The state of confusion does not mean that there was or is any lack of interest in the problem. An Association of Library and Information Science Education conference dedicated to the topic in 1984 resulted in a special issue of *Journal of Library and Information Science Education* for Fall, 1984. Partly as a result of this conference and other pressures, an attempt was launched to rewrite the *Standards for Accreditation* (American Library Association, 1972). The result was and remains consternation among those in library science and librarianship, reopening the philosophical and practical meaning of accreditation. The discussion reached the point that a number of schools voted to opt out of accreditation in a straw poll. The precursor to this straw poll was a group of deans and directors meeting under the aegis of the Council for Library Resources.

Compounding the issues surrounding accreditation are the problems facing library science programs, especially in research-oriented institutions. The recommendation for closure of the Columbia University program seemed to galvanize ALA into action. It charged a special committee with examining the issues related to the closure of library science programs and to address the ALA Council resolution that a broad-based commission be established to study these matters.

The Shank Report (Shank, 1990) was received by the association with little enthusiasm. Its conclusions seem to run counter to the prevailing mood of the association. In its findings, the Shank Report noted the following:

1. Lack of relevancy of library science programs within universities
2. Library science outside the core activities of the university
3. Small size but high maintenance costs
4. Undeveloped alumnae networks
5. Lack of appeal in the competition for the best students
6. Communication problems with the profession about the mission of education
7. Female dominated programs and professions, including library science, which traditionally do not fare well in academia

Those who deal with library science and its placement in the academic environment will note the parallels with other reports and research investigating the problem. Paris (1986) identified many of the same characteristics. Indeed, the majority of reports come to approximately the same conclusions. The conundrum is that few in library science or in librarianship seem to have the vision to see the writing on walls or in reports.

In the face of ALA's inability to move library science (and by extension librarianship) into the quality position, what has accreditation accomplished? The process of accreditation is a major contributor to shaping the content and structure of the curriculum in library science. But the process has some other consequences. McClure and Hert (1991, p. 10) note that, "it may be an embarrassment to the program since it must then 'explain' to university administrators the basis for COA's very traditional recommendations." As was noted by an interested but involved outsider to librarianship, "Accreditation is a powerful social force for either improving the quality of service rendered by a profession or for the entrenchment of tired people in an old system who are waiting for time and outsiders to create a new profession" (Beasley, 1984, p. 68). An honest assessment of accreditation may fall somewhere in the middle of Beasley's range.

In certain circumstances and in the proper places, accreditation may be a valuable tool to arrest the attention of certain university or college administrations. The range of programs accreditation attempts to cover under one umbrella is entirely too broad. There are major differences between the program mounted by a Research I institution and a program mounted in a liberal arts college. Each has its strengths and each has its weaknesses; the point is that they are different programs with different expectations of students and faculty. Any process that initially assumes they are equivalent is doomed to fail.

Accreditation has served a worthwhile purpose. It does bring the profession of librarianship into closer contact with educators in library science on a regular basis. It has engendered or further enhanced the discussions of the quality and shape of library science, some would say, to the point of pathology. The current debate about the nature and content of the proposed standards is endemic to this discussion.[1] It is also natural for any profession to wish control of those who desire entry. In this light, librarianship needs to assert its rightful duty. But accreditation is not the answer. Accreditation speaks to maintenance of program quality. Accreditation cannot raise program quality, of itself, because accreditation is a leveling agent. It speaks most clearly to minimalist standards. Although the current *Standards for Accreditation* speaks about increasing the quality of programs, what level of quality is intended? The answer is a minimalist level. Standards are not elitist and must be set low enough to accommodate the majority of programs in place at the time of promulgation, otherwise they would never be accepted. This is a point librarianship seems not to understand.

The profession wishing to control entry must have some means of certification. Williamson called for certification in 1923 for this reason, and McClure and Hert (1991, p. 19) joined his call. Moving toward certification would disengage the philosophical problem that now plagues accreditation. However, certification is neither a panacea nor an easy solution. The accreditation problem is difficult and there is no reason to suspect that the solution to the problem will be any less difficult.

Conjoined with the accreditation problem is the issue of institutional context. This is the predominant environmental factor facing library science. It is also the factor least understood within the accreditation process and by librarianship.

Organizational theory sees organizations as systems. Systems have either open or closed characteristics and in the educational context, they must be open systems. Open systems are characterized by their exchange with their environment (Dessler, 1976). For library science, the exchanges that must take place are the same as other academic units within the educational framework. In return for recognition by the university or college, library science must supply something. That something is library science's contribution to the educational mission of the system, the university.

---

[1] At the time of writing, the *Standards* were still proposed. They have since been approved by vote of ALA Council.

At the outset, a vary large and pernicious assumption needs to be addressed. Placement in an academic setting is not a mandated right for any unit, including library science. This is not to say that library science should *not* be included in academic environments, but only that there is no chair at the table with library science's name emblazoned on it. The placement and the maintenance of that placement in academia is a privilege, not a right. Both library science and librarianship are prone to forget this very important concept. Even when they do remember it, they tend to use traditional or historical arguments for retaining their place in academia.

When the Columbia University library science program was under fire, one of the arguments librarianship and library science marshalled was that Columbia was the historical seed for library science programs. Although true, the argument does little, if anything, to counter the problem. Arguments to the heartstrings do little within academia.

A second argument often used by library science, and other disciplines for that matter, is the argument that any good educational system should have a library science program. This is a variant on the argument that higher education is critical to political units such a cities, states, and the nation. Although we all may believe this, increasingly the argument comes back from those in control of the purse strings: "Prove it!" For library science, the problem is one of demonstrating worth within the framework of the institution of which they are privileged to be a part. This involves considerably more than protestations, regardless of validity, that library science is a worthy discipline for consideration in higher education

Simplifying matters, there are basically two types of institutions of higher education; research-oriented and instruction-oriented. This black–white dichotomy is seldom as clear cut as it is presented here, but the distinction does serve a purpose in presenting the argument from two different frameworks.

The research-oriented institution is interested primarily in the synthesis, production, and dissemination of information and knowledge. Instruction does not necessarily become second-rate in such an institution; indeed, there are those who suggest that it is enhanced by the research thrust. The point is that there are certain expectations of units existing in research-oriented institutions. Among these are the following.

1. An emphasis on scholarship and the production of the results of scholarship in peer-refereed media
2. An emphasis on graduate education as opposed to undergraduate education
3. A greater emphasis on the provision of external funding from grants and contracts
4. A greater emphasis on the academic nature of its premier units

The instruction-oriented institution is more interested in the following characteristics.

1. A greater emphasis on the quality of instruction in the institution
2. A greater emphasis on the undergraduate component of the institution
3. A justifiable pride in the ability of its graduates to move to research-oriented institutions as graduate students
4. Development of a close and continuing alumnae base from which it will seek support

The suggestion here is that there are at least two models, each with different assumptions and expectations. Library science programs exist in both types of institutions and should exist in both types of institutions. The issue is the placement of library science programs in higher education constructs. Being a part of an institution means that in some way the unit accepts and adjusts its goals and mission to that of the parent institution. This appears to be difficult for library science.

In the research-oriented institutions, library science is normally seen as a weak link, contributing little to the overall mission of the institution. This stems from at least two sources.

First, the library science program is normally more attentive to the instructional components than to the research components. Library science has a tradition of investing its intellectual resources heavily in instruction and for this we should take some deserved praise. We have done so, however, out of step with research institutions. At the time research institutions are now rediscovering the benefits of the instructional components, library science is out of step because we do not have the tradition of research that other units in the institution have garnered.

The second reason library science is often considered a weak link in the research-oriented institution is its professional-school focus. Professional schools are for the most part ill-understood within research-oriented institutions. The strength of most research-oriented institutions does not lie in its professional schools and where there are strong professional programs; the clear emphasis is on both academic quality and quality research.

Within the instruction-based institutions, library science is sometimes considered an anomaly. Part of the reason for this lies with the fact that there is no undergraduate program leading to the master's degree program. In an institution that places its emphasis on undergraduate instruction, programs such as library science appear to be incomplete. It should be noted that this phenomenon is also a problem for research-oriented programs.

Both types of institutions want to see quality programs survive in their respective schools. Doing so requires that library science conform instead of insisting on its vested right to be a professional school when it wishes or to be an academic unit when that suits its purpose. At some point, the decisions need to be made. How they make those decisions will have a great deal to do with how well, or if, they are able to survive in any institution.

Two models exist for library science programs in academic institutions. The first is the professional school approach and the second is the academic program approach.

The professional school approach is an outgrowth of the history of library science and its educational roots. Williamson (1923) noted that there was a great deal of education and training being performed in the larger public and academic libraries. The apprentice mode of learning was a comfortable concept for librarianship. This evolved into a mind-set of professional education, especially in the years following Williamson. The advent of the master's degree in lieu of the B.L.S. in the 1950s was an outgrowth of librarianship's desire to become more acceptable within the academic community. This was a time marked by the rise of professional schools in colleges and universities, and it is understandable that librarianship and library science wished to take advantage of this opportunity.

Adapting to the professional school model was not difficult for library science, fresh from the apprentice school model. Although professional education at that time, as it is now, was less predicated on training and more attuned to education, library science was characterized as a training program. The philosophy and mission of a training program are less well developed than those of an educational program. A training program assumes that the primary goal is the inculcation of skills useful for a profession at the point of entry. The insistence on the primacy of formats and not the rationales for formats is one mark of training programs. A concentration on the pragmatic and not on the philosophical is another mark.

Library science was very adept at moving its apprentice programs into a training program under the umbrella of higher education. It has been much less adept at noticing that higher education and especially professional schools in higher education have progressed beyond the models they used in the 1950s. The mind-set of most library science programs and of those in librarianship who stand in judgment of these programs is firmly rooted in the 1950s.

Virtually every professional program in higher education has made its program more academically based, with the exception of library science. Professional schools gained stature on campuses because of their well-developed alumni and alumnae networks. Professional schools in higher education are marked by their ability both to generate significant amounts of external funding and to attract a high level of student. Library science has done little, if any, of this. Library science, as a professional program, has been left adrift. When economic times were less stringent, library science programs could continue to exist, but in stringent times, they become targets. Professional school status does not and has not conferred any special station on library science. Portions of library science now recognize this fact, but librarianship still has not realized the shift.

The second model for library science is the academic model. This model assumes that library science is an academic unit and will operate under the same rules and on the same playing field as other academic units. The consequences for library science are both good and bad. On the positive side, library science can take its place as an equal with other academic units in the university or college. On the negative side, library science now must follow the same rules for approbation as other academic units and library science has seldom had to play by these rules.

A consequence of the academic model is that library science is not normally a separate and distinct school. In short, it gives up some autonomy. At the risk of being harsh, it never really had the autonomy it purportedly is relinquishing, except in very specific settings. Specific settings are those in which the library science school was the premier unit in the local setting. Such would be the case in a small college in which the library science program was either the only graduate program or one of a handful.

The distinction between the two models may be considerably more blurred than presented here. A professional program may be very academically oriented. The issue is less one of what label is attached than what philosophy is underlying the unit. If the unit is convinced that it is contributing to the university or college in the same manner as the other academic programs, then it is following a more academic model. If the program is attuned more to fulfilling the needs of a profession that offers entry level positions, then it has a more professional or training approach.

Which approach is better? Either one is perfectly acceptable provided it is in keeping with the mission of the parent institution. The academic model is the more acceptable to most research-oriented universities, and the professional model may be more acceptable to other parts of higher education. In either case, the model presumes some changes, some of them major, in the library science programs in higher education. Whether these programs have the fortitude to make the changes is the question.

If accreditation and the institutional context define the present circumstances of library science, the ability of these two concepts to work in harmony is a particularly important issue. In point of fact, they do not work well together at all.

Survival for any academic unit is predicated on its internal not its external validity. If a unit is not accepted in its home university or college, no amount of accreditation strength will overcome this lack of acceptance. Accreditation and its proponents do not seem to understand what the inherent and very real pecking order is in library science. It is internal first and only secondarily, is it external.

Accreditation does take cognizance of the institutional variables, but the issue is one of primacy. Perhaps some schools need to be reminded on a 7-year cycle that they should meet some range of minimal standards. The majority of schools already have a review process in place that assists the parent institution in maintaining its standards. For a research university aiming for a place among the top twenty of the research universities in the country, standards will be significantly higher than those of any specialized accreditation scheme, such as library science. This is a generalization, to be sure, but one based on both empirical evidence and common sense.

That the library science accreditation process does take into account institutional factors is a distinct plus. Accreditation is reasonably sensitive to governance and codification of local options, especially at the levels above the library science program. The process appears less sensitive to innovation and experimentation at the library science program level, although the data on which this statement rests are anecdotal. The number of deans and directors who perennially complain about this problem, however, would seem to suggest that something is amiss.

The overall misuse of accreditation by librarianship leads to a conflict with library science, especially those programs in Research I or high-visibility universities and colleges that already have quality controls extant. This conflict is manifest as an attitude on the part of accreditation. This attitude seems to take the form of a requirement to find something *amiss* that requires a recommendation. An example of this attitude and its manifestation is the current ALA Committee on Accreditation's (COA) interest in multicultural and multiethnic faculties.

No university or college in the United States can operate without an approved affirmative action plan in place. Individual biases and feelings aside, library science is remarkably sensitive to the issues of affirmative action, even more so than the majority of academic colleagues. Library science and librarianship are committed to affirmative action both in practice and in theory. A practical demonstration is the hiring practices of schools of library science.

The current COA attitude seems to be to interpret the existing standards in such a way that schools of library science are required to have faculty with multiracial and multiethnic makeups. Such goals are laudable, but there are three concerns here. First, COA is replicating the work of the local institution. To what end? There does not appear to be an answer to this question, and no response is forthcoming from COA.

The second problem with this is the apparently cavalier manner in which COA may interpret the standards, with no oversight from either librarianship or library science. This is the eternal problem of who is watching the watchers. In this case, there appears to be no one and no one with any interest in doing so.

Finally, there is the problem that COA recommendations are seen and read by university and college administrators. Any college or university administrator who is astute enough to retain his or her position for 10 minutes is intimately familiar with the requirements for affirmative action and the consequences of failure to meet those requirements.

Why does COA think it is doing schools of library science a favor in focusing attention on an issue that the local institution can handle better? In a time when library science is being examined closely in higher education, why plant seeds of potential problems where no problem exists? This is the attitude problem. Accreditation appears to be more interested in finding items with which to browbeat programs than in strengthening programs. Put another way, accreditation needs to understand the implications of the actions taken under its umbrella. Accreditation can have a devastating effect, unintended perhaps, but no less damaging. Quality programs are directly threatened by inferior accreditation.

The current state of library science is uncertian. The uncertainty springs from a variety of areas, but can be laid into two broad areas: accreditation and the institutional context. Realistically, accreditation of library science programs will not materially change most institutions in which library science programs are found. However, institutional context is changing the face and character of library science programs or at least those programs astute enough to notice they must change. Accreditation and librarianship need to recognize the relative ranking of power and do more than pay lip service to this recognition.

Library science programs have an excellent opportunity to retool and recast themselves into programs that fit more closely in and are contributors to the university or college environment to which they belong. These are positive times as long a library science is committed to progress. The lack of ability to progress will be a determining factor in the eyes of university and college administrators as to whether library science programs belong in higher education

This can also be a positive time for accreditation. The system badly needs overhauling and although draft standards are now proposed, it needs to move beyond the puerile accreditation that now characterizes library science. Accreditation that is recognized as meaningful by university and college administrators should be our goal. The proposed standards do not accomplish this and, as a result, both librarianship and library science will pay the price. If universities and colleges are unimpressed by the attempts at accreditation, they will transfer this lack of impression to the quality of the library science programs. If higher quality programs and higher quality graduates are desired, the mechanisms must be built that will achieve this end.

Accreditation, library science, and librarianship all have good futures, provided some time is spent examining the desirable future position. Then the resources and mechanisms can be developed to ensure that position. Maintenance of the status quo, a favorite enterprise of library science, librarianship, and accreditation, will not transport them to any level of quality. Maintenance of the status quo is the best recipe for mediocrity. Where are we going? It depends on our will to change. On the assumption that there is both the rhetoric and the will to change, the following section presents at least one vision of the future.

V. Models for the Future

Prognosticating about the future of library science using the crystal ball of the past and knowledge of the present offers a view that is distorted but still the best view possible. The following are competing views of the future for library science. Before embarking into the future, however, it should take stock of where it is and where it wishes to be.

That it is not where it wants to be is the underlying assumption here. This is a healthy sign. There are some signposts from the past that suggest where we should be heading. The economic and political climate for library science or any other struggling discipline is not as robust as we would like. Perhaps the future is right where we want it—just waiting to be seized.

Impulsively reaching for whatever appears first or impresses us as potentially beneficial is part of the reason library science is in the position it is today. Calling its educational institutions professional schools, for example, does not innately confer legitimacy on library science. This should be one lesson it has learned. Moving to a master's degree did not gain materially more respect for librarianship. This is a second lesson we should have learned. The goal now is to examine some of the options available as we consciously and intelligently build our future. Not all options will be available in every institution or will work in others. Fashioning the future of library science is partly a contingency approach based on prior and present events and partly a conscious decision to move forward. Moving forward presupposes first, a decision to move and second, a knowledge of what direction is forward. The assumption is that both library science and librarianship wish to move forward.

Two basic models currently compete for the future direction of library science. The first is the professional school approach and the second is the academic approach.

McClure and Hert (1991) give a succinct, excellent argument for the professional school approach. They see the majority of library science and information science programs offering limited graduate-level degrees in a discipline-based mode. They suggest that some programs may actually flourish in this mode, but only because of institutional inertia. In the view of McClure and Hert, the proper place for a library science program is one in which the school offers multiple degrees and some specializations at both the undergraduate and graduate levels. Further, they argue, the school must be more in what they term the "information professions, professional school based," areas (McClure and Hert, 1991, p. 2). Along with their suggestion that schools move into this area, they are critical of schools that stay in the discipline-based mode and that offer only limited degrees. In their view, such a school would do a disservice to librarianship by fostering isolation, especially from other information professions.

McClure and Hert (1991) have an interesting argument and it is all the more interesting given the context in which it was presented. The paper was a presentation at the Conference on Specialization in Library/Information Science Education sponsored by the Committee on Institutional Cooperation (CIC) schools of library science. It was this group that took a straw poll in the fall of 1991 to determine if they wished to continue accreditation by ALA. The result of their nonbinding vote was to forego accreditation by ALA. It may be, however, that the model presented best fits Syracuse University and it is not necessarily a model for the rest of library science. The model may also fit the theme of the conference more closely than it fits library science in general.

If the goal is to develop niches for librarianship within the growing pantheon of information professions, one of the ways to accomplish this is to specialize. The problem with specialization is that it is a moving target. The larger problem, that of niches, is that the information professions keep growing at a very rapid pace, making the delineation of anyone's niche difficult. Difficulty should not be a reason for failure to investigate a potential solution to a problem, and McClure and Hert (1991) offer an intriguing solution.

Every organization wishes to find a comfortable and secure home for itself. Educational organizations and units within those organizations are no different. Educational institutions are composed of two types of units, the discipline-based and the professionally based programs. In theory, each of these units has proposed to the parent institution what and where its niche is in the organization. A part of this proposal to the parent institution is a description of the pool of potential students from which the program will draw and where the graduates of the program will go. A reasonable way to approach thinking in these terms is to think in terms of a new program proposal to the university or college administration. The McClure–Hert proposal is one means of building this new program proposal within the existing framework of other professional programs. One example is the framework of business and public administration schools.

A second model is the academic unit approach or what McClure and Hert call the discipline-based approach. This approach assumes that library science has a definable intellectual niche within the university or college structure. One of the major differences between the two approaches is readily apparent. The professional school approach focuses on increasing the knowledge and skill level of graduates who will fill specific positions—positions that were defined a priori. The discipline-based approach has as its goal increasing the knowledge and skill level of graduates who may fill a multiplicity of positions, none of which were defined a priori.

A professional school approach has a number of benefits that suggest it is a model worth consideration in library science.

First, the professional school approach allies library science with some of the strongest programs in any university or college. Schools of medicine, law, and engineering normally have high stature on most university and college campuses. This stature is a direct outgrowth of medicine, law, and engineering being able to articulate their mission well and succinctly and how their mission dovetails with the mission of the university or college. Library science should be able to articulate its mission and how its mission fits into the schema of the university or college. What library science lacks that medicine, law, and engineering possess are (1) a strong and vocal alumni and alumnae network; (2) a history of visible contributions in terms of students, faculty productivity, and external funding; and (3) a mechanism for determining acceptability to the profession that is not a part of the educational mission.

Professional schools such as business, nursing, and music have slightly less cachet in higher education than medicine, law, or engineering. Business, nursing, and music do not have the political clout in academia that medicine, law, or engineering have. Primarily, this is because of the relatively low ranking in possessing the three elements noted in the above paragraph. It is most often business schools, however, with which schools of library science are compared.

Comparisons of schools of library science with schools of business can be very worthwhile for the university or college and beneficial for both units. Most business schools have some component or unit within their structure that focuses on information and its handling in the for-profit sector. The relatively narrow audience, business, and the affinity of those in business schools for quantitative methods give business schools an edge over most library science programs. Library science programs are not known for their use of quantitative methods. The opposite is true of business schools. The consequence of this affinity is that business schools can more easily assimilate information science constructs into their curricula. Business schools can also more easily assimilate the methods of engineering and computer science, which are perceived as more erudite than qualitative examinations of information constructs.

Business schools are primarily concerned with the for-profit sector, although a large number have public policy and public administration aspects to their programs. Library science and librarianship can learn a great deal from self-examination of what they do and how they do their jobs by looking at them from a business school perspective. Service organizations other than libraries have used such examinations to their benifit. Library science and librarianship have traditionally been adverse to this sort of examination, suggesting that their mission in some way transcends the business approach. This is a seminal philosophical point and one that business understands much better than do library science and librarianship.

Libraries are merit goods in the United States. They are a benefit to all and are supported by all. A point of divergence between business and librarianship is that business does not subscribe to the immutability of that concept. This is not to say that business cannot hold worthy philosophical positions such as believing in merit goods. Business, however, is intent on improving the share of the resources that accrue to their enterprises. Library science and librarianship believe this, too, but for the most part do nothing proactive to increase the resources available. Part of the rationale is bound up in the belief that the population at large will grace library science and librarianship with resources because they are a "good" for society. Business takes a much more cynical attitude. As long as library science and librarianship continue to believe that their mission transcends the struggle for resources, they will continue to receive fewer resources than they rightfully need. This includes the intangible but critical resource of goodwill.

Business has much to offer library science and librarianship in the areas of streamlining services. Libraries are notoriously difficult to use for the general public; they are often organized for the benefit of librarians rather than the public. As a service organization, this is an unhealthy attitude. Librarianship has an incredible array of data that suggests they are not doing what their users wish them to do. An example is the range of the catalog-use studies going back to the 1950s. Libraries do not act on these data, however. Small businesses, and especially service-oriented businesses, would act forcibly and swiftly considering such data. Libraries would be different and perhaps better places if they were operated using some of the principles of the for-profit sector.

The issues involved in libraries being very different if operated more in a for-profit mode are less important than if libraries operated in a mode that would better articulate their mission. Typically, the for-profit organization must carefully think out its niche in the economy. Careful and thoughtful delineation of the mission of libraries would be a benefit to society, library science, and librarianship. It would require a refocusing of the profession and of the educational structure assisting the profession, however.

Part of the refocusing of the educational structure involved in such a shift would be the movement to a wider array of degrees and specializations within library science. The single terminal degree or the concentration on only graduate-level study would be seriously examined and found wanting. A range of degrees, such as is common in business schools, would be the result. Specializations would be more common and more easily justified within the business school environment. One reason for this is that business schools have no great difficulty in prescribing a longer master's degree program than is the norm in academic units. This may be attractive to some proponents of extended programs in library science and to some in librarianship who argue for greater and more extensive specialization. Such a move would also have the benefit of injecting a larger amount of management coursework into a library science program, reagardless of length.

For all the discussion about moving to a professional school approach such as business, librarianship does not appear to be ready to pay the price of such a move. The price is a rethinking of the mission of the library and how librarians work within this organization. The movement of library science into a school of business would be the easier of the problems to solve. It too has its difficulties, especially in reconciling the attitudes and proclivities of faculty members who are more attuned to qualitative than quantitative methodologies. Such a move would have the benefit of sheltering library science in a relatively healthy environment in academia. It would also have, as a detriment, the loss of autonomy for the majority of library science programs. There are mixed blessings in any move into an existing professional school.

A second alternative for library science is the academic unit approach. Like the professional school approach, it has some implications for library science and librarianship. Movement to an academic approach would mean that library science must be able to articulate its intellectual contribution to the university or college in unambiguous terms. In most cases, this will mean an articulation based on the trinity of teaching, research, and service. A consequence of such a move would be that library science would be compared with other academic units on an equal footing.

Being placed on an equal footing with other academic units is a distinct problem for library science. The Williamson Report and the selective implementation of that report placed library science in a role that consciously moved library science out of the academic unit mind-set. Library science has fought for years to maintain its independence and autonomy in the university or college structure. Such a strategy may appear desirable when resources are abundant, but it is at best shortsighted in times of resource scarcity. It also has the unfortunate consequence of allowing library science programs to operate outside the normal intellectual mainstream of the university or college. Regardless of the type of unit, professional or academic, operating outside the mainstream of the university or college is a singularly dangerous activity.

If library science is primarily concerned with why people approach information entities and how they use these entities, then library science is a social science. Library science can be viewed as concerning itself with the social interactions that occur when people seek information. Sociology, psychology, philosophy, communication, political science, geography, and linguistics all have much to offer library science in terms of joint and common research and teaching areas. Library science's association with these academic units places library science very close to the intellectual center of the university or college. For those who believe that libraries, and, therefore, library science is more centrist than a cloister, this approach is very appealing.

Library science has some difficulty in meeting at least one of the qualifications for active involvement in the social sciences. The social sciences are marked partly by scholarly production. Robert Hayes' (1983) study clearly points to the problem of scholarly production in schools of library science. Universities and colleges are convinced that scholarly productivity is one measurement of quality of a program. This is not just a "more is better" argument but it is also based on some empirical evidence that good graduate students and good faculty are attracted to an academic unit that is demonstrably alive intellectually. Library science has some research available that suggests that geography is the primary decision point for students entering our programs. There are always some students from outside our "geographic boundaries." It is these students we seek to attract. The best argument, however, is that prospective excellent faculty members will be more attracted to a school that is productive than one that is not.

Part of the argument that library science faculties are not engaged as much as they should be with scholarly production is the nature of their mind-set regarding publication. Colleges and universities have a very clear definition of what constitutes scholarly production: publication in a peer-reviewed journal, preferably one with the best reputation in the field. Publication in a house organ such as *American Libraries* or *Library Journal* is not discouraged but does not fulfill the definition. This is a change in outlook for a number of library science faculty members. It will also have some impact on the nature of the literature in both library science and librarianship.

There is some inherent risk involved in moving into the model of the academic unit. Library science is presently oriented toward graduate programs, especially master's level degrees. The current mood in academia is shifting to the undergraduate side of the equation. Few library science programs have undergraduate programs, making library science programs more anomalous.

The lack of undergraduate programs also has some consequences for how library science is perceived in the mix of academic units. The majority of the social sciences (and the majority of programs in most universities and colleges) require an entering graduate student to have an undergraduate degree in the discipline in which he or she wishes to do graduate work. There are exceptions, and those exceptions are normally in closely allied areas or in areas where the student is required to take certain courses to make up deficiencies. Library science does not have an undergraduate feeder program and only rarely are students admitted who are required to fulfill deficiencies. These differences are not lost on university and college administrators, who wonder how library science can give a legitimate master's degree without that which they consider appropriate undergraduate preparation. Movement to the academic model would require library science programs to assess the potential and political need for undergraduate degree programs.

The academic model would mean a wider variety of degree programs and options available to the student. Besides undergraduate degrees, some serious consideration regarding doctoral programs would need to take place. This is especially true in Research I institutions. For a program to stop at the master's level, there must be a reason. Because the program is preparing graduates for a professional career is not a valid reason under the academic model. Professional careers are the choice of the graduate, not the direction of the program.

An interesting result of moving to the academic model would be the reduction in importance of professional accrediting bodies, especially specialty accreditation bodies such as COA. If library science is a social science like sociology and communication, for example, then library science should be judged in precisely the same manner. Overall accreditation of the university or college suffices for the social sciences and is usually coupled with some form of internal program review process. If such procedures are sufficient to maintain the world-class standing of any number of academic programs in the United States, they might be acceptable to library science programs.

The academic model would mean greater variety and less specialization, depending on the characterization of specialization. A master's degree that requires the student to take a certain number of courses outside the library science program may be viewed by some as specialization and by others as a dilution of the program. Viewed from the standpoint of the profession, such a program may be met with skepticism. The academic model has a different output standard than does a professional program. The output standard for an academic program is an educated person who has advanced knowledge not only about library science but also advanced knowledge in a secondary area, the academic minor discipline. It means that the gatekeeping function of librarianship is now shifted to the profession and out of library science. In no way does the academic model translate to the inculcation of first-day job skills.

Movement to an academic model would have as one of its potential results a reduction in the number of students accepted into a master's degree program. Administrators in higher education have some difficulty in believing that quality graduate-level education is possible when an average library science faculty of 10 has a master's program enrollment of 400. The academic model presupposes that the student in a master's degree program can "pick the professor's brain." This is difficult at best with a student-to-faculty ratio of 40 to 1 at the graduate level. Most universities and colleges have an unwritten benchmark of 10 to 1 as a reasonable ration of graduate students to faculty. At the same time, these universities and colleges often have deliberate ratios of overall students to faculty. The ratios seem to hover nationally at approximately 20 to 1. If library science is to use the academic model, it must play by the established rules.

The major benefit of the academic model is that it would move library science into the mainstream of the university or college. The drawback is that library science would lose a large measure of its autonomy as a separate unit with the organization. The gain would more than compensate for the loss.

There is much to recommend the academic model. It may not be appropriate in some cases, however. Library science and librarianship are both enamored of what can be called the one-way myth; that is, there is only one way of doing something. In those organizations where the professional school model is more appropriate, that is the model that should be used. There is no inherent goodness in either model—they are means to an end.

At the present, the professional school model is used more often than is the academic model. Higher education, however, seems to be moving away from specializations and toward a return to the basic core of education. Higher education is giving greater attention to the social sciences and humanities than it has in some time. This may augur well for those programs that are academically oriented.

Even if the professional school model is used, library science programs clearly must become more academically focused. There is no particular reason that the models proposed here cannot be combined in varying weights, contingent on the requirements of the institutional environment. Library science programs must exist within this environment, regardless of their success in meeting the demands of librarianship.

There is a final means of dealing with the future that is always a choice—doing nothing. In an eductional environment, this is deadly. Continuation of library science programs in the mode of the past will see greater numbers of schools closing and the remaining schools weakening by association. Choosing to remain static is an abrogation of educational and professional responsibilities. It is not a viable option, but it is one that too many schools and too many librarians will choose.

In the following section, prognostications are made about the future of library science in higher education. These are educated guesses, using the past, the present and what little glimmer of the future that is available. They are also tinged with an element of hope that library science may move in these directions in the very near future.

VI. Future Trends in Library Science

The closing or the threatened closing of a number of schools of library science recently has galvanized both library science and librarianship to consider the fate of the educational system that supplies the profession with new members. In some cases, the rhetoric is characterized by more heat than light, but the positive point is that there is an ongoing discussion about the future of library science. The models presented in the previous section can be used to good advantage by schools of library science. In that light and with the object of continuing the discussions on the future of library science, the following prognostications are made.

1. More schools of library science will be examined very closely by their parent institutions. Those schools that can articulate their place in the academic environment will have a greater chance to survive and potentially flourish.

2. More schools of library science will close and the majority of these schools will be in Research I or research-intensive universities. Because of the tenacious traditionalism of library science programs, they will have greater difficulty in making a case for retention in such institutions.

3. Undergraduate programs will become common in library science units. This will result from two compelling forces: the need to develop a feeder pro-

gram for graduate programs and the need to expand the overall faculty-to-student ratio consistent with other academic units in the university or college.

4. Accreditation, as practiced by COA, will cease to be a major force for library science programs. Universities and colleges see specialized accreditation as generally wasteful of resources. This is especially true when standards for accreditation do not engender quality.

5. Increased interest on the part of librarianship will develop in the concept of certification. Librarianship will see certification as a means of self-policing itself as accreditation wanes.

6. Regardless of model used, greater emphasis on academic components of the library science program. Academia is increasingly more concerned with output measures for its faculty. For library science this will mean greater emphasis on scholarly production in peer-reviewed media.

7. Greater acceptance of and implementation of the academic model, especially in Research I and research-intensive universities. By their nature, Research I and research-intensive universities focus on the academic programs or on those professional programs that are more academic than training centered. Library science programs in such environments will be forced to move toward more academic orientations.

8. Greater use of faculty without a Ph.D. in library science because of the inability of present doctoral programs to meet demand. The quality and quantity of doctoral student output in library science is insufficient to meet the demands of library science programs. Ph.D. holders from other disciplines will be needed to fill the positions coming vacant in library science programs.

9. Temporary increase in the number of doctoral programs offered by schools attempting to fill the demand for more library science faculty. Such programs will fail relatively quickly because of the lack of quality students entering the programs.

10. Greater dependence on distance education and nontraditional education models in library science programs in parallel with the same movement in higher education. The shift from the full-time student to the part-time and the mature student in higher education will require use of new models and technologies. The assumption of the student moving to the institution is rapidly being replaced by an aggressive outreach program on the part of universities and colleges.

11. Development of a two-tiered system within librarianship composed of those with a bachelor's degree and those with a master's degree in library science. Those with bachelor's degrees will become line librarians and those with master's degrees will be department heads and run small to medium-sized libraries.

12. Reduction in the scope of the information industry claimed by library science and librarianship. Greater articulation of the niche of library science and librarianship.

13. Reduction in the number of students entering and receiving a master's degree in library science. This will result partly from the availability of the bachelor's degree and its acceptance by the profession.

14. Greater interest in specialization outside the master's program, especially in technical and management areas. This will be offset partly by courses at the bachelor's degree level.

15. Greater meshing of library science with other social science units in universities and colleges. As library science becomes more academically oriented, it will develop linkages with other academic units.

16. Increase in scholarly production on the part of faculty members in library science programs to meet university and college requirements for continued status in the organization.

The preceding items are neither all equally probable nor will they occur in synchronization. The process of change and mutation will occur in fits and starts. The process will not always be easy nor will it be without some debate and rancor. The key to ensuring the future of library science is that it must be willing to take the opportunity to change. Library science is not alone in missing opportunities, but as part of the information profession we have fewer excuses than most for missing those opportunities. The mark of a profession is its appetite for positive change. We need to whet this appetite and move forward. Library science has a bright future in academia, but only if the opportunity to articulate its place in the university or college is not squandered.

References

American Library Association, (ALA). (1972). *Standards for Accreditation.* ALA, Chicago.

Beasley, K. E. (1984). Issues in library accreditation. *Journal of Education for Library and Information Science* **25**, 67–81.

Butler, P. (1933). *An Introduction to Library Science.* University of Chicago Press, Chicago.

Cole, J. C. (1990). *Report of the Provost on the School of Library Service at Columbia University.* Columbia University, New York.

Colwell, E. C. (1949). The role of the professional school in the university. In *Education for Librarianship: Papers Presented at the Library Conference, University of Chicago, August 16–21* (B. Bevelson, ed.). American Library Association, Chicago.

Dessler, G. (1976). *Organization and Management: A Contingency Approach.* Prentice Hall, Englewood Cliffs, New Jersey.

Grover, R. J. (1985) Library and information professional education for the learning society: A model curriculum. *Journal of Education for Library and Information Science* **26**, 33–45.

Hayes, R. M. (1983). Citation statistics as a measure of productivity. *Journal of Education for Librarianship* **23**, 151–172.

Houser, L. J., and Schrader, A. M. (1978). *The Search for a Scientific Profession: Library Science Education in the United States and Canada.* Scarecrow Press, Metuchen, New Jersey.

Mason, R. O. (1990). What is an information professional. *Journal of Education for Library and Information Science* **31**, 122–138.

McClure, C. R., and Hernon, D. P. (1991). *Library and Information Science Research: Perspectives and Strategies for Improvement*. Ablex Publishing Company, Norwood, New Jersey.

McClure, C. R., and Hert, C. A. (1991). "Specialization in library/information science education: Issues, scenarios, and the need for action." Paper presented at the Conference on Specialization in Library/Information Science Education, Ann Arbor, Michigan, November 6–8, 1991.

Paris, M. (1986). Library school closings: Four case studies. Doctoral dissertation, Indiana University, Bloomington.

Richardson, J. (1982). *The Spirit of Inquiry: The Graduate Library School at Chicago, 1921–51*. American Library Association, Chicago.

Robbins-Carter, J., and Seavey, C. A. (1986). The master's degree: Basic preparation for professional practice. *Library Trends* **34,** 561–590.

Rothstein, S. (1966). The ideal faculty member: Qualifications and experience. *Journal of Education for Librarianship* **16,** 173–182.

Schlessinger, B. S., Schlessinger, J. H., and Karp, R. S. (1991). Information science/library science education programs in the 1990s: A not-so-modest proposal. *Library Administration and Management* **5,** 16–19.

Shank, R. (1990). *ALA Special Committee on Library School Closings: Report*. American Library Association, Chicago.

Vondran, R. F. (1990). Rethinking library education in the information age. *Journal of Library Administration* **11,** 27–44.

White, H. S. (1991). New educational values and employability—Closing the gap. *Journal of Academic Librarianship* **17,** 209.

White, H. S., and Paris, M. (1985). Employer preferences and the library education curriculum. *Library Quarterly* **55,** 1–33.

Williamson, C. C. (1923). *Training for Library Service: A Report Prepared for the Carnegie Corporation of New York*. Carnegie Corporation, New York.

The European Communities: Reference Works and Documentary Sources of the Spanish Parliament

Rosa María Grau
Miguel Angel Gonzalo
Research and Documentation Library
Congress of Deputies
28014 Madrid, Spain

I. Introduction

The creation of the European Communities (EC) in the Spring of 1951, after the signing of the European Coal and Steel Community (ECSC) treaty, heralded the beginning of a long process toward European unity. Six years later, in 1957, two new treaties consolidated and expanded ECSC beyond its initial purpose of economic unity, solidarity, and security; the treaties making up the European Economic Community (EEC) and the Atomic Energy Community (Euratom) were signed in Rome. In 1965, EC took a step toward integration when a treaty was signed creating a Joint Council and a Joint Committee. Since 1965—with some fluctuations in the level of activity, depending on the periods of time—EC have carried out constant activities, as shown by the many treaties of modification, decisions, resolutions, agreements, and acts that were signed. Among these, the Act of 1976, related to the election of the representatives in the Assembly of the Peoples of the States forming the Community (European Parliament), stands out. By this act, election would be by direct universal suffrage in 1979 and, with this, the goals that had been present in the constitutional treaties themselves and that had gone through different stages, were now fulfilled. Some of these goals had been of great importance, such as direct elections, proposed by Dehousse. The concept of a European parliament, elected by universal suffrage, was thus confirmed. This idea was the essential element for progress through integration and strength, based on a democratic framework and a balance among the various institutions of the Community.

The founding countries (Federal Republic of Germany, Belgium, France,

Italy, Luxembourg, and Holland) were successively joined by Denmark, Ireland and the United Kingdom, and Northern Ireland in 1972, Greece in 1979, and Portugal and Spain in 1985. In January 1986, the current Community of the Twelve was finally shaped. It does not appear that, for the time being, an increase in member nations will take place, although there are countries, such as Austria, that show an interest in joining. The only alterations that have taken place recently have been the result of the unification of both Germanies that, although it has not modified the number of nations, has meant an increase of 16 million in the number of EC citizens, adding to the 63 million already in EC from the Federal Republic of Germany.

From the mid-1980s, the main aim of the Communities has been the achievement of an internal market. With the signing of the Single Act in 1986, based on the 300 measures proposed by the Commission in its white paper of 1985 and immediately ratified by the Twelve after Spain and Portugal joined, one of the main projects of the Communities ever since its creation will be fulfilled: the single internal market in 1992. This date has lost whatever power it had as a myth, and it has become somewhat disquieting. Basically, this act refers to the elimination of all controls and formalities between borders of the member states, the right of all Community citizens to settle, work, and study in all countries of the Community, the freedom of movement for all capital, the suppression of the treasury frontiers, and establishment of similar direct taxes (basically, value-added taxes), as well as the harmonization of Community law. In sum, the elimination of all physical, technical, legal, and fiscal barriers among its member states will occur. Whether these objectives are fulfilled in their entirety in 1992 is irrelevant because the important thing is that the will and the commitment of the Twelve toward a process of integration is producing highly significant changes. However, the events taking place in the early 1990s in Eastern Europe will open again the issue of enlargement of the Community, which, throughout its history, has been adjusted in accordance with the concept of integration.

II. Community Documentation

The main institutions in the process of decision-making in EC are the Commission, the Council of Ministers, the European Parliament, and the Court of Justice. The Economic and Social Committee and the Court of Auditors (similar to the General Accounting Office of the U.S. Congress) should be added. The existence of these institutions and the successive incorporation of the member states generated the creation and subsequent increase in the Community's documents. As a result of its objectives of coordination, cooperation, and harmonization, a close and complex relationship arose among its states and also between these states and the community institutions. This relationship results in a specific type of document generated by EC (directives, regulations, COM [Commission] documents, decrees, etc.), by the member countries (laws, decrees, etc.), and by other international organizations and nonmember countries. In addition, the number of its official and nonofficial publications is very high, since 1986 nine languages are used, and their contents have been enriched as other countries have joined the Community, tightening the bonds between them and introducing new economic, social, and legal factors.

The purpose of this article is to describe the documentary sources of the Spanish Congress of Deputies as they relate to EC and the type of information that the Community makes available to its member users. Before describing the sources, we devote the remainder of this section to the definition and classification of the general type of documents of the Community. As we are aware that we must be brief, we refer the reader to the book written by Thomson (1989), where the subject is given detailed treatment.

A. Definition

The Community documents share, of course, the characteristics of the documents generated by other international organizations, such as, to mention a few, the European Council, the Interparliamentary Union (UIP), and the Western European Union (WEO), but at the same time they bear the signature of national documentation. International organizations, essentially a product of the twentieth century, are based on the union of two or more nations to promote a continuous activity between members, generating, as a rule, a multilingual official documentation that creates commitments and obligations between its members and also reaches a wide audience, even if it is only due to the fact that a considerable number of countries take part in it.

However, a part of the documentation of EC has an aspect that makes it look qualitatively different from the documentation of other international institutions. That is its legislative character and, as a result, the requirement on the part of all its member nations to fulfill the regulations. This fact should be pointed out because of the effect on each of the countries that must either apply the contents of the documentation directly, as in the case of regulations, or, in turn, make laws based on the rules established by the Community, as in the case of directives.

What then do we call Community documentation? In the few handbooks that deal with this topic, the term "Community documentation" is applied to the group of documents generated by Community institutions, including all official and nonofficial publications. The latter take the form of articles for general knowledge, preparatory documents, annuals, magazines, leaflets, statistics, etc., most of which are financed by the Office for the Official Publications of the European Communities (OOPEC) which acts both as publisher and distributor. OOPEC was created in 1969 and coordinates the tasks related to printing, sale, and distribution of the material from the Community institutions. Although the printing is often done in non-Community printing houses, probably for economic reasons, the sale and distribution falls completely within OOPEC. It would appear logical that OOPEC and the institutions retain their own capacity for printing to be able to handle confidential material, urgent requirements, failures in the contracts and, if necessary, for simple convenience. All this material can be gathered together roughly, in the following way: (1) the official EC journal and (2) EC material other than the official journal. This would then be Community documentation in the strict sense. However, any documentalist specializing in this subject needs to handle documentary sources that go beyond those mentioned above. It is worth noting where the line between Community and non-Community documentation is placed. Besides scholarship and studies about EC from all parts of the world, Community documentation is also generated by the governments of the member countries such as laws of adaptation or documents produced within the national parliaments, such as the proceedings of sessions of the parliamentary committees that deal with the subject of integration. In fact, the database CELEX, includes national measures to implement EC legislation and incorporates regulations from the different member countries.

The control of the documentary sources implies, therefore, not only the handling of all those documents produced by the Community institutions, including the agreements with nonmember countries and the official policies about this matter, but also all documentation that the member states develop as an obligation of being members of the Community.

Community documentation is defined by a number of features:

1. It forms a legislative network that goes from the Community institutions to its member states in a continuous attempt to harmonize their legal arrangements.

2. It is supranational, as there exists an executive branch, a parliament, and a court of justice that bring together 12 nations, forming a body that executes the tasks of direction and control over them.

3. It is multilingual as it is a documentation that is officially published in nine languages (German, Danish, Spanish, French, Greek, Dutch, English, Italian, and Portuguese). At a national level, this fact does not produce significant problems from the documentary point of view, as it is normally received in the language of the particular country and, perhaps, in an additional language, but in the case of the European institutions, its handling is more troublesome and, above all, costly. To make it easier, all documents

and publications have a different color for each language. For instance, Spain's distinctive color is red.

4. It is international because of the power that EC have to establish relationships with other international bodies or with third countries.

5. Its documentary typology is varied, making necessary the usage of various sources: official and nonofficial publications, databases, internal documents, bibliographies, directories, etc.

B. Classification

All of the documentation that we have referred to before can be classified, apart from the official and nonofficial, in the following way:

1. Legislative documentation, the source of which is the Official Journal of the European Communities, composed of the "L," "C," and "S" series. It contains the primary documentation (treaties), the secondary documentation (regulations, directives, decisions, and recommendations), the agreements with third countries (conventions) and the supplementary legislation of each of its member states in connection with EC, as published in their respective, official government journals.

2. Jurisprudence established by the Court of Justice of the European Communities and jurisprudence established by the courts of the member states in which the community regulations are directly applied.

3. Documentation of the legislative process (COM documents, debates of the European Parliament (EP), reports, and a variety of documents many of which are not published.)

4. Nonofficial publications and those for general distribution.

5. Scholarship, in the form of monographs and periodical publications emanating from EC themselves or from specialists in this field.

III. Information in Europe

One cannot speak about Community documentation, however, without referring immediately to the information policy of EC. As explained in Section II, the documentation about EC is diverse and comes from different sources (libraries, documentation centers, databases, etc.). We should add to this fact that all information produced by the Communities must automatically be treated in such a way that it can be rapidly distributed among the member states and their 320 million citizens with their different and heterogeneous problems. In addition, the people responsible for information have had to organize themselves to ensure that Community action occurs within a unified program of research and development. For that purpose, the Community institutions have established technical, scientific, educational, and cultural programs, supported by the new information technologies that permit diversification and widening of the field of action.

The four Community institutions (Council, Commission, Court of Justice, and EP) are engaged, in one way or the other, in the policy of diffusion or distribution of the information. The Commission prepares proposals, the EP informs, the Council makes decisions, and the Court plays the role of jurisdictional control. These are the channels of decision. However, among the 22 top departmental offices of the Commission, four directorate generals (DG) are particularly concerned with information:

1. The DG IX: Personnel and administration, on which the library depends
2. The DG X: Information, communication, and culture, operates the SCAD database in Brussels, EUR-OP in Luxembourg, and the press offices established in each of the member states and in certain countries such as Switzerland, the United States, Japan, Australia, and Venezuela
3. The DG XII: Devotes itself to R & D
4. The DG XIII: Telecommunications, industries of information and innovation; takes care of the major technological programs

Of all services that make up these four top departmental offices, four of them are particularly interesting:

1. The Central Library of the Commission of the European Communities, which reports to DG IX. It is located in Brussels and has a branch in Luxembourg; its essential objective is to give aid to and provide information to the Commission. Its database, created in 1978, is for internal use and is called ECLAS.
2. The Central Service of Automated Documentation (SCAD), which is complementary to the Central Library. Its database was created in 1983. It has both an internal and external task; it provides information to the personnel of the Community institutions and to the public in general, directing the public toward its available services.
3. The Official Publications Office of the European Communities (OOPEC) which reports to the DG X. We referred to this office in Section II,A.
4. The databases with information on EC, of which there are currently more than 850, can be found in the database DIANE, disseminated by the European commission host organization (ECHO).

Historically, plans of action were successively proposed by the Commission in the years 1975, 1978, and 1981, as a result of which EURONET

(Community communications network, now eliminated) was created and DIANE was developed as an information service. Plans for sectoral information have also been proposed for agriculture, environment, medicine, and health, followed by a Community program for market development of specialized information in Europe, adopted by the Council on 27 November 1984.

The IMPACT programs (information market policy actions) represent the last stage for the time being. IMPACT 1 was approved by the Council on 26 of July 1988 (Decision 88/524/CCE), and its objectives were to create an internal market of information services, to promote and strengthen the capacity of competitive offers by the European suppliers, to foster the use of advanced information services, and to intensify the efforts jointly deployed for guaranteeing the cohesion of the Community on the subject of the policies about information services. The first activities intended to achieve these objectives were prepared in close contact with the consultant group of top executives of market information services and were carried out during the years 1989/90.

The program IMPACT 2, proposed by the Commission to the Council 23 January 1991 (COM (90) 570 final), was approved by the European Parliament on 11 July 1991 and was adopted by Decision 91/691/CEE on 12 December 1991. In this new IMPACT program, the general objectives of the previous program and the majority of the specific objectives continue to be maintained.

The experience and the changes operating in the information market, however, require a certain reorientation of Community initiatives. The common objective of the various functions of IMPACT 2 is to integrate the market in the Community area, overcoming any technical obstacle, reducing the regional differences as regards the supply and use of modern services where information is concerned, and promoting European cooperation among suppliers of information. The different activities proposed include one addressed to the libraries of EC to improve both the efficiency of the interchange of information among them and the conditions for applying new information technologies in the library field.

The current European position in the world market of electronic information services is evidently still weaker than it should be. Considerable market fragmentation exists, partly caused by disagreements among the member states themselves. This discrepancy is illustrated by the simple fact that a single member state produced nearly one-third of the databases of the Community in 1988 and carried out 74% of all exports of Community databases to the United States. Another example is that at the present, business volume of the European market of online information services (excluding videotext) represents one-third of the volume of the market in the United States. In 1988, EC produced only one-half as many online databases as did the United States.

All this leads us to believe that the policy of the Community institutions with regard to the information market results from a need to simplify access to the European sources of information and meet the competitive challenge put forth by the United States and Japan.

IV. Spain and the European Communities

As early as 1962, Spain began negotiations as a first step toward attaining full integration in EC. Negotiations continued throughout the 1960s. In 1970, a commercial agreement between Spain and EEC was signed in which the involved parties committed themselves to "consolidate and expand the existing economic and commercial relations" and to establish "the basis for a progressive expansion of mutual interchanges." This agreement, which was based on article 113 of the EEC Treaty, predicted a first stage of at least 6 years during which the essential obstacles to the interchanges would be progressively eliminated. The second stage, undefined, remained subject to subsequent negotiations between the parties.

Shortly after the agreement came into force, the Spanish authorities and the Community worried about the effects the 1973 entry of new countries would have on the Community as well as the entry of Great Britain that was to take place in 1972. Great Britain was, as a matter of fact, the main market for the export of Spanish agricultural produce, which was not fully covered by the agreement. Spain would also be affected by the raising of British tariffs that had to be consistent with those of its new partners in the Community. Negotiations were difficult, breaking down at different points.

After the coronation of King Juan Carlos I, on 22 November 1975, negotiations were restored and at the beginning of 1976, the Spanish government expressed its willingness to join the Community. The process, however, was to last longer than expected. On 28 July 1977, the month after June parliamentary elections (the first since 1939), the Spanish Minister for Foreign Affairs officially submitted to the President of the Community Council an application for Spain to join the Community. This application took place 2 years after that of Greece and 4 months after that of Portugal.

Despite the favorable opinion of the Council of Ministers, the Commission, the Parliament, and the Economic and Social Committee, negotiations lasted from 1979 to 1985. Difficulties first arose in 1980, basically because of agriculture, which caused a new delay until 1984 when the Community submitted to Spain a negotiation position for the agricultural sector. Finally, the negotiations were closed on 6 June 1985; they had lasted 7 years.

The membership treaty for joining the Community is composed of only three articles in which the EC members express their willingness to establish the systems whereby Spain and Portugal could become members of EC.

The membership act, which is a technical appendix to the treaty, is composed of four parts. The first part includes the principles; the second, the adaptation of the treaties; the third, the adaptation of the acts (secondary legislation) adopted by the institutions; and the fourth, the transitional measures.

Without a doubt, the repercussions coming from the entry of Spain into EC are important. Since January 1986, Spain has had to incorporate into its legal structure Community laws and make an effort to harmonize its economic and social policies with those of the rest of the Community. From an institutional point of view, it means that from the beginning, official organizations must be created to deal with the Community. Among these, one can cite the Joint Committee (Congress and Senate) for the European Community, to which we refer in Section VI,A.

As is logical, this change manifested itself in many other sectors, both official and private, such as industry, agriculture, fishing, international relations, all economic and financial issues, customs and tariffs, free passage of citizens, services and finances, and so forth. One must include in this long list both scientific research and the creation of libraries and research centers that would allow for access to information required by all sectors.

Because EC was the result of a long process of negotiations that created interest in the Communities everywhere, there were already centers in Spain specialized in Communities research. When Spain joined EC in January 1986, it was decided to accelerate the process of creating centers dedicated exclusively to the Community matters and to increase bibliographic and document collections. The universities expanded their plans of study and created centers for Community documentation as did all the sectors that were connected with or influenced by the incorporation of Spain into EC.

V. Organization of the General Secretariat of the Congress of Deputies

The Cortes Generales is formed by the Congress of Deputies and the Senate, as established by article 66 of the Spanish Constitution of 1978, in force since 1 January 1979. Each chamber has its own general secretariat, with a practically identical organization. The rules of the Congress of Deputies were approved in 1982, and they replaced the provisional rules of 1977 and established in article 60 that "the Congress will have the necessary resources in personnel and material for the development of its functions, especially technical services, documentation and consultancy." The rules established, as well, in article 31.1, that it is the duty of the Board of the Congress (steering committee) to "adopt whatever decisions and measures are required for the organization of the work and for the internal ruling of the Chamber." The board, in its turn, can authorize the general secretary to develop those measures.

Since 1977, the organization of the General Secretariat in Congress has been modified on different occasions, one of them a few months after the approval of the rules that have been in force since 1982. The growing activity of Congress and the parallel increase in its administrative–parliamentary functions made the successive reorganization necessary.

To complete the directives established by the constitution regarding this matter, it is neessary to mention the decision of article 72.1: "The Chamber establishes its own rules, approves its budgets with total autonomy and, in mutual agreement regulates the Statute of Personnel of the Parliament. . . ." To fulfill this mandate, the Cortes Generales approved the Statute of Personnel of the Cortes Generales on 26 of June 1989, which left the 1983 directive (and its subsequent modifications) noneffective. On 27 June of the same year, the payroll and organizational rules of the General Secretariat of Congress were approved. All this was published in the *Boletin Oficial de las Cortes Generales* (official journal of the Spanish Parliament) on 25 of July 1989, Series E, No. 199.

According to what was established in the Statute of Personnel of Parliament, in addition to the temporary personnel and to the personnel belonging to the state administration for missions of security who do not report to the corps of personnel of parliament, the personnel are, with required qualifications, the following:

1. Corps of lawyers (5-year university degree in law)
2. Corps of librarians-archivists. (5-year university degree in either philosophy, literature, law, science, politics, economics, sociology, or mass-media sciences)
3. Corps of consultants (5-year university degree, according to specialization)
4. Corps of shorthand writers and stenographers (3-year university degree or equivalent)
5. Corps of technical-administration personnel (3-year university degree or equivalent)
6. Corps of administrative clerks (high school, technical education, or equivalent)
7. Corps of ushers (primary school, lower technical education, or equivalent)

The General Secretariat of Congress of Deputies is structured as a series of higher bodies and management centers. They are the following:

1. *General Secretariat.* The lawyer in charge of the General Secretariat is appointed by the Board of the Congress of Deputies on the basis of the proposal of its president. Her or his duties include those of managing the assistance, support, and legal advice, as well as technical and administrative help, to the various bodies of the chamber and also to the higher leadership of the administrative services of Congress. These tasks are carried out under the authority of the board.

The services of immediate assistance to the General Secretariat are structured in a cabinet for legal and technical advising for documentary support and a secretary of administrative assistance. The legal body and the press service report directly to the secretary general, as do the security services of congress.

2. *General Assistant Secretariat.* The general assistant secretary, appointed by the board as a result of a proposal by the general secretary, offers support to the general secretary in the carrying out of his duties and directs the immediate leadership of the administrative services of the chamber.

There is a thesaurus coordinating office reporting to the general assistant secretary. This office is to be run by a librarian-archivist and, at the present time, this post is vacant. The duties are to study, evaluate, propose, standardize, and disseminate the systems to be followed by all users for employing terms, establishing the descriptors of the EUROVOC Thesaurus development, which is now being used for the indexing of the Congress's databases. This office is concerned with the maintenance of Congress's EUROVOC Thesaurus in agreement with the principles establiched by OOPEC, assessing the value of incorporating the new issues and the costs of enforcement.

3. *Management Office of Parliamentary Technical Assistance.* The duties of this office include assistance to the general secretary and, if necessary, to the deputy general secretary in those tasks of preparation, advising, and execution of the subjects that are part of the activities of the plenum of Congress, the board, and the committee of spokesmen of Congress of Deputies. In this office, the department for legal advice, the writing of the proceedings of session, and the register and document distribution are integrated. In the latter, the service for administrative processing of databases and official publications area are incorporated.

There exists a position for a civil servant of the corps of librarian-archivists, who would be assigned to management and whose duties are to offer documentary support to the management. This person is to carry out the indexing of the documents introduced in the ARGO database, as well as the speakers' speeches in the parliamentary sessions. He also would develop the indexes of the official publications, using the ARGO database.

4. *Committee Management Office.* This department carries out the tasks of parliamentary assistance, support, and advice to the chamber committees.

5. *Studies and Documentation Management Office.* The responsibilities of this office include studies and research pertaining to parliamentary activity, as well as the formation of the necessary documentary base. Its structure is the following:

A. Manager's Secretariat
B. Department of Studies, including a unit for legal and parliamentary studies and the area of economic studies
C. Department of European Community Studies and Comparative Law. In this department, a number of special tasks directly related to EC are carried out. The questionnaires from the European committee and parliament sent to the Spanish congress are answered in this department. Also, texts are translated and the *Boletin de Derecho de las Comunidades Europeas* (BCE) is prepared. The information sheet with the summary of the activities of EP during each session is also published in cooperation with the Senate.
D. Documentation Department, which comprises the storing and processing area (periodical publications) and the distribution area. This area has responsibility for units of European Community and Spanish documentation, foreign documentation, and economics documentation. In the unit of European Community and Spanish documentation, the tasks of gathering information related to EC is carried out. In addition, the processing of EC documentation is dealt with, excluding the periodical and monographic publications
E. Library Department, which comprises two areas: bibliographic information and technical processing
F. Archives Department, that comprises two units: the parliamentary collections and the administrative collections
G. Publications Service, on which the offices for internal and external distribution depend

6. *Economic Affairs Management Office.* This office deals with the matters related to contracts, grants, facilities, budgets, and accounting of the chamber.

7. *Parliamentary Relations Management Office.* This office takes care of the management, organization and preparation of the parliamentary relations of the Congress of Deputies and those of the Cortes Generales (Congress and Senate).

8. *Internal Government Management Office.* The duties of this office include the management, advising, and control in matters related to the personnel who work in the general secretariat of Congress.

9. *Data Processing Management Office.* This office is concerned with the data processing system installed in congress.

10. *Auditing.* This department has the rank of management office and carries out the tasks of auditing in its different modes and the accounting of

all events, documents, and proceedings of the general secretariat from which rights and obligations of economic character are derived.

VI. Documentary Sources

A. Parliamentary Documentation Pertaining to the European Community: The Joint Committee for the European Community

The Cortes Generales maintain a specialized body for relations with EC and for debating every matter related to the European integration, the Common Market, and Spanish policy in Community matters. This body is the Joint Committee for the European Community. Parliamentary documentation in connection with EC must go through this Joint Committee, which was created on 27 December 1985, by Law 47/1985, for the purpose of reporting to the government in regard to the application of EC's law (*Boletín Oficial del Estado*, No. 312 of 30 December 1985 and No. 49 of 26 February 1986; this is the state's official journal), through the first paragraph of article 5, which established that "a Joint Committee of the Congress and Senate will be constituted and it will be named the Joint Committee for the European Communities."

During 1985, the Congress of Deputies European Communities Department had prepared a survey on the special committees of other national parliaments responsible for study and follow up of EC matter (Daranas, 1985a). According to Law 47/1985, it was responsible for creating the European Communities Joint Committee. It also established the European Communities' member states international treaties ratification procedure (Daranas, 1985b).

The Joint Committee was originally formed with 15 members, 9 of whom belonged to Congress and 6 to the Senate; the members were appointed at the beginning of the legislature by the parliamentary groups in "numbers equivalent to the numerical importance of those in the Chamber." However, with the extensive modifications undergone by the Joint Committee in the third legislature (with the appearance of the so-called "associations," i.e., unaligned deputies who participate with a mixed group and, based on their ideology, form "agrupaciones" or associations) and the need to offer opportunities to parliamentary political forces for participating in the Committee, a reform of the 1985 law was required. This reform took place through law 18/1988 of 1 July, and was a modification of article 5 of law 47/1985 of 27 December, which gave power to the government to create laws in application of EC law (*Boletín Oficial del Estado*, No. 161 of 6 July 1988).

From the date of this reform, the number of congressmen and senators that make up the Joint Committee was established by the boards of the chambers in joint session at the beginning of each legislature, guaranteeing in any case the presence of all the parliamentary groups and also, if required that of the "associations." The scope of the committee is as follows:

1. To be informed, immediately after their publication, of the effects on article 82.6 of the Spanish Constitution of the legislative decrees issued in application of law derived from community law
2. To be informed by the government of all issues requiring legislation from EC that would contradict standard Spanish law
3. To receive available information from the government about the activities of the institutions of EC with respect to the application and practical steps of the entry of Spain into the Community
4. To be informed by the government of the rationale for its politics within EC and of the decisions and agreements of the Council of Ministers of EC

To these original responsibilities, the following ones were added in 1988:

5. The committee can prepare reports based upon the proposals of regulations, directives, and decisions that the Commission of the European Community presents to the Council of Ministers.
6. The Committee is responsible for establishing cooperative relations with the bodies of EP. It can also hold joint meetings with the Spanish congressmen in EP.
7. The Committee has a duty to maintain interaction and collaboration with the existing committees in other national parliaments of the member states of EC whenever they have similar responsibilities.
8. Through the regular channels, the Committee can submit to the boards of both chambers reports and technical evaluations that contain subjects that may be considered of special interest to, and the responsibility of, the Joint Committee.

From a documentary point of view, it is important to point out that the Committee has an obligation to submit a report about the activities carried out in the recent past to both chambers at the beginning of each period of sessions.

The Joint Committee was constituted in the second legislature during which it held two sessions: 12 February and 9 April 1986. Its activities can be monitored using two different sources: the ARGO database of information on parliamentary activities and, the "Cronica de las Sesiones Celebradas por la Comision Mixta" (chronicle of the sessions held by the Joint Committee), which is prepared periodically by the librarian/archivist of the Cortes Generales and which is published in the *Revista de Estudios e Investigacion de las comunidades Europeas* (REICE) (Magazine for studies and research on the European Community). The "Crónica" consists of two parts: records of the activity and subjects treated and information about any required personal participation, the purpose of the persons's appearance, and the parliamentary group that requested it; and the "Diario de Sesiones" (daily sessions) in which the discussions of the Committee are reported.

The "Crónica" started publication with issue 3–4 1988 of the REICE and began with a summary of the activities of the Joint Committee from the start of the third legislature until March 1987. It also included the chronicle of the sessions held from March until the end of 1987: issue no. 5 1988 covered the sessions held on 2 and 3 March 1988; issue no. 9, those of 1 and 22 February 1989 and of 7 March 1989; issue no. 10, those of 5 and 12 April 1989; issue no. 11 and 12, those of 10 and 31 May 1989; issue no. 14, those of 14 March and 10 May 1990, and issue no. 15, those of 7 June 1990.

The ARGO database allows us to follow the complete activities of the Joint Committee as well as the rest of the parliamentary administration. We deal here with a reference database created by using the documentary package called MISTRAL, which is supported on a Bull DPS-8 computer. ARGO permits following the parliamentary course of any initiative submitted by the Joint Committee as well as locating the "Diario de Sesiones" in which a predetermined speech is recorded. As an indexing language, EC's EURO-VOC Thesaurus is used.

Rules on computer access to the congress documentary database of 17 January 1991, published by the *Boletin Oficial de las Cortes Generales, Series E* of 31 January 1991, facilitate access to the existing information, provided that it is not of a restricted nature. The rules provide authorized access for public institutions such as the Senate, government, Constitutional Court, General Council of the Judicial Power, the ombudsman, the Court of Accounts and the Central Electoral Office, and the legislative assemblies of the autonomous communities. However, this list does not entirely exclude access of other bodies and public or private entities that may be authorized by the Board of the Congress Deputies, through an application addressed to the General Secretariat of Congress of Deputies.

The rules regulate the conditions of access, which include payment for the connect costs, although the possibility exists that this particular condition will not be applied if an agreement of reciprocity is established in the interest of Congress. This rule does not apply to the connections made by the government from computer terminals located in those areas of the chamber used by the Congress of Deputies.

From the point of view of the documentation services the Joint Committee is a valuable receiver of important documentation from the government. For example, during the third legislature (1986–1989), the government sent (among others) the following documents to the Committee:

1. Documentation on Spanish and European community legislation from 12 June 1985, when Spain and Portugal signed the membership treaty, legislation that complements the treaty itself, and information about the legislative and community plans submitted by the Ministry of Foreign Affairs in its appearance before the Committee on 9 April 1986

2. Summary of the aid legislation by the Ministry of Agriculture, Fishing, and Food in favor of the agricultural/food industry and, also, the aid furnished by the EEC through the Fondo Europeo de Orientación y Garantía Agrícola (FEOGA; European Agricultural Guidance and Guarantee Fund) to improve conditions for the processing and marketing of the agricultural and fishing products, as submitted by the general director of agricultural and food industry

3. Annual report of the court of accounts of EC pertaining to the year 1986

4. Report from the European council in Brussels of the 11–12 February 1988: consolidated conclusions of the European Council and the working program for the execution of the conclusions of the European Council

5. A summary note about the agreements reached in the Brussels Summit on the agricultural stabilizers introduced by the Minister of Agriculture, Fishing, and Food

6. Summary file cards of documents on interest-group policies of EC, presented by the Minister of Foreign Affairs in his appearance before the Committee 13 October 1988

7. Record of the meeting of 16 February 1989 in the interest-group conference convened by the Minister of the Public Administration, with the object of debating the implementation of the motion approved by the Congress of Deputies, to discuss ways to permit the participation of autonomous communities in the process of formulating the Spanish position on EC matters, and to design a working plan for executing the agreed mechanisms as submitted by the Minister of the Public Administration

8. Report about development of the East–West security relations of Western Europe, submitted by the Committee of General Affairs of the Assembly of the Western European Union

During the third legislature, the Committee held 34 ordinary sessions in a total of 105 hours. Its constitutional session took place on 10 September 1986 and the last legislature's session was on 31 May 1989. During this period, 7 non-law proposals were examined, 54 oral questions discussed, and 61 appearances were made (36 government appearances, 23 authorities and civil servants, and 2 retired people).

B. Documentation on the European Communities

Before the membership treaty was signed, the Spanish Parliament had worked out a complete document and study series for both the Members of Parliament and the information of the general citizens. Much work was done on the electoral systems in the members states to elect their representatives in EP (Ruiz-Navarro Pinar, 1985). Another accomplishment was the "dossier" (Membership Treaty. . . . 1987) that was worked out by the Congress of Deputies European Communities Department on the parliamentary debates held in every member state's national chamber and in EP dealing with the Spain–Portugal membership treaty. This work includes the session's journal collection, proper parliamentary committees' decisions and reports, and introductions of bills that, after being approved by member state's parliaments, allowed both Iberian countries to become EC member states.

Sources of information and documentation about EC that are available in the Congress's Documentation Department follow.

1. Diario Oficial de las Comunidades Europeas (DOCE) (Official Journal of the European Communities)

This journal is the main documentary source. It was created by means of the EC council's decision made on 15 September 1958 and, since 1968, it is divided into two series and one supplement.

1. *"L" Series (Legislation).* This series includes all derived law (Section VII,B,3) and is divided into two sections: I and II. Section I refers to "acts whose publication indicates they are rulings." In the index, acts printed in fine letters are those of current management and have been adopted in the frame of the agrarian policy; they have, generally, a limited period of validity. The rest of the acts are printed in the index in bold characters, preceded by an asterisk. Section II contains those statements whose publication does not indicate a ruling: directives, decisions, recommendations, technical evaluations, atypical events, and so forth.

The Congress of Deputies General Secretariat prepares a publication called *Boletín de Información* (Information Bulletin), which is distributed among congressmen and senators on those days when plenary sessions are held; it contains a permanent section called "European Communities," prepared by the Documentation Department in which the most significant decisions appearing in the "L" Series since the last plenum of the Congress of Deputies are mentioned.

2. *"C" Series. (Communication and Information).* This series is also divided into three sections with three subsections corresponding to the institutions (Council, Commission, Parliament, Court of Justice, Court of Auditors). Section I "Comunicaciones," its subdivision "Commisión" contains mainly announcements for bids, communications about the applications of custom-duties preferences, aid systems, etc. The subdivision "Parliament" contains written questions with replies; in this section, however, the official records of the monthly sessions of EP are published with its self-approved texts. In

the subdivision "Court Of Justice," sentences issued by the court in its diverse deliberations are published (this would be the first official jurisprudence publication of the court). Section II, "Actos jurídicos preparatorios", (preparatory legal actions) contains fundamental committee proposals: directives, regulations, decisions, and other actions; economic and social committee technical evaluations are also recorded. Section III, "Información," (also with a triple division) records, among other activities, announcements for bids, opposing bids, and solicitations.

3. *The "S" Supplement of the Diario Oficial.* This series is published separately and contains mainly announcements of public bids concerning markets for civil works and supplies for the public bodies. In the Documentation Department, the complete collection of the *Diario Oficial* is available (except for the "S" supplement) in French from its start until the entry of Spain in the Community and, from then on, in Spanish. (This official journal also includes an annex in which EP debates are published; in the department, there is a record of all debates since 1984.)

The entry of Spain into the community represented a considerable transformation in the tasks of documentation. Evidence of this is the *Edición Especial del DOCE* (Official Journal of the European Communities Special Issue), which includes the official translation of all actions adopted before that entry, covering the period between 1952 and 1985. This solution was chosen because it was more economical and more practical than translating the DOCE in its entirety from its beginning. Thus, the references of the *Repertorio de la Legislación Comunitaria Vigente* (Directory of community legislation in force) (an issue that is brought up to date every 6 months) with respect to derived law in force before 1985 are made to the volumes of the *Edición Especial*.

Since 1986, the department has used microfiche as a storing method and as a complement of the DOCE printed edition. The Documentation Department also uses CELEX database of EC as an instrument for searching the information described up to now. Considering that primary documents are available, access to the document is easy, once its publication references have been obtained.

2. European Commission

The work of the Commission can be followed in the Congress Studies Management Office through various sources. First, the series of COM documents contain Commission comunications and Commission proposals prior to the publication of the DOCE "C" Series. Second, the *Boletín de las Comunidades Europeas*, published monthly, furnishes information about principal events and the activities of the institutions. In this bulletin, one can find, for instance, texts adopted by the different European councils. Its thematic order allows a monthly follow-up on the legislative evolution of EC in different fields. The last a source contains information of great practical use, the Informes de Actividad (activity reports) (general, agriculture, and competitiveness).

3. The European Parliament (EP)

In addition to what has been said in connection with the DOCE, the Parliament's activity can be followed through the *Documentos de la Sesión*, which are composed of three series (Paesa, 1987b): (1) "A" Series, which includes reports prepared by the various committees that are the object of debate in the plenum; it also includes the corresponding resolution proposals; (2)"B" Series, which covers resolution proposals submitted by parliamentarians; and (3) "C" Series, which includes documents submitted by the Community institutions (mainly the Commission).

The A Series is kept in the Documentation Department. Other informative publications about the Parliament are the *Actas Provisionales de la Sesión* (Provisional session acts), which are brought from each session of EP by a member of the corps of lawyers of the Cortes Generales, once each session is finished. This lawyer normally accompanies the Spanish euro-congressmen to the EP. Also three additional publications are brought: Clarín y Ecos de la Sesión ("Bugle and Session Echos"), prepared by the EP itself including matters to be treated and the results of the debate, respectively, and one information sheet, prepared by the general secretariats of Congress and Senate. The *Actas* include a summary of every partial period of the sessions. Searches pertaining to EP take place through the database system of EP which is called EPOQUE.

4. Economic and Social Committee (CES)

The CES documents series covering technical evaluations prepared by this body are also received. In the *Boletín de Información*, which is prepared by the general secretariat of the congress, COM documents, session documents, and CES documents are given a code number as they are received in the Documentation Department. These three types of documents (COM, CES, and EP) are stored by using microfiche as a support. They are preferably in Spanish but also in French for those periods that could not be completed.

5. Court of Justice of the European Communities

The official document *Recueil de la Jurisprudence de la Cour de Justice* is received by the department. From 1986 on, this report has been published in Spanish. In this publication, the material is expanded; therefore, the court sentences, the origin of the law, and the reports by the general lawyers are included.

On the other hand, in the *Repertoire de Jurisprudence et Droit Communautaire* we find, in the "A" series, the jurisprudence of the Court of Justice relating to the constitutional treaties of the Communities and also the derived law. In this publication that covers, up to now, the period 1977–1985, the jurisprudence of the court is analyzed by referring to an index of subjects.

The "D" series of the publication includes jurisprudence relative to the Brussels Convention of September 1968 that covers the judicial competence and the recognition and execution of the legal resolutions in both civil and commercial matters. To accomplish this, the department holds two publications:

1. The *Actividades del Tribunal de Justicia de las Comunidades Europeas* (European Court of Justice proceedings) (weekly), which has been published in Spanish since the entry of Spain. This publication is divided into four sections:
    I. Court sentences, which appear either as complete texts or only as verdicts
    II. Judgements, which include matters that are still in the judgement stage
    III. Sentences awaiting final hearing
    IV. New matters
2. The *Bulletin Périodique de Jurisprudence*, published semiannually, analyzes jurisprudence in accordance with a table of subjects, similar to the Repertoire of Jurisprudence.

6. Monitoring the Application of EC Directives

The integration of EC requires a commitment to adapt Community directives to the internal law of every member country. The documentary follow-up is carried out, in this aspect, through the IBERLEX database (*Boletin Oficial del Estado*, 1986). One refers to a documentary database in complete text from 1986 to the present and has only reference entries for the period from 1966 to 1986. It is accessed using the MISTRAL management package. It has references to a database of the Spanish legislation that uses "General Measures" from the *Boletin Oficial del Estado* as a source of information for Part I. In the field called "REFPOS," the measure used has references to the corresponding Community directive.

The state secretariat for EC in the Ministry of Foreign Affairs periodically publishes some reports of practical use concerning application of Community directives.

C. Documentation of Scholarship

Documentation of scholarship on EC is divided, because of its documentary processing, into monographs (processed by the Library Department) and articles in serial publications (processed by the Documentation Department).

The Documentation Department of the Congress of Deputies handles more than 1000 magazines, in both Spanish and foreign languages. A part of this important collection consists of periodical publications exclusively devoted to EC. (see Table I).

It should be pointed out, however, that most of the law, economy, and social science magazines dedicate special attention to EC. As a result, they are the object of a special follow-up within the department to ensure their correct dissemination, which will be explained later. The documentation department has four works of reference that can be updated:

1. *The Mercado Comun Dictionary* of the CISS Publishing House, which combines expository studies with the reproduction of measures and sentences. It is organized around the following main areas:

Volume I:	Treaties and Institutions
Volume II:	The Fiscal System (VAT)
Volume III:	Trading Corporation Law
Volume IV:	Establishment Right
Volume V:	Economy and Transport
Volume VI:	Industry and Energy
Volume VII:	Agriculture and Fishing
Volume VIII:	Competitiveness Right
Volume IX:	Regional Policies and Environment
Volume X:	Foreign Relations
Volume XI:	Free Circulation of Goods (Customs)

2. The *Dictionnaire du Marche Commun* (The Dictionary Of The Common Market) consists of six volumes of interchangeable sheets containing Community legislation, jurisprudence, and development legislation.

3. The *Law of the European Economic Community Dictionary* is based on the articles of the founding treaties and the regulations of each of the sectors defined by them.

4. The *Handbuch des Europaischen Rechts* is composed of 23 volumes on interchangeable sheets and contains abridged Community legislation and explanations for its correct application.

VII. Reference Services

A. Library and Documentation Department Services

1. The Library Department

a. History. The Congress library has a long history. Its origins go back to the primitive Cortes (parliament) of Cadiz in 1810. It is located in the Palace of the Congress in which, since its inauguration in 1850, it has had its

Table I Periodical Publications Concerning the European Communities Available in the Spanish Congress

Country	Publication
Spain	*Boletin de Derecho de las Comunidades Europeas*
	Carta (la) Europea
	Euronoticias
	Gaceta Jurídica de la CEE
	Movimiento Europeo
	Noticias CEE
	Repertorio de la Comunidad Europea
	Revista de Estudios e Investigación de las Comunidades Europeas
	Revista de Instituciones Europeas
European Communities	*Boletin de las Comunidades Europeas*
	Comunidad Europea
	Documentos CEE
	Dossier de l'Europe
	Economie Europeenne
	Europe Social
	Europe Vert (L')
	Eurostat Review
	Eurostatistiques
	SCAD Bulletin
France	*Revue du Marche Commun*
	Revue Trimestrielle de Droit Europeen
United Kingdom	*Common Market Law Reports*
	Common Market Studies
	European Law Review
	Yearbook of European Law
Belgium	*Cahiers de Droit Europeen*
	Documentation Europeenne
	Europe
	Europeen, les
	Rapport Mensuel sur l'Europe
	Telex Mediterranee
Italy	*Comuni D'Europa*
	Rivista di Diritto Europeo
Netherlands	*Common Market Law Review*
	Europe Aujourd'hui
	European Economic Review
Federal Republic of Germany	*Europaische Grundrecht Zeitschrift*
	Europarecht
Portugal	*Assuntos Europeus*

own space. The historic collections correspond to the uneven stages of its history. In 1977, it recovered its role as a Congressional library, and the process of modernization and updating of collections was accelerated. To illustrate these facts, the number of works incorporated in 1976 did not reach 1000, whereas currently about 4000 are added every year. Since 1 September 1989, the library has been directed according to operating instructions issued in the *Boletin Oficial de las Cortes Generales*, Series E., No. 204.

b. Users. The following users have access to the collections: (1) congressmen and senators, (2) personnel of the Congress and Senate, (3) authorized personnel from the parliament groups, (4) mass-media representatives who regularly cover parliamentary activities, and (5) researchers, subject to previous application.

c. Status of Its Collections. Besides its ancient collections, which are rich in variety and wealth, books on both law in all its branches and economic, political, social, and historical subjects have a tendency to predominate in the modern collections. Although these are the most common, the purpose of the library is essentially encyclopedic in the sense that it keeps up-to-date in the rest of the fields of knowledge such as philosophy, religion, literature, and geography, to mention only a few. It is a library with a considerable degree of self-sufficiency, as is proved by the fact that interlibrary loan is infrequent.

The library has historical catalogs of printed materials of the past century and of the beginning of this one for special collections. The so-called "modern collections" (Martin-González, 1989) refer to the books received from 1943 until now and they maintain bibliographic control through three catalogs (topographic, authors, and subjects). The classification of the subjects is hierarchial and alpha-numeric, based on the diverse fields of knowledge. Group 9 is devoted to law and, within it, 9.K (international law) contains the area that is EC, with paragraphs and subdivisions for various matters: general studies, history of the integration, law legislation, and economy institutions. Computerization of the collections started in January 1992. Since then, the EUROVOC Thesaurus has been used.

The number of works received every year is approximately 4000 of which 5% (about 200) are given over to EC in its different aspects. Many of them are self-publications of the EC proper. It must be borne in mind, however, that in the Spanish law books, as in those of any one of the member countries, it is a matter of course that those aspects that have been modified or adapted to the European law are included. Therefore, this 5% would be considerably more if all books in which Community matters are dealt with were included. This phenomenon takes place not only where law is concerned but also in many other fields such as sociology, economics, and so forth.

Among the reference works, the library owns the *Repertorio de Legislacion de las Comunidades Europeas*, Pamplona, Aranzadi, 1986–, which annually includes all the Community legislation since 1986. In the reading room, and, therefore, with direct access, the *Diario de Sesiones de las Cortes* from 1810 up to now can be found. The *Diario Oficial de las Cortes Generales* (Congress and Senate) is also available there. This is a work that is continuously consulted, and, without doubt, the one that attracts the greatest attention. Through these journals of sessions and bulletins, Community matters can be studied from the Spanish parliamentary perspective.

The library prepares a monthly bulletin recording all the works received, and there is a special chapter devoted to EC.

d. Usage of the Collections. Works consulted in the library proper, those in the reading room as much as those that are not directly accessible, during the period of 1986–1989 (Third Legislature) accounted for 14,944 uses (about 5000 every year). Although it is difficult to determine what percentage would be concerned with EC matters, we can confirm that the interest in these matters was high and has increased considerably in the past few years. The number of bibliographic enquiries was 7380 for the same period.

The book loans are reserved only for congressmen, senators, and personnel of the Cortes Generales. Researchers, personnel authorized by the parliament, representatives of interest groups, and the mass media can only do consultations in the reading room. Reproduction of bibliographic material must be requested, provided that the copyright law is respected. The number of books loaned out during the period 1986–1989 was 8516 (about 3000 per year).

The number of researchers who are issued cards varies between 150 and 200 per year. The most frequent topics of research are: parliamentary history, biographies of congressmen, and parliamentary debates concerning specific subjects, which often is related to EC (membership history, adaptation of community law, and so forth). Researchers that carry out studies on EC are, in many cases, foreigners who are enjoying scholarship grants to complete specific research or people who belong to some official body that is interested in compiling information on a specific subject. The countries represented in this type of work have been, during 1990 and 1991, France, the United States, Austria, and Germany.

The use of the library collections is improved by the requests, inquiries, and suggestions made by users in the documentation and archives departments. The library is open from 9 A.M. to 9 P.M. Monday through Friday. From the library, one can access the following data:

1. Database of the Library of the Congress of Deputies
2. Database of periodical publications in the Library of the Congress of Deputies
3. ARGO, with the Congress of Deputies activities
4. GELABERT, with the Senate activities
5. CALEX, with the Spanish autonomous communities legislation, contributed to by the Senate
6. IBERLEX, for access to the *Boletín Oficial del Estado*

2. Documentation Department

The Documentation Department includes, as mentioned before, a unit of Spanish and European Community documentation. Reference documentation searches on EC are of two types: one, searches performed in answer to requests submitted through the department by outside users (we point out that this department, as opposed to the library, is not open to researchers) and two, those searches made by members of the department itself. Regarding the first, reference will be made to the 1989 first half-year statistics (these are the only ones available at the present moment). Thus, between January and June 1989, a total of 852 requests for documentation were received. They were distributed as follows: 405 were for Spanish documentation; 201 were addressed to the periodical publications unit and were primarily oriented toward magazine articles; 48 were for foreign legislation; 46 were for documents of international bodies; and finally, EC documentation was the subject of 131 inquiries.

We will now examine the monthly distribution of the inquiries. Spanish documentation received: Janaury, 445 requests; February, 81; March, 77; April, 87; May, 60; and June, 55. The periodical publications section attended to 16 inquiries in January; 40 in February; 35 in March; 42 in April; 33 in May; and 35 in June. Attention was paid to 6 inquiries concerning foreign legislation in January; 14 in February; 14 in March; 4 in April; 5 in May; and 5 in June. International bodies documentation was the target of 9 requests in January; 8 in February; 14 in March; 9 in April; 3 in May; and 3 in June. Finally, regarding EC documentation, 17 requests were dealt with in January; 38 in February; 35 in March; 34 in April; 15 in May; and 13 in June. In a more detailed examination of the 131 requests for EC documentation, data are also available on the origin and type of the requested documents and matters. Regarding the origin of the requests, 68 requests were made by parliaments, 48 by congress and senate civil servants, 11 by Spanish or foreign official bodies; and 4 by private institutions.

Requested materials are widely varied and reflect the multiplicity of problems discussed by the parliament. Special concerns, based on the large number of requests made, were environment, social policies, institutions, agricultural policies, regional policies, internal market, structural funds, laws relating to the free circulation of workers, tax policy, competitiveness policy, and to a lesser degree, telecommunications, sport, industry, science and technology, drugs (regarded as medicines), and tourism. Finally, with reference to documentation type, the requests for Community legislation prevail, while documents about the Commission, European Parliament, and the European Court of Justice take second place.

At the department's initiative, a number of measures for general distribution have been undertaken and these include working out "dossiers" of documentation that accompany the process of the parliament bills considered as the most relevant. A "dossier" incorporates all the Spanish legislation in force (sometimes the historic legislation already repealed is also included). It also incorporates legislation of the autonomous communities, Constitutional Court jurisprudence, and Supreme Court, foreign legislation equivalent to the main countries in our political environment, main resolutions emanating from international institutions, a bibliography and, finally, documentation of EC concerning texts of the treaties, derived law, preparatory acts of the institutions, and jurisprudence of the Court of Justice.

For the distribution of the department's bibliographic material (the collection of the periodic publications to which we have referred), a *Boletin de Sumarios* is worked out; it is structured in the typical manner (index of articles is included as well as abstracts). An appendix is also included for which references of interest to the parliamentarians are selected each month by specialized personnel, whether it is because of the subject itself or for an in-depth study of subject in question. This appendix has a permanent section devoted to EC in which the most important articles published in the previous months are included. These consist of not only those articles appearing in the specialized magazines mentioned earlier, but also in the whole of the works received. References selected this way are incorporated in a database for future automated searching. At the present time, the final steps are being taken to begin computerization for the entire collection of magazines.

The Cortes Generales are in the process of preparing a non-official publication that will be of great use for reference tasks. We refer to the *Boletin de Derecho de las Comunidades Europeas* (BCE), which includes not only the legislative review of the Spanish legislation as it appeared in the *Boletin Oficial del Estado* in connection with EC, but also the most significant rulings that have found their way into the *Boletin Oficial de las Comunidades Europeas*. The review is presented according to the instructions of the *Repertorio de la Legislacion Comunitaria vigente*. The BCE includes fixed sections devoted to the Community institutions (Council, Commission, and European Parliament) providing information about their activities. BCE ends with a section devoted to studies.

There is a second distribution channel for the magazine articles. The Senate department of EC participates in the preparation of the aforementioned publication of the Cortes Generales, (BCE), which contains a permanent section run by the librarian-archivist and consists of reviews of the articles and monographs concerning EC that have been received in the collections of the Senate Documentation and Studies Management Office. They are indexed with headings extracted from EC EUROVOC Thesaurus.

The Senate, through its EC Department, prepares various monthly bulletins that are distributed among a selected number of users. For one, *Boletin de Prensa* (Press Bulletin) picks up Community activity news as it appears in the domestic press. For another, a selection of the COM, CES, and EP documents is made and the bibliographic references are presented in two monthly bulletins indexed with EUROVOC headings. The user who has a special interest in obtaining the complete document has only to apply for it to the aforesaid department.

B. Automation

To solve the big problem of searching and retrieving EC documentation, EC must take advantage of the numerous existing community legal databases (Paesa, 1987a). The documentation department has access to the following databases, produced by different institutions in EC, which are capable of satisfying practically all user information requirements.

1. Celex

CELEX (Communitatis Europa LEX) is the system of computerized documentation of Community law. It is produced by EC institutions (Commission, Council, European Parliament, Court of Justice, Economic and Social Council, Court of Auditors, European Bank of Investments, etc.) From the moment that it became compulsory for EC documents to be published in the member countries' official languages, there is a version of CELEX for each Community language. Since March 1991, versions have been made available in French, German, Dutch, Italian, Danish, and also pilot versions in Greek and in Spanish.

CELEX is composed of eight sections which are listed by number, as follows:

1. Original treaties, membership treaties, and the Single European Act
2. Agreements and other resulting actions of the external relations of the Community or the member states with nonmember states and with international bodies

3. Derived law (regulations, directives, decisions, CSEC decisions and recommendations, opinions, EEC and EURATOM recommendations, resolutions, and some communications, programs, reports, etc.)

4. EC secondary legislation (decisions of the representatives of the governments of the member states after holding meetings in the Council, also international agreements between the member states for implementing what was established in the treaties, etc.)

5. All preparatory work: proposals of the Commission, communications, reports and programs, resolutions of EP (opinions, resolutions of own initiative, resolutions on budget preparations, technical evaluations from the economic and social council, etc.)

6. European Communities Court of Justice jurisprudence

7. National measures for application of EC directives. This section is of particular importance to the reference tasks of the Documentation Department because CELEX furnishes information on the application of EC directives in each of the 12 countries in a unified way so that other sections of CELEX need not be accessed. Unfortunately, this section is in an experimental stage and its thoroughness cannot be guaranteed

8. Parliamentary questions

2. SCAD

The database called "Systeme Communautaire d'assess à la documentation" (SCAD) is of great use for reference tasks. It contains four types of documents:

1. "A" Documents: preparatory works and community acts (derived law, Committee proposals, EP's resolutions). These documents are indexed by using a keyword list.
2. "B" Documents: official publications and public documents of the European institutions
3. "C" Documents: reports on periodic publications related to EC institutions activity
4. "D" Documents: position-taking papers and social mediative opinions

SCAD was created in 1983. Its growth is estimated at some 15,000 entries per year; it is updated weekly. It uses Mistral V5 as a search language (the same as CELEX).

There is the possibility of using the MISTRAL macroprocedures called "actualités 1992" to be able to visualize, almost automatically, a selection of facts and publications considered to be the most important, the most recent, and those that really affect the achievement of the internal market.

3. EPOQUE

In 1987, an agreement was signed whereby access to EPOQUE by the Congress of Deputies was permitted. It covers the following: session documents produced by EP, such as the reports that appear in the "A" series and also the proposals of resolutions that are found in the "B" series; debates; adopted resolutions; petitions; parliamentary questions, both written and verbal or originating in "question time"; documents originating in other institutions and that are published in the "C" series; studies prepared by either the EP or the other national parliaments; and a catalog of the EP library. It also contains references from the simple document to the complete dossier of parliament procedure.

EPOQUE can be searched in two ways: (1) it allows for a guided search through a number of menus that require answers to simple questions proposed by the system itself (this procedure is, at this moment in September 1991, inoperative for technical reasons); and (2) it allows a more detailed search that implies a knowledge of the search language, CCL (common command language).

4. ECHO

Recently, a contract was signed by which the Congress Studies Management Office has been converted to a user of the ECHO services. ECHO offers "online" access to more than 20 bases and databanks. It was created in 1980, aiming to foster the use of the automated documentation of EC. This service reports to the General Management Office XIII/B (telecommunications, information industries, and innovation). Some of the databases that are consulted (free of charge) in the Documentation Department through ECHO by using the CCL language are the following:

1. BROKERSGUIDE: Has supplied information since 1986 about the information brokers that regularly operate in EC member states, whether they are individuals, companies, or organizations such as national libraries, database producers, and so forth
2. CORDIS: Short for Community research and development information service. Its main objective is to furnish information concerning the Community research and technological development (RTD). The majority of the information available through CORDIS comes from the Committee services, as a result of Community activity.
3. DIANEGUIDE (Direct information access network for Europe): Supplies information about database producers, bases, and databanks, and special details about them (name, type, coverage, number of documents, etc.)
4. DOMIS (Directory of materials data information sources): A directory of information sources and services available in Europe for the various industrial fields
5. DUNDIS (Directory of United Nations databases and information systems): Shows how to access the United Nations documentation, its technical studies, and its gray literature

6. EABS (Euro-ABStracts EC research programmes): Contains references to the published results of the scientific and technical investigation programs, totally or partially sponsored by EC
7. ELISE (European local initiatives system of exchanges): Part of the ELISE network, devoted to the promotion of initiatives for local employment. Analyzed documents are reference monographs, proceedings, studies, and so forth.
8. EURODICAUTOM: The cross-terminology database containing technical and scientific terms, acronyms, and abreviations with their meanings
9. MISEP (Mutual information system on employment policies): Set up in response to member states delegations' request for information as background both for members' decision making and for the Commission's coordinating role

C. Resources of Other Spanish and Foreign Offices

1. The European Parliament Office in Madrid

The Office of Information of the European Parliament in Spain is located in close proximity to the Congress offices, and it has (Rodríguez Bouyssi, 1986) a section devoted to social mass media and culture, a publications secretariat, and a documentation division. The staffs of these two offices maintain a cooperative relationship and an open exchange of information.

2. The Commission Information Office

The Commission Information Office in Madrid operates as a representative of EC in Spain (Saez de Calzada, 1983). Its divisions include exhibitions and Community education, press and information, visual teaching material, communication and culture, documentation and administration. The documentation center receives all the publications and documents of EC institutions.

3. European Documentation Centers (EDC)

The integration of Spain into EC has, as it has been pointed out throughout this article, generated an increase in the information requirements concerning this organization; thus research centers in Spain have met this demand through the creation of specific documentation centers (Euroconfidentiel, 1991). As can be seen in Table II, most of them belong to universities or major economic organizations such as the Chamber of Commerce. The Documentation Department logically maintains contact with several of these EDCs to make access easier to those documents, which are stored in one center and are not available elsewhere.

Table II European Documentation Centers in Spain

Location	Center
Alicante	Cámara de Comercio, Industria y Navegacíon
Badajoz	Cámara de Comercio
Barcelona	Escuela Superior de empresas (ESADE)
	Universidad Autónoma de Barcelona, Facultad de Económicas
Bilbao	Universidad del País Vasco, Facultad de Ciencias Economicas-Departamento de Economía Aplicada
	Instituto de Estudios Europeos, Universidad de Deusto
Córdoba	Arcos de Europa, Facultad de Derecho
Granada	Palacio de los Condes de Gabia
Madrid	Universidad de Alcalá de Henares, Colegio de San Pedro y San Pablo
	Universidad Autónoma, Facultad de Ciencias Económicas y Empresariales
	Universidad Complutense, Instituto de Estudios Europeos, Facultad de Derecho
	Centro de Estudios y Documentación Europea (CEYDE), Universidad Politécnica
	Centro de Documentación Europea de la Comunidad Autónoma de Madrid
Murcia	Universidad de Murcia
Navarra	Universidad de Navarra
Oviedo	Centro de Documentación Europea
Palma de Mallorca	Centro de Documentación Europea
Salamanca	Universidad de Salamanca, Centro de Documentación Europea
San Sebastián	Centro de Estudios Europeos
Santander	Universidad de Cantabria, Centro de Documentación Europea
Santiago de Compostela	Universidad de Santiago, Facultad de Económicas y Empresariales
Sevilla	Universidad de Sevilla
Tenerife	Universidad de la Laguna, Facultad de Derecho
Toledo	Cámara de Comercio e Industria
Valencia	Universidad de Valencia, Facultad de Económicas
Valladolid	Universidad de Valladolid, Facultad de Derecho
Zaragoza	Universidad de Zaragoza, Facultad de Derecho

4. The State Secretariat for the European Communities

The State Secretariat for the European Communities is the body of the Minister of Foreign Affairs in charge of carrying out policies regarding Spain's relationship with EC. From the documentation point of view, the Congress

Studies and Documentation management offices has access to the database fed by the state secretariat. The information is distributed into three databases:

1. ARCE, which holds references of documents from 1987 until 20 May 1990 (116,000 references)
2. SECE, which includes references from 20 May 1990
3. LEGC, which covers regulations published in Chapter I of the *Boletín Oficial del Estado* (BOE General Measures) since 1987; parliamentary initiatives published in A,B, and C series of the Congress and Series II of the Senate since 1987; the legislative measures that have appeared in the L series of DOCE since 1957; analysis of significant interest documents of C series of DOCE since 1957; and, finally, the COM documents since 1987.

Databases can be accessed through the IBERPAC network and have been created using BRS software. Inquiries are assisted by a system of menus composed of simple question-and-answer commands.

References

Boletín Oficial del Estado. (1986). *Base de datos de informática jurídica del Boletín Oficial del Estado (Iberlex). Legislación de disposiciones Generales.* Boletín Oficial del Estado, Madrid.
Daranas Peláez, M. (1985a). *Los Parlamentos Nacionales de la Europa Comunitaria y el Parlamento Europeo.* Congreso de los Diputados, Madrid.
Daranas Peláez, M. (1985b). *Procedimiento de ratificación de los Tratados internacionales en los Estados miembros de las Comunidades Europeas (Adhesión de España y Portugal a la C.E.E.).* Congreso de los Diputados, Madrid.
Euroconfidentiel. (1991). *1991 Directory of EEC Information Sources.* Euroconfidentiel, Rixensart, Belgium.
Martín González, A. (1989). La Biblioteca del Congreso de los Diputados. *Revista de las Cortes Generales* **18**, 227–267.
Paesa, M. (1987a). Bases de datos jurídicas existentes en la comunidad Económica Europea. *Revista de las Cortes Generales* **11**, 283–293.
Paesa, M. (1987b). Fuentes para el estudio del Parlamento Europeo. *Revista de las Cortes Generales* **12**, 379–392.
Rodríguez Bouyssi, J. (1986). Panorama de las fuentes y servicios de documentación en las instituciones de las Comunidades Europeas. *Boletín de la ANABAD* **1–2**, 91–99.
Ruiz-Navarro Pinar, J. L. (1985). El Parlamento Europeo: sistemas electorales de los diez y alternativas de la futura ley electoral española. *Revista de las Cortes Generales* **6**, 341–416.
Sáez de la Calzada, M. (1983). El centro de documentación de una oficina de prensa y documentación. La oficina de las Comunidades Europeas. *Boletín de la ANABAD* **1**, 91–99.
Thomson, I. (1989). *The Documentation of the European Communities. A Guide.* Mansell, New York.

Bibliography

Bravo i Pijoan, *et al.* (1986). El Comité d'informació i documentació científica i técnica de la Comunitat Econòmica Europea. Paper presented at the Segones Jornades Catalanes de Documentació de la Societat Catalana de Documentació e Informació, Barcelona, 1986.

Englelfield, D., ed. (1990). *Parliamentary Libraries and Information Services: A Directory of the Member Legislatures of the European Communities.* Camera dei Deputati, Ufficio publicazione, Rome.

Fernández García, J. L. (1981). La Información en la C.E.E. *Documentación de las Ciencias de la Información* **5,** 243–258.

Gómez Caridad, I. (1986). Información y documentación científica en las Comunidades Europeas. *Revista Española de Documentación Científica* **1,** 63–65.

Grau Guadix, R. (1991). El usuario en las bibliotecas especializadas. In *Seminario Hispano-Británico sobre cooperación bibliotecaria,* pp. 115–141. Centro de coordinación bibliotecaria, Madrid.

Hopkins, M. (1981). *Policy Information in the European Communities. A Bibliographical Guide to Community Documentation. 1958–1978.* Mansell, London.

Huber, W. (1981). Los Servicios EURONET/DIANE y su utilización. *Revista Española de Documentación Científica* **1,** 25–40.

Jeffries, J. (1981). *A Guide to the Official Publications of the European Communities.* Mansell, London.

Lodge, J. (1983). *The European Community. Bibliographical Excursions.* Frances Printer, London.

Official Publications of the European Communities. Aslib Social Sciences. Information Group. (1980). Exchange of experience seminar. London, 10th December 1979. *Aslib Proceedings* **9,** 335–367.

Pau, G. (1990). A practical introduction to sources of information about the European Communities. *Aslib Proceedings* **11–12,** 427–436.

Pelou, P. (1990). *L'Europe de l'information: Programmes, marches et technologies.* ESF, Paris.

Tratado de Adhesión de España y Portugal a las Comunidades Europeas: (documentación parlamentaria de los doce países de la Comunidad y del Parlamento Europeo sobre la ratificación del Tratado de Adhesión de España y Portugal). (1987). Congreso de los Diputados, Madrid.

Index

ISBN 0-12-024616-3

90018

9 780120 246168